THE EMPTY CAGE

THE EMPTY CAGE

Inquiry into the Mysterious Disappearance of the Author

CARLA BENEDETTI

Translated from the Italian by William J. Hartley

Cornell University Press
Ithaca and London

*Cornell University Press acknowledges with thanks
the translation grant from the Italian Ministry
of Foreign Affairs, which aided in the
publication of this book.*

Originally published as *L'ombra lunga dell'autore: Indagine su una
figura cancellata.* © Giangiacomo Feltrinelli Editore Milano. Prima
edizione in "Campi del sapere" settembre 1999

First published 2005 by Cornell University Press

Printed in the United States of America

Design by Scott Levine

Library of Congress Cataloging-in-Publication Data
Benedetti, Carla, 1952–
    [Ombra lunga dell'autore. English]
    The empty cage : inquiry into the mysterious disappearance of the
author / Carla Benedetti ; translated from the Italian by William J.
Hartley.
        p.   cm.
    Includes bibliographical references and index.
    ISBN 0-8014-4145-5 (alk. paper)
    1. Authorship—Philosophy   I. Title.
    PN175.B4613 2005
    801—dc22
                                2004023904

Cornell University Press strives to use environmentally responsible
suppliers and materials to the fullest extent possible in the publishing of its books. Such materials include vegetable-based, low-VOC
inks and acid-free papers that are recycled, totally chlorine-free, or
partly composed of nonwood fibers. For further information, visit
our website at www.cornellpress.cornell.edu.

Cloth printing   10 9 8 7 6 5 4 3 2 1

To Robert Dombroski, a great Gadda scholar and dear friend. Upon its publication in Italian, he was the first to review this book for English-speaking readers and believe in its value. Now as this English translation appears, my first thoughts are to him. I only wish he were here to see it.

CARLA BENEDETTI

"E alle stecche delle persiane già l'alba."
—Carlo Emilio Gadda, *La Cognizione del Dolore*

This translation is dedicated to Robert S. Dombroski. As you did so many times throughout a life of committed intellectual endeavor, bringing us together, you made the work happen. With deep gratitude and great affection for my mentor and friend . . .

WILL HARTLEY

How well I would write if I were not here!

SILAS FLANNERY

CONTENTS

1. Is the Author Dead?   1

The Author without Text   2

A Late-Modern Myth   5

Authorialism   8

The Author and the Work   12

War against the Author   16

Late Modernity   20

Authored Merchandise   23

2. The Author without Genius   26

The Triumph of Poetics   27

The Artist and the Label Pusher   30

Reflectivity of Art   34

Over and Over Again   38

Anticipatory Poetics   39

Aisthesis and *Noesis*   41

Conceptual Literature   44

The Strategic Author   48

Author-Image   51

Empty Cage   54

3. **The Author as Condition of the Work**   57
   Useless Precautions   58
   Wayne Booth's Implied Author   62
   A Second Self   65
   Guardian of Meaning   67
   Having an Author   70
   Being Authored   74
   Authored (*d'autore*) versus Generic (*di genere*)   77
   Film and the Birth of the *Auteur*   78

4. **From Genres to Authors**   83
   The Ancient Functions of Genres   84
   The Identity of Literature   89
   A New Perverse Function   91
   The Cunning of Convention   98
   The Surviving Genres   100
   Literature as Genre   107

5. **The Differential Logic of Modernity**   111
   Novels and Genre Criticism   111
   Literature Observes Itself   114
   What Is an Artistic Technique?   116
   The Exhaustion of Literary Forms   119
   Differential Sensations   123
   Variation, Transgression   126
   Art and the Self-Referential   128
   The Spiral of Self-Consciousness   132

6. **"This Is Literature!"**   136
   What Makes Literature Literature?   137
   The Aesthetics Solution   139
   Breaking Away from Aesthetics   141
   The Impossible Return to Aristotle   144
   Dissecting the Body in Search of the Soul   146
   Fish's Experiment   150
   Profiting from a Tautology   151
   Dispute   154

7. **Malaise and Its Remedies**   158
   The Eye inside the Author   158
   Bound Writings   161
   Artificial Genres   166
   Genius Returns as Game   168
   Recipe for a Work of Art   169
   Return to Meter   174
   "Long Live the Chain!"   177
   Grace and the Apocryphal   182
   Desecration and Reenchantment   185

8. **Endless Mourning**   188
   The Two Deaths   188
   A Medicine against Genius?   191
   Internalized Epigonism   194
   The Absent Work and the Already Inscribed Word   196
   Claustrophilia   199
   Literature "Reconfigured"   203
   Late-Modern Learning   205
   History Reconfigured as Labyrinth   207
   Double Bind   209

   Bibliography   213
   Index   223

THE EMPTY CAGE

CHAPTER 1

Is the Author Dead?

A few years back, the pale face of an author who goes by the name Alfonso Luigi Marra started popping up in the book sections of several newspapers. An entire page of *La Repubblica,* then of *il manifesto,* and finally of *La Stampa* was taken up by his advertisement: the photograph above, below it a long extract from the book being promoted. Marra has written a number of books, not at all easy to classify judging by the titles that followed (for example, *Cucciolino, La Storia di Aids* [Cucciolino, the Story of AIDS]), nor by the pedantic tirades on presumably difficult themes which covered the page. These were written in a strange mélange of legalistic and countercultural styles that left the reader with little or no understanding as to the book's subject matter. The insert kept on appearing, at more or less regular intervals, over the span of a year or two. Outside of that full-page ad, however, no one ever mentioned Marra. His work was not an event, and his advertising campaign (the cost of which one can only imagine) reminded me of that "soundless din" which Theodor Adorno said he would find each morning in the pages of the daily papers.

What, then, were those books all about? In order to find out more, I once made inquiries at the newsstand: no one had ever heard of them. I went back to check the advertisement: it promised the book would be available "at the newsstand" by a future date. A few months later an-

other full-page ad announced a new book by Marra, again with publication put off for a later date. I began to suspect that the obscure Neapolitan publisher (whose address was given) was fictitious, that Marra had
never written a single book, and that those full-page ads with the long
blocks of text constituted his entire opus. It was a tempting hypothesis,
but then a friend of mine assured me that he had held at least one of
those books in his own hands; it had been distributed free at some
demonstration in Naples.

Yet even if those books do exist, it doesn't change much. Marra's work
continues, and probably will continue, to be ignored by most readers; it
is just the same as if it didn't exist. His author-name, on the other hand,
certainly does exist and is perhaps still well-known to many. It is a curious case of a literary disappearance in which, contrary to some literary
theorists, it is not the author who vanishes, but rather the work. We
could call it the "Marra effect" in homage to the extravagant Neapolitan
lawyer who squandered his inheritance on self-promotion.[1]

The Author without Text

The Marra phenomenon epitomizes the situation of an astonishing number of authors in our time (including those who have no need to pay for
their own advertising campaigns), a condition extending to essayists,
philosophers, and artists as well. They exist as authors insofar as they
are talked about in that virtual salon constituted by the system of designated sites, from the talk shows to the culture sections of newspapers,
rather than as the authors of works which have actually been read, appreciated, concretely experienced. This phenomenon runs counter to
what literary theories of the last decades, from structuralism to semi-

---

1. But did he in fact squander it? Marra was later elected to the European Parliament
as a candidate of Forza Italia. [For one of Marra's ads, see photo insert.] After the Italian
edition of this book had already been prepared to go to press, another case of self-
promotion, even more dramatic in its outcome, caught the attention of Italian reporters
(if not book reviewers). To promote his last novel, *Il cerchio* (The Circle), Franco De
Longis, a Genovese business consultant and self-published author, thought up an unusual sales network. He solicited orders from private companies and corporations, which
were entitled to recover the cost of purchasing the books as gifts to employees through a
tax write-off. Meanwhile, in the local newspapers a blizzard of advertisements presented
the book as a best-seller and an internationally acclaimed masterpiece. On the same day
that his last advertisement appeared, De Longis disappeared by committing suicide.

otics, from hermeneutics to deconstruction, right up to the new theories of computer hypertext, have been predicting for some time. All they do is repeat over and over that authors have been eclipsed by the anonymous presence of texts and by "creative networks," that what counts for the reader is not the author but the text, in its internal architecture and in its reference and relation to other texts. And yet things seem to be going somewhat differently. Today, what reaches the reader by means of the intricate circuits of communication is not the *text without author,* but the *author without text.*

Authors without texts are not simply names. They may have full "structured" lives, populated by facts and opinions. What we know about them are their faces: faces that stare at the hesitant reader from the covers of their books. And we know about their opinions: their "authoritative" voices speak to us from culture sections and from television screens, greedily solicited or spontaneously volunteered. They talk about their own books, what they mean and how they should be read; they also talk about other writers' books, great authors of the past, and the fortunes of literature. Sometimes they even talk about customs, war, and where the world is heading. But there is one thing above all else that we know about these authors: how they fit into the great scheme of literature. Their names fill the culture sections grouped together and counterpoised, with so many diagrams, categorized according to literary genealogies and poetic typologies. In other words, what we know especially and always about them is their "poetics," that concept which supposedly encapsulates the meaning and value of their artistic work. Sometimes it is an author's self-declared poetics; more often, though, it is a brand attributed by the publisher for promotional purposes, or by cultural journalists and critics caught up in their day-to-day disputes.

The phenomenon of knowledge disseminated by means of fame has been an everyday institution for centuries. People can become indirectly familiar with innumerable classical authors without ever having read a single line of their work, either through descriptions in school textbooks or by word of mouth. But what I am talking about is more peculiar. The textless author is himself his body of work. His name is a sign, or to borrow somewhat provocatively a term that semiotics has reserved for the literary text, a "hypersign," rich with internal references ("also the author of . . .") and external ones ("in the tradition of author X," "totally different from author Y"). The author's name as hypersign is presented to the reader insofar as it is endowed with its own "differentiating marks": what distinguishes one author from the others; what kind of project-making defines his or her work; why he or she is considered new or original. The author's differentiating mark can even be conveyed by association with a particular generation, as has been the case with the category of "young narrator" in Italy since the early 1980s. It is this bundle of references to the author, and by the author to others, that makes the text exist for readers and purchasers, as the publishing industry well knows. In the marketplace, construction of the author's image is crucial for promotional purposes. Peculiarities about the writer, real or fictitious, that can be spread across the culture sections (the author's corporeal effigy, or contrariwise, a mysterious invisibility; an opinion, a political position, some biographical fact) are the most commonly used ingredients in sales strategies. Analogous phenomena are also found in other sectors of the culture industry, from painting and sculpture to cinema.

Alfonso Luigi Marra is an author without works, but one merely belonging to the lowest depths. That is why he was never mentioned in the book reviews: the simplest way to punish an uninvited guest is for the rest of the party to ignore him. On one occasion, however, a well-known journalist took it on himself to deliver Marra a sounder thrashing. In the pages of a nationally distributed newspaper, the journalist issued a stern reprimand affirming the seriousness of literary communication, which does not allow itself to be detoured by paid advertising. Despite the attempt at self-promotion, the journalist suggested, Marra would never sell a thing. It was as if to say: "Everything is working for the best. Successful authors (i.e., the ones we have decreed to be successful) can hold their heads high. Publicity does not the author make. Readers know how to tell the difference." But on the basis of what? one might ask. Certainly not on the basis of the texts, which do not "appear" except through what the cultural custodians say about them.

The hypocrisy of cultural journalists goes hand in hand with the peaceful dreaming of theoreticians who nowadays talk only about texts and readers, and never about authors. It is as if the author no longer exists for them, whereas, the pillar of today's literary institution is precisely the author. It is the author that supports its various moments, from production to promotion, from criticism to the act of enjoyment. The Marra effect might be able to awaken them at least enough to introduce a doubt: if the author really is dead, who then is this figure who continues to wander, like a ghost, over the old literary continent? And what if that network of texts, hypertexts, and intertexts with which their dreams are crowded is merely a literature of authors without works?

A Late-Modern Myth

If we ask ourselves how it is possible, in the face of such macroscopic evidence, that literary theory has so long been able to remove the author from its studies (and from its visual field), it will be necessary to go back to the years when one of the most peculiar myths of our epoch began to take shape. Here it is concentrated into a single, highly charged sentence by Roland Barthes: "The author enters into his own death, the writing begins."[2]

What makes this into a "myth" is not only the magic stroke of the eraser that rubs out the cumbersome entity of the author, but also the fact that it speaks volumes about this disappearance. Here is the strange account, in epic tones, of a funereal celebration, whose undisputed protagonist remains the author, even if only in the role of the dead body. Its motto is "what matter who's speaking?"[3]—since it is always language that speaks; "what matter who's writing?"—since writing opens up the space in which the subject is dispersed; "what matter whose signature is appended?"—since what is important in the text is its internal structure, or its references to other texts.

As a matter of convention, we can trace the birth date of this myth to the 1960s, even though it is necessary to go back further, and in multiple directions, in order to discover its genesis. When Barthes was writing *La Mort de l'auteur* in 1968, New Criticism in America had already been attacking the notion of "the author's intention" for some time; Emile Benveniste had already begun his studies on the subjectivity of language, which had a strong impact on the myth; and Maurice Blanchot had already woven together his epic on writing as an impersonal, anonymous space in which the writer experiences his own death.[4] But it is in the late 1960s that the death of the author theme explodes in essays of philosophy, criticism, and poetics. Its epicenter is France, where it is also tied to the names of Jacques Derrida, Julia Kristeva, Philippe Sollers, and amplified by the concomitant reflections of Jacques Lacan on the "subversion of the subject."[5] From there it flows into a plethora of literary theories,

2. Barthes 1968, p. 49.
3. A reference to the third section of Samuel Beckett's "Texts for Nothing"; see Beckett 1967, p. 81.
4. Cf. Wimsatt and Beardsley 1946; Benveniste 1956 and 1958; Blanchot 1955.
5. Cf. Sollers 1968; J. Lacan, "The Subversion of the Subject and the Dialectic of Desire in the Freudian Unconscious," 1960. English translation in Lacan 1977, pp. 292–325.

from semiotics to deconstruction, giving birth to a theoretical dogma from which we have yet to free ourselves. According to this dogma, in order to understand, interpret, and evaluate literary texts the author is not a necessary term of reference. Even hermeneutics, the other philosophical koine of our times, is linked to it. Despite its own nineteenth-century, Diltheyan tradition (which understood comprehension as the psychological reconstruction by the reader of the author's intellectual horizon), hermeneutics has developed an analogous rejection of the category of the author. With Hans-Georg Gadamer's so-called "linguistic turn," even hermeneutics unburdens itself of the necessity of examining the author's intentional consciousness and begins to speak only about the intention of the text, in full consonance with the myth. Thus, even for hermeneutics, the reader no longer maintains a dialogue with authors, but only with the network of headless texts.

According to the theories into which it has been integrated, in place of the author, the myth variously prioritizes language, writing, reading, but in any case, the text and texts. The concept of *literary work* (*l'opera*), a notion that can't help but imply an author insofar as it is created by someone, is now replaced by the concept of *text* (a tissue of connections, with neither organs nor muscles, whose system of nerves lacks a centralized brain). The text is then conceived as existing in contact with a myriad of other texts, which together form a strange organism, pulsating with its own life, like a mass of unicellular beings which absorb one another and reproduce through parthenogenesis. This reticular organism goes by the name of *intertextuality*. The idea of intertextuality, which each theory describes in its own way, though all taken together constitutes a homogeneous ideology, corresponds to the theme of the death of the author. Intertextuality ratifies the irrelevance of the creative subject and celebrates its eclipse. Literature turns into a tightly woven network of texts, each referring to the others and all caught up in the dialogue of intertextuality.

In more recent years, the myth has been taken up again by the sirens of the new information technologies, who, having appropriated some poststructuralist concepts, give them a kind of "empirical validation" and the potential for mass diffusion. According to many, the so-called interactive reader created by hypertext has given the coup de grâce to the agonized figure of the author. By giving the reader the possibility of choosing his own path through the metatext, of annotating texts written by others, and of creating links between them, many of the author's traditional prerogatives become useless (authority, autonomy of the work, intellectual property), and any approach to texts based on the author's role is rendered obsolete.[6] And there are those who straightforwardly claim that "the network is the future of creative writing."[7] Thus, today, wherever one turns, people now talk only of texts, hypertexts, intertexts, and metatexts, of readers who dialogue with the texts, and of texts that dialogue with other texts. The author no longer exists; or rather, we speak as if that were the case.

The main purpose of this book is to liberate theory from the dogma just described and from the hypocrisy that feeds it. The author obviously has not disappeared, and her function has never been as strong and central as it is in today's literary communication. No matter how devoid of works or reduced to little more than an image, a bodiless semblance, some may be, it is precisely the author who holds up the institution of literature and, more generally, the institution of art. Such a claim will naturally need to be argued out patiently, through an analysis of those features that can be considered specific to modern art, and the manner in which late modernity has reelaborated them. Proceeding in that direction, we will also be able to answer the question that has probably already arisen in the mind of the reader: how to explain the fact that contemporary culture, even as it gives such a strong and central role to the author, has, at the same time dreamed and theorized his or her demise? How can we explain such a discrepancy between the facts and their description by theory? What was the myth of the author's death really all about? Poststructuralist literary theory has left outside its purview an incredible quantity of phenomena tied to the author, her role in the techniques of classifying and ordering artistic communication, her exploitation, her transformation into an image; and above all, as we shall see, it has wiped away with a single stroke the deep sense of malaise that such phenomena have produced in artists. Thus, its whole theoretical arsenal can only appear suspect to us. Indeed, not only is it deficient in various ways, it is hardly "innocent" insofar as it remains in denial. Of course, no theory is innocent, but the theory of the author's death, with its whole corpus of notions and correlated methodologies (all of which flow into the redefinition of literature as intertextuality), drapes this fact in an

---

6. Cf. for example Landow 1992. It is also significant that the American professor, in arguing for the importance of hypertext for the teaching of literature, describes it as "embodying" the theories of Barthes and Derrida. The description of hypertext in De Carli 1997, is more problematic.

7. This is what the four authors of *Q*, an Italian novel published under the pseudonym of Luther Blisset (Turin, Einaudi 1999), declared in an interview released to *La Repubblica* (March 6, 1999). See also p. 9, n. 9.

even heavier veil. A rampant ideology can never be regarded as innocent.

Here then is the other objective that this book proposes for itself: to show how behind that "blindness" of literary theorists lies a set of beliefs, and a rather partial (though widely shared) idea of literature, which over the last decades has gradually asserted itself through their efforts. The myth of the author's death has produced not only theories, concepts, and critical (though not neutral) methodologies, but also a peculiar, absolutely novel manner of conceiving literature: a literature withdrawn into the infinite network of self-reference, in whose nodes the writer still exists but is reduced to the role of *bricoleur,* of "scribe," of the "eternal copyist" of what has already been inscribed. In short, the author never did disappear, but the myth of the author's death has nonetheless produced something: it has left us its legacy of the epigonal idea of literature (for more about this, see chapter 8).

Authorialism

Many of the phenomena that I have already mentioned are largely tied to the way books are sold. That might lead us to think that the hypertrophy of the author is only an epiphenomenon provoked by the culture industry. This is, moreover, the most commonly held opinion, which is to say, the one most commonly held among the few who have looked into the problem over the last twenty years. One interesting example is the distinction traced by Bernard Pingaud between the role of the *author* as a public figure (one that is fed to the media and the advertising campaigns) and the *writer,* whose characteristic is instead that of "disappearing behind the text." There is thus a conflict between the two roles, and for the writer who is prevented from disappearing by the culture industry, there would be no other recourse than to abstain from any kind of intervention, even from talking about his writing, so as not to be transformed into a "publicity agent for his own work."[8] Such a diagnosis, even if not limited to books and art, is not far removed from the more radical no-copyright policy practiced among the postsituationists, or the invention of an author whose name anyone can assume, like "Luther

---

8. Pingaud 1977, p. 78. For the *Tel Quel* group, too, the fact that writing, which in itself is anonymous and plural, is personalized in an author's name, was nothing more than "a market effect" (cf. *Tel Quel,* 1968, p. 41).

Blisset."[9] The author is still considered to be no more than the consequence of the economic-legal system based on the property rights to one's work; by suppressing copyrights, one suppresses the author as well. Finally, there is the opinion according to which the author is the product of the old printing press technology and allied publishing interests, and therefore on the verge of being eclipsed as the new technologies of computer hypertext gradually spread.[10] The persistence of the author, according to the foregoing views, is typically seen as a monstrous excrescence engineered by the culture industry, booksellers, and the art market, and thus as a phenomenon to be studied in the field of the sociology of literature. Though carrying so much weight in literary communication today, the author is viewed as no more than a thin layer of mildew superimposed on the fabric of art from without. Internally, however, art and literature go on being something quite different: sheltered from commercialism and industry (assuming that such shelter exists), the only thing that counts is the text.

My opinion differs, as do, moreover, those of many artists and writers who have experienced the phenomenon, especially those who have expressed a more or less explicit uneasiness regarding it. Italo Calvino, for example, intuits with extraordinary acuity how the figure of the author and her persistence in image are not only a market or copyright phenomenon, but are rooted and inscribed in the very mechanisms of the enjoyment of reading. As Calvino has the writer Silas Flannery say in *If on a winter's night a traveler,* "Readers are my vampires." Even Barthes, in his later reflections, realizes that the figure of the author, far from being canceled out, is kept alive precisely by the reader and his "desire."[11] I believe then that the hypertrophy of the author, before being a market effect, is a specifically artistic phenomenon that has its roots in certain traits peculiar to modern art and in the type of enjoyment that it induces. If the author, in the guises of author-image and author-strategist, has become such an important function of art and contemporary literature, it is due not only to the dust-jacket photographs, or the way names are promoted like car models. The culture industry, with which this book is only marginally concerned, does nothing more than amplify and exploit

9. "Luther Blisset" is the collective pseudonym adopted by European situationists as a protest against copyright laws.

10. Cf. Landow 1992.

11. Concerning Calvino's obsession with his own author image, see Benedetti 1998; we will return to Barthes in chapter 2.

for its own ends something that already exists in modern artistic communication. It is something that dates back at least two centuries, but which in the twentieth century intensified to the point of becoming problematic. It has often been felt by artists to be oppressive, experienced subterraneously as a threat to art, but never described with precision, and therefore never named. First of all, then, we must give it a name. We shall call it *authorialism*.

Authorialism is a particular investment in the author-function which has the effect of making it impossible for a work of art to exist except as the product of an author. It is not simply a matter of the work's paternity (knowing who produced it and when), nor of its correct comprehension (knowing what the author wanted to express), but above all of its artistic valorization (knowing if this object before me is or is not a work of art). In order to attribute the status of art not only to a text, but also to a painting, a film, a photograph, or a video installation, we need to consider each as the product of an artistic intention. Only on this condition can we approach objects, performances, and texts as works of art. We will then speak of them, and not merely by chance, as being *authored* (*d'autore*).[12] The nexus established between artistic value and being *d'autore* has become so close in the modern period as to have precipitated out linguistically in this common Italian expression.

Classical works were also clearly viewed as the product of an artistic intention. Even premodern man knew, for example, how to distinguish sculpture (the product of the chisel, manual dexterity, and imagination) from the beautifully fluted seashell, the work of nature, whose "production" was not preceded by any artistic intention. But what occurs in the modern epoch is more peculiar. Today even a seashell might be viewed as a work of art as long as it is displayed in a gallery, in other words, as long as it is perceived through the artistic intention that has "precipitated out," not in the object, nor in its making, but in the act of displaying it. In short, anything can be art if, and only if, whoever enjoys it may suppose there are artistic reasons behind the artist's decision to exhibit it, whether it is something found in nature untouched by a sculptor, or just an object of everyday use such as Duchamp's bottle rack. The reasons may be provocational or paradoxical, but as long as they are reasons of art, no matter how indeterminable, the viewer is forced to question

---

12. In Italian, *d'autore* means "high quality" and can be applied not only to books, paintings, and films but also to any item, such as *pasta d'autore*. It derives from the notion that an object coming from the hand of a known artist can be assumed to be of value. [trans.]

them, and thus to suppose that they exist. Granted, this example is rather singular, and it will rightly be countered that modern art amounts to more than this. But it is precisely in this extreme possibility of transforming an object not intrinsically artistic into a work of art that we can measure the broad scope and incredible power that artistic intention has acquired through modern art. And wherever there is intentionality there has to be a subject. The modern author is nothing other than that required element or hypostasis to which is attributed that artistic intention without which there is no work of art.

So if the contemporary author persists, it is not simply because the publishing industry or the art market prevents him from disappearing, but because his function is required by the very modalities of artistic valorization. What makes a text into a piece of literature? What makes an object into a work of art? Here is the necessary starting point for posing the entire question since, in the turbulent sea of modernity, it is to this rock that the author is moored. What keeps him or her alive today are the very modalities of artistic valorization, whereas premodern literature and art had other modalities of valorization. Formerly there were "objective" marks, intrinsic to the object, signaling its status as art. Not only certain qualities of its fabrication, but also and especially the marks of genre: a sonnet, a tragedy, or a depiction of the Holy Family. In modernity, on the other hand, the valorization of the supposed authorial intention at the work's origin primarily, and in certain cases exclusively, determines what is art and nonart. There is no work of art in and of itself. The work of art must be constructed by artistic communication. And the processes through which it is constructed require processes of attribution to an author, that is, the supposition that there is, at the work's origin, an artistic intention (whether conscious or not), a meaningful selection among artistic possibilities capable of providing sense and value to what we are reading or viewing.

Furthermore, the artistic intention that modern art has long valorized is of a particular type: it is not simply the intention to make a work of art, but to make it *different*, surprising, something that goes beyond the current canons. A work is invested as art, in short, insofar as it is the bearer of a *differential value*. It is especially here that authorialism reveals itself as a specifically modern trait, tied to the insertion of works of art into a sequential order, in which there is evolution, accumulation, and differentiation. Modernity is not capable of conceiving art other than through its history, nor does it conceive artistic value that is not based on difference. Thus arises that peculiar dialectic centered on the new and the original, and the strong role attributed to poetics. Each work is always interrogated not only in regard to its artistic intention, but also with respect to how it differs from others, how it distinguishes itself from what has already been seen, why it might be considered original, etc. The author serves as the framework on which such a differential value is supported.

The term *intention* should not necessarily make one think of selections that are programmatic or conscious. Even if the artist subjectively does not choose, the reader nonetheless approaches the work and takes it in as the product of an authorial choice: a selection out of what is artistically possible based on the artist's expressive need, or realized on the basis of the "poetics" which guides her artistic practice and which the work implicitly embodies. When we speak of choice, we locate ourselves within the purview of the act of enjoyment, and therefore of *attribution* (which, as will soon become clearer, is something other than *reception* as conceived by hermeneutics, which presupposes no attribution to an author). It is the reader or viewer who transforms the artist's selections, which in themselves may even be random or compelled, into subjective choices endowed with intentionality: that intentionality that is capable of providing meaning and artistic value to what we are viewing or reading. From this perspective, the term *unconscious choice*, to which criticism often has recourse in order to hold its aporias at bay, may be useful for the act of enjoyment, but is not so for theory. There is no need to call on the artist's unconscious. The choice of the author is nothing other than a choice attributed to him by the reader on the basis of certain characteristics of the object, to which he gives value in considering it as a work of art. In the same way, all the other conceptual mediations required by modern enjoyment so that a "product" may be considered artistic e.g., poetics and style), and involving the supposition of a choice on the part of the writer, are to be considered as phenomena of attribution.

The Author and the Work

So understood, the author has little to do with the intending subject, the provider of meaning, to whom prestructuralist critical practice (or hermeneutics before Gadamer) referred, and about whom today, after a long ostracism, people are timidly beginning to speak again.[13] This no-

13. An example of this is Compagnon 1998 (who refers back to Hirsch 1967); we shall have occasion to deal with him further on.

tion, which was nodding on the sidelines for years, has been abruptly roused from its slumber and called back onto the field by theoreticians and philologists as the guarantee for a correct interpretation of the text, against the interpretative drift of poststructuralism; it is meant to serve as a kind of *guarantee of the signified* and criterion for the proper interpretation of the text. Even in this defensive use it is tied to an idea of the author unlike the one I am trying to describe here. The intention that I am referring to, besides being one that is attributed, is also of a rather different type because it is not simply an *intention of meaning*, but an *artistic intention*. It is not so much a matter of what the author *wanted to say*, but of what she *wanted to do* artistically. It does not merely bear on the meaning of the text, the signified which the author supposedly deposited there and for which the interpreter searches. Instead, it bears on how the work is made, the form in which it is incarnated, the style, the poetics, and all those other characteristics to which one can attribute artistic value. In other words, the problem of the author goes beyond the problems of interpretation of the text to grapple with those of the work's artistic valorization. And no matter how determined the interpreter is not to be bound by what the author meant to say (as many today maintain), it is impossible to do away with his artistic intention, his artistic project, factual or supposed as it may be, since without presupposing it, the text in question would not even exist, that is, would not be a literary/artistic work.

Nor does the concept of author that I am talking about coincide with those notions that have in some ways "survived" in the literary theory of the second half of the twentieth century. I am referring to the "implied author" found in narrative studies and to the "ideal author" of semiotics. Such notions are not utilizable for the purposes of our inquiry (see chapter 3) because they make the author into merely a *function of the text*, considered by structuralism and semiotics as a kind of "axiom," a self-evident fact of literary communication. For me, the author is instead a *function of the work.* And the work does not coincide with the text: it too is the product of processes of attribution. Neither the author nor the text can be considered the primary element in the system of modern art, and even less can they constitute the basis for a theory of art. The only basis possible for such a theory is the lurching deck of the ship on which one is sailing (as Gadda, speaking about cognitive activity, once wrote), which is to say, communication itself considered as a process. The system of modern art as it is being described here is founded neither on the author nor on the text, but is composed of communicative processes alone, which reproduce themselves on the basis of preceding communications. Author and work are both constructs, the products of attributions, and each of them presupposes the other. The processes through which a modern work of art is "constructed" require processes of attribution to an author: attribution of an artistic intention, of a choice, of a project, conscious or unconscious, of a poetics, of an idea of literature, or even of a style (a notion which those theories even claimed to have eliminated). And for such processes of attribution there is nothing whose relevance is automatically excluded: at times even an author's biographical data might be called on to support an artistic value. To devotees of structuralism and semiotics that has the ring of blasphemy.

As a function required by the processes of constructing the work, the author would seem to be, at least as long as we hold to this type of artistic logic, something that can never disappear. It is not enough to render the texts anonymous or pseudonymous in order to do away with that "being who reasons" and makes projects, whom we name author, and to whom we attribute choices, intentions, programs, or even merely unconscious selections; that is because his function is rendered necessary by ties that are broader in range, regarding the system of artistic communication within the laws of its operation and in its very condition of existence. Nor is it enough, on the part of the critic, to place the biographical or psychological data of the artist between parentheses, to give up searching through the writing for the symptom or sign of what someone intended to say, to concentrate exclusively on the architecture of the texts (their recurrent elements and their variations). Whatever decision the critic (or interpreter) may make, it will start nevertheless from the presupposition that the texts about which she speaks are literary works, and no matter how absolutely she abolishes every reference to the author from her discourse, the very notion of the work still implies that author, whom she claims to have banned from her explanation and critical interpretation. As Michel Foucault well demonstrated, it is not sufficient to repeat the empty slogan that the author has disappeared for the author to really disappear. The very notion of the work (*l'oeuvre*) presupposes that of the author. Even the notion of writing (*écriture*), which was supposed to depose the author from his throne, instead "sustains the privileges of the author through the safeguard of the a priori."[14] The utopia of the author's death and the dispersion of the subject meets here its

14. Foucault 1969, p. 120 (for variants introduced into the English version of 1980, see Foucault 1994, vol. 1).

strongest critique, and at the hand of a philosopher who certainly sided with neither author nor subject.[15]

Foucault's brief essay, though, remains merely the outline of an analytical study neither elaborated by him nor pursued by others. While often invoked as an obligatory bibliographical reference by those who study literature, as we shall later have occasion to note, it was more often misunderstood than properly utilized. Even Maurice Couturier (to be discussed below), in an otherwise interesting attempt to reintegrate the author as a necessary partner to that exchange between two subjects which is reading, ends up by having Foucault say, or rather "predict," that the author-function is destined to disappear from literary discourse just as it has already disappeared from scientific discourse. Foucault, on the contrary, does not predict anything, he simply historicizes, and thus renders *contingent* that to which Couturier seems to want to attribute a metahistorical necessity: "No matter how much is said, the author-function will remain of primary importance."[16] Literary theory is often guilty of metahistorical generalizations. The author function that we are describing is instead, in the spirit of Foucault, altogether historical, tied to the artistic system that we have witnessed in modernity.

Ideally this book proposes to continue Foucault's inquiry, though focusing exclusively on literary discourse (which was for Foucault, on the contrary, only one particular instance among the various possible discourses endowed with author-function). This choice of material, obviously owing to what is of specific interest to us, is not simply made to restrict the field of study. Indeed, in a certain sense we are extending the field. For Foucault, the author-function is involved in all *discourses* characterized by certain modalities of circulation and valorization, whereas for us it refers to all works of art, not only those that are verbal. By searching out the sites in which the author-function is inscribed in literary texts as works of art, we shall end up investigating something on which Foucault's discourse did not touch: the processes of attribution by which an artistic value is conferred. In modern literary texts, what

15. Foucault's intention was rather to deprive the subject of its role as originative foundation, analyzing the subject as a variable and complex function of the discourse (ibid., p. 137), a role that, in his opinion, the structuralists continued to concede to it despite having reduced it to an intralinguistic function. Furthermore, the reason why Foucault grew truly angry when he was categorized as a structuralist is that, as Blanchot writes, "he could sense in structuralism a traditional whiff of transcendentalism" (Blanchot 1986, p. 71).

16. Couturier 1995, p. 245.

makes reference to the author a necessity is, according to my hypothesis, indissolubly tied to their artistic valorization, that is, to precisely what makes them works of art rather than ordinary discourses. And this necessity is one which literature shares with the other forms of modern art. The strong mediating role played by poetics, for example, is a phenomenon found in many areas of artistic production. Authorialism goes well beyond the verbal arts and can be equally detected in the plastic arts, the performing arts, and the cinema, even though it has specific characteristics in each one.

Insofar as it is a phenomenon that cuts across the boundaries of different artistic practices, authorialism brings us back, willingly or not, into that enclosure which gathers together all the arts and which formerly constituted the domain of aesthetics. In the twentieth century, concrete artistic phenomena obliged literary theory (as well as the other theories of art, separated according to their different "media," language, and image) to reintroduce that broader perspective into the sphere of its inquiry. These days, the various arts seem to participate equally in many of the "fundamental questions." For example, the need to actively set up a method of distinguishing art from nonart, which used to be mainly a problem for literature and much less so for painting and sculpture, is now shared by all the arts, including, as we shall see, cinema. The procedures through which such a distinction is made do not greatly differ from one field of art to another. Reference to the author as subject of an artistic intention, as responsible for choices made within the range of the artistically possible, thus as subject of a choice of poetics, is the very condition for being able to attribute artistic value to a text, a painting, a video installation, a film, or a photograph.

War against the Author

It goes without saying that this particular artistic logic based on the author and his or her supposed choices of poetics no longer runs as smoothly as it once did. A whole series of "symptoms" show us that contemporary art now perceives it as worn-out and confining, something to be opposed or avoided. With its rejection of univocal poetics and its ironic detachment from the idea of the authenticity of style, the postmodern has been the most visible signal of this trend. But there are many other signs, that indicate how that mode of artistic logic had started to "cause trouble" since the beginning of the twentieth century. The onset of those symptoms, which are none other than the signs of a problematization of the author, coincides with, according to the scheme that I am proposing here, the onset of late modernity.

Authorialism is like a chronic and progressive disease of modernity. It leads art to the impasse of a totally reflected and "rationalized" practice. The author as project-maker assumed to be at the origin of the work has now replaced the genius; the author as strategist squanders every margin of nonreflective activity conceded to artistic practice; the writer, reduced to eye that observes itself, is caught in the cage of her own self-observation. That effect is experienced by many artists as a source of paralysis. Then, as a further cause for uneasiness, there is also that author image constructed in the act of enjoyment and hyped by the strategies of promotion, which turns back on the writing subject, entrapping him or her in an annoying, petrifying, unwanted identity, as is paradigmatically illustrated in the "lived authorial experience" of Calvino, who was constantly under pressure to wear a mask and simultaneously to reveal his controlled identity.

Yet, for the very reason that it provokes malaise, authorialism also incites a search for "remedies." In the attempt to loosen the dominion of authorialism, twentieth-century artistic practice set up an array of techniques and devices that operate precisely in the "zone" of the author, where the artist's "choice" supposedly takes place, making it problematic, and at times, paradoxical. This involves stratagems, maneuvers, evasive tactics, all of which are aimed at freeing, at least partially, the creative act from the hegemony of the author as project-maker; otherwise, they are aimed at preventing the reader from presupposing the author to be at the origin of the work, thereby making it complicated, if not completely impossible, for the former to construct the latter's image. Consequently, we call them tactics of deauthorialization to make clear their reactive nature. Even so, they often become true and proper poetics, shared by many writers and endowed with a certain complexity and internal articulation, which are repeated and perfected over time, and which sometimes cross over into other areas, capable of being applied equally to literature, figurative arts, and even music. Generally speaking, we can place them in three broad categories: bound writings, the search for grace, and the apocryphal effect (see chapter 7). Naturally these three solutions cannot pretend to have exhausted the artistic panorama of the twentieth century. However, I am convinced that many aspects of late-modern literary production can be fruitfully looked back on as attempts to oppose the hypertrophy of the author as strategist and the author as

image. Among the factors that put the dynamics of late-modern art into
motion, authorialism is surely one of the most important, especially as a
negative element, spurring the invention of remedies against the paralysis which authorialism itself had brought on.

So if in this book it is asserted that the author is not dead, it is not only
for the pleasure of proving a dogma wrong, but because the myth of the
author's death risks covering up much of what is troublesome about the
art of our time. If one declares irrelevant exactly that function which
artistic practice has sought in various ways to explode, lighten, or neu-
tralize, generating a luxuriant phenomenology of techniques and writings in so doing, one will hardly be able to understand the experiments
of the twentieth century: from those first rude outbursts on the art scene,
set off above all by dadaism, to the more matured manifestations of the
last few decades. Even the practices of writing commonly called postmodern (the ironic detachment of the author from his or her own voice,
the display of a clearly inauthentic style—a style not "used" but only
"mentioned," cited, as if it were that of another, in other words, the apocryphal effect) can be better understood and evaluated if read as a particular type of deauthorializing practice. The apocryphal effect is just an attempt to randomly cancel out every "differential value" of style or
poetics, to frustrate the very idea of original artistic intentionality, something which the reader-enjoyer can't help but assume lies at the work's
origin.

What actually went on in the twentieth century was therefore not, as
myth would have it, the cathartic disappearance of the author (tragic for
the subject, but liberating for art); it is instead the persistence, in no way
cathartic, of the highly resistant and hypertrophic author as project-
maker (and, consequently, of the author as image), against whom artistic
practice wages guerrilla warfare. All of which goes to show that the author not only plays a central role, but also has now become the problematic which frames the field of art.

From the time when works of art ceased to circulate anonymously, the
notion of author enjoyed for centuries an obvious and untroubled existence: where there is a work, there is surely someone who created it.
Early in the twentieth century, however, this notion was for the first time
removed from the nonproblematic background of the preceding epochs
only to become increasingly controversial and "painful." That transformation is precisely the object of our inquiry. In these pages we will not
concern ourselves so much with when the notion of the author in art and

literature was born,[17] but rather with when it began to "make trouble," and with the reasons why such a thing might have happened. As Foucault, from whom I draw the concept of *problematization*, writes, in order for a system of notions or of practices to enter the visual field of thought, it is necessary "for a certain number of factors to have rendered it uncertain, caused it to lose its familiarity or provoked a number of difficulties concerning it."[18] This is exactly what takes place around the notion of the author in the twentieth century. A combination of factors, which we will describe by and by, has borne the long familiar and discounted notion of "author" into the eye of the cyclone so powerfully that artistic practice has declared war on it, while theory has scrutinized it under a series of byzantine distinctions (among them, implied author, real author, ideal author) and has ended up making the author's disappearance into the object of a myth.

Even the "birth of the reader," that is, the reader's elevation to nearly undisputed protagonist of contemporary literary theory, is proof of the problematization of the author. As Gadamer noted, the concept of genius disintegrates with Valéry's famous line: a work is never completed, it is abandoned. With that gesture, Valéry transfers to the reader that "authority of absolute creation" which until then had been considered the prerogative of the author, and which he or she seemingly would no longer exert. In effect, the author now passes the work over to the reader and the interpreter, who are expected to complete it through a labor that

17. Concerning the genesis of the notion "author," which has been the object of diverse studies, Foucault's hypothesis, which places the factor "punishment" prior to that of "appropriation of a benefit," seems convincing to me in a general way: "Speeches and books were assigned real authors, other than mythical or important religious figures, only when the author became subject to punishment and to the extent that his discourse was considered transgressive" (Foucault 1969, p. 124). But specifically regarding works of art, I believe that another factor must be placed first: that which Benjamin describes as secularization of the cultural value of artworks. The aura (or uniqueness) of a work was originally the expression of a cult founded on a ritual, and inseparable from it. But when the cult is detached from its ritual function in order to become a profane "cult of beauty," the uniqueness of the work "is more and more displaced by the empirical uniqueness of the creator or of his creative achievement." In other words, artistic value is based on the work's "authenticity" (Benjamin 1936, p. 244 and p. 244 n.6). See also the studies collected in Chamarat and Goulet 1996.

18. *Polémique, politique et problématisation*, in Foucault 1994, vol. 4, p. 597. Nonetheless, Foucault did not think of the author as a problematic field; his concept referred to other fields of inquiry, such as madness, sexuality, truth, etc. The concept of "problematization" is tied to a particular way of "writing history," which some have criticized: cf. Castel 1994.

has "the rank and rights of a new production."[19] This then is where the aesthetics of reception gets underway. Beyond, however, what Gadamer would like to substitute for the aesthetics of unconscious creation (and which for us is unacceptable; see chapter 8), what seems to me important to emphasize is his "diagnosis." If the reader triumphs, it is because the author is now *without genius*. Or, to put it into our own terms, problematizing the notion of author comes about because the equilibrium between reflection and unconscious creativity, summarized in the eighteenth century and in the romantic notion of genius, has been lost. In other words, the "problematization"[20] of the author comes about because the very act of creation has turned uncertain, problematic, even impossible as viewed through the melancholic eye of late modernity.

Late Modernity

Authorialism is the product of modern artistic logic. But it is only late-modern art that settles accounts with authorialism in a conflictive and self-critical manner. This turning reflective of what until then had been part of the "silent mechanism" of art can be explained within a more general process that emerged in the early decades of the twentieth century: art becomes aware of its own mechanisms. It is a kind of deutero-learning,[21] through which, artistic logic, centered on the rotation of poetics, the compulsion to be original (in diction, image, form), and the valorization of the author as subject of a poetics, and which until that point had guided art, suddenly gets laid bare. In the cold light of self-awareness come the crises of paralysis and the need to escape them. This self-critical awareness (which, however, is simultaneously self-paralyzing) is what distinguishes late-modern art from modern art. Born with romanticism, modern art is simply *reflective*, that is, mediated by its concept, as demonstrated by the ever stronger role it attributed to poet-

19. This process, Gadamer continues, amounts to "an untenable hermeneutic nihilism" (Gadamer 1995, p. 95).

20. This expression will be used hereon as equivalent to the Italian *problematizzazione*, a nominalization of the verb *problematizzare*, to indicate the designation of an issue or area of study as worthy of theoretical attention and elaboration. [trans.]

21. Gregory Bateson gives this name to the type of learning that involves a jump in the level of logic; the subject learns to resolve not only the individual problem but also the entire class of similar problems (cf. *Social Planning and the Concept of Deutero-Learning*, in Bateson 1972, pp. 159–176). I also borrow the notion of "double bind" from Bateson, understood as a situation in which a paradoxical order (command) results in a blockage or paralysis of endeavor (ibid., pp. 271ff).

ics. Late-modern art is instead reflective and *self-critical,* in other words, aware of its own mechanisms and of the blind alleys down which they lead, yet unable to call the premises of those mechanisms into question. Self-criticism does not mean that that logic has been surpassed: it means only that artistic practice now lives in conflict with something it still can't do without, something inscribed in the very condition for the existence of art as such. So late modernity is also a terrain strewn with ambivalence and double-binds.

In regard to periodization, approximate and conventional as all periodizations are, I take dadaism as the milestone signaling the beginning of late-modern art. Dadaism is really not a vanguard movement like those that preceded it; it is already the expression of a critical problematization of the notion of the author and of modern artistic logic (see chapter 8) and is therefore a late-modern phenomenon. Such a periodization is quite dissimilar to the one embedded in the great debate over postmodernism. Even in the midst of so many discordant opinions (about what the postmodern is, about how to define or evaluate it), that debate has produced consensus on at least one point. There is widespread agreement that an epochal turning point divides the twentieth century around the decade of the 1960s, though some would have it earlier, and others later. I believe, in contrast, that the true discontinuity in artistic phenomena lies elsewhere. The point of transition was much earlier. It occurred precisely with that deutero-learning manifested in the first decades of the century, whence begins the paralyzing self-criticism of modernity, of which the postmodern is no more than an extreme episode. The postmodern is thus contained within the same time frame as late modernity, which for me is a more inclusive concept. And that means the postmodern still falls within the time frame of the modern.

Of course, I do not intend to deny the formation at the end of the sixties of that particular stylistic-ideological koine, based on the manipulation of traditions (or, as I am proposing to call it here, the apocryphal effect), commonly referred to as "postmodernism." What seems to me to be erroneous, however, is to consider it as the inception of a new epoch of art. If late-modern art is that in which the malaise of modernity (toward which art itself becomes critical while searching for remedies and escape routes) begins to be felt, the postmodern is nothing but the last of these remedies. But for that very reason it is not a new epoch of art marking a leap beyond (or outside of) the modern. There is a substantial continuity that binds the remedy to the malady. Authorialism is a phenomenon engendered and nourished by the dialectic of modernity, but the remedies that late-modern art and literature conjured up to fight it do not constitute an exit from that dialectic. Nor do bound writings, nor does the search for grace, nor does the apocryphal effect. The postmodern does not therefore represent a true leap forward with respect to what it claims it has left behind, but rather a reaction (and, as we shall see, a pathological one) to the malaise of modernity.

The "late modernity" formula thus literally expresses my periodization hypothesis since the phenomena about which I am speaking, the postmodern included, really have to do with a late phase of modernity, not something that comes after it. As for the "postmodern," I shall use the term only to indicate that particular class of remedies, developed since the late sixties (comprising the apocryphal effect, the ironic distancing from the idea of creation, and that particular self-description of art that contemplates its death as if it had already taken place; see chapter 8), but which, despite its prefix, remains for us only a chapter of late modernity.

I said "*despite* its prefix," but it might be more accurate to say *because of* it. If one digs a little further into the term, there is something curious to be read there. "Postmodern" is a paradox. Or better, it is the linguistic incarnation of a double-bind, one of so many double-binds strewn across late modernity. The modern is an eternal present that keeps shifting with us; it is a kind of temporal deictic, like the adverb "now," to which it is etymologically related:[22] anyone can say he or she is modern, today just as one hundred years ago. Postmodern, thanks to its prefix, directly attacks this presumption of the modern as being on the crest of history's wave, and forever advancing with it. After "now" there will no longer be another "now." From now on, there will no longer be the possibility of saying "now" again. We come on the scene late, after the very possibility of saying that we exist "now," that we are "new," that we are "modern" has already been exhausted. That is the message that the term *postmodern* implicitly disseminates. Yet, for the very same reasons, the postmodern cannot even claim to have *superseded* the modern. If it were to do so, the postmodern would be revealed as a new movement, a new "now," equal in every way to those which have come and gone in the modern age, and so fall back into the same artistic logic from which it claims to distance itself. With this paradox inherent in its notion (only if it is not new is it new, but if it is new, then it really isn't, ad infinitum), the postmodern certainly does criticize the bad infinity of the modern, but at the same

22. The Italian *moderno* is derived from the Latin *modo*, meaning "right now." [trans.]

time, the former remains eternally prisoner to the latter. The double-bind enclosed in its name says it all: you can't go beyond the modern, since everything that goes beyond it is still modern.

Late-modern learning, as we shall come to ascertain, produces double-binds. And you can't get out of a double-bind until you jump out of its premises. If you search for a way out, you end up back where you began, the road still blocked off and more discouraged than ever, as in a labyrinth, which, moreover, is the guiding image of late modernity. Late modernity is a long series of attempts to escape a labyrinth which it has constructed, and from which, by definition, there is no exit (not, at any rate, by walking through it). The postmodern does not lie outside of this picture; it is a false exit out of the modernity from which it never succeeded in breaking away. But even worse, it is a pathological *adaptation* to such paradoxical conditions. Its special "contribution" has consisted in the euphoric elevation of everything that until then provoked fear and anguish: the death of art, the end of creation, our supposed condition of epigones. The myth of the author's death has played a pivotal role in all of this. Without it, the epigonal idea of literature, which theorized and "normalized" the labyrinth, transforming it into a steel-barred prison, turning its historical contingency into an irreversible destiny, could never have been elaborated. When will the postmodern end? Its very concept admits of no end. Thus, the postmodern can be considered as the traumatic arrival point of late-modernity: if it has calmed any anxieties, it is only through the idea that there is no way out, and there will never be one.

Authored Merchandise[23]

The artistic logic based on the author and on his or her supposed choices of poetics has caused trouble since early in the twentieth century. Even so, there remains one site in which it continues to function without hindrances or conflicts—the culture industry, which has incorporated authorialism into its own mechanisms. By making the author and his supposed poetics into an efficacious means of promotion, the culture industry does nothing but repeat, grotesquely amplified through its own circuits, those typically modern traits that contemporary art has become allergic to.

23. *Merci d'autore* in the Italian, which is to say, "high-quality merchandise." [trans.]

This, too, is in some ways an irony of history. The culture industry has appropriated that which originally was used by art as a way of opposing that very same industry. The category of "authored literature"[24] began with an oppositional function; specifically it stood in contrast to *feuilletons*, serial novels, the "lowbrow" literature produced for the public at large, degraded to an object of consumption. This concept thus stood in opposition to the products of the culture industry of that time. But if in the nineteenth century, "being authored" was a sufficient criterion to distinguish art from merchandise, by the time Adorno introduced the expression,[25] cultural merchandise was presenting novel characteristics. Every product, Adorno wrote in 1963, is offered as "individual," so that

> adopting Benjamin's designation of the traditional work of art by the concept of aura, the presence of that which is not present, the culture industry is defined by the fact that it does not strictly counterpose another principle to that of aura, but rather by the fact that it conserves the decaying aura as a foggy mist.[26]

The products of the spirit stylized by the culture industry were no longer, even then, merely mass-produced commodities, something which would later become even more obvious in the aestheticized merchandise of the post–Fordist era. Today's culture industry has changed a lot compared to that of the earlier era of mass production. In its sample case of products can be found not only serial novels or *telenovelas*;[27] nowadays there are *d'autore* products of all kinds, and of great prominence: *d'autore* stories, *d'autore* paintings, *auteur* films, *auteur* video. Indeed, one might almost say that what the industry promotes is above all else the author, his or her image, artistic project, artistic intention, "poetics."

It is often said that the postmodern has called into question the opposition between mass culture and elite culture. But it would be necessary

24. The Italian *letteratura d'autore* is similar to the English concept of "literature" according to its description as "artistic writings worthy of being remembered" (cf. *Random House Dictionary of the English Language*, 2d ed. unabridged, 1987). [trans.]

25. Adorno and Horkheimer 1947 introduced the expression "culture industry" as a substitute for "mass culture," which they judged to be false and mystificatory, insofar as it passed off as originating in the masses what instead is only a product imposed by commercial interests. (See also Adorno 1991, pp. 98–99.)

26. "The Culture Industry Reconsidered," conference held at the Internationale Rundfunk Universität der Hessischer Rundfunk in 1963; English translation by Anson G. Rabinbach in Adorno 1991, pp. 101–102.

27. *Telenovelas* is the Spanish word for televised soap operas. [trans.]

to add that the opposition has simultaneously been nullified by the art industry. Mass literature has incorporated its opposite: it can be "authored" just like so-called serious literature. And the latter, in turn, at times pretends to distinguish itself from that with which it now nearly coincides, by standing on the same pillar. Artistic institutions (museums, theater, literature) today no longer have the prerogative of being the designated site for aesthetic experience. On all sides the aesthetic can be experienced outside of art: in the media, on television, in advertisements, in fashion, in pop music, in the incessant spectacle of the metropolis. It is found above all in the myriad objects with which we enter into daily relation: cars, teakettles, watches, cookie packaging. In the postindustrial era, *styling* has entered the sphere of mass production, and the consumer has become an "appreciator" of its products. Today's consumer can enjoy the beautiful, or to put it better, the new, the *up-to-date*, the *trendy*, if not in art, at least in objects of consumption. But in the same context in which the aestheticization of the living world has dissolved the traditional confines of the aesthetic, the survival of art as a specific institution is more than ever guaranteed by the author-function. Thus we have on the one side authored merchandise (*merci d'autore*), like leather jackets, purses, or even coffee-makers bearing the signatures of world-renowned designers such as Yves St. Laurent, Calvin Klein, Giorgio Armani (and thereby endowed with value), while on the other we have fetishized authors and their fetishized works (*feticci d'autore*), like the latest book to hit the bestseller list due to the name-recognition of the author rather than the intrinsic value of the work itself.

CHAPTER 2

The Author without Genius

Carlos Argentino Daneri has an Aleph in his cellar. Despite that, or perhaps just because of it, he is a mediocre poet. Borges depicts him as intently at work on an endless poem, titled *La Tierra*, in which he would like to set down a description of the entire planet in verse. He reads several stanzas to a friend who is visiting for a completely unrelated purpose; the friend is bored but keeps it to himself. Nevertheless, in his enthusiasm for his own work, Daneri not only recites but also provides detailed commentary, illustrating for his listener the supposed qualities of each line. He points out, for example, how "the second [line] flows from Homer to Hesiod (generous homage, at the very outset, to the father of didactic poetry), not without rejuvenating a process whose roots go back to scripture—enumeration, congeries, conglomeration."[1]

The friend, whose name is Borges, and who is also the narrator of the story, silently listens to the poet's commentaries, which turn out to be much more sophisticated and complex than their object. And he comes to a surprising conclusion: the work of this poet does not consist in writ-

---

1. Borges 1970, p. 18. [Translator's note: In the story, the Aleph is described as "one of the points in space that contains all other points" and "the only place on earth where all places are—seen from every angle, each standing clear, without any confusion or blending." See Borges 1970, p. 23.]

ing stanzas, which are often merely the product of diligent labor, patience, and chance. His poetic work consists instead in attributing virtues to these stanzas, or rather, inventing them: "I saw, however, that Daneri's real work lay not in the poetry but in his invention of reasons why the poetry should be admired."[2]

Daneri writes mediocre verse, and so his self-commentaries make us smile. But we do not laugh at those of a poet such as Montale or of a writer such as Calvino, which are set down with philological scruple in the best editions of their works. Naturally, whether we are dealing with a mediocre or a great talent makes a difference, but in either case the phenomenon is the same. For the poet, there is a "secondary labor"; indeed, going by the slightly paradoxical formulation of Borges, the poet's work consists precisely in this. Furthermore, it should not be forgotten that this very same mediocre poet, as Borges informs us in the "Postscript" that closes the story, is later awarded the Second National Prize for Literature. Evidently, even the readers, critics, and juries who hand out literary prizes know how to "invent" the reasons why a poem may be considered admirable. This set of reasons why a work should be admired, that is, the conception which presumably contains within it the meaning and value of an artistic practice, is what we call poetics.

The Triumph of Poetics

Have you ever tried to do a totally silent reading of a sentence? It is next to impossible. The sounds of words follow right on their being read, even if only in a soundproof corner of the mind. And now try reading a contemporary literary text without asking yourself what meaning the author intended to convey through his work. Inevitably we pose ourselves certain questions. Why, for example, did he or she choose such an unusual form, or, on the contrary, why such an obvious and traditional one in comparison to the extravagant narratives that we have become accustomed to? The effort to suppress or ignore such thoughts is also nearly impossible. And yet with these simple queries you have already summoned up the mediation of poetics.

Try reading *If on a winter's night a traveler* without asking yourself why Calvino wrote a novel made up of ten beginnings of a novel which interrupt each other; or the later short stories of Gianni Celati without asking

2. Ibid., p. 19.

why he employs such a simple, minimalist style in them, almost that of oral storytelling. Then try reading a "cannibal"[3] without asking why it is so overloaded with foul language and devoid of verbs in the subjunctive mood, or why there are so many short paragraphs. For questions of this nature, there will always be someone capable of inventing a reasoned answer.[4] But whether that answer is provided or not, and whether it is the poet, the critic, or the reader who happens to provide it, what entails the specificity of modern artistic communication is its being mediated by such questions. Nonetheless, it is quite probable that such "secondary labor" would not exist for the poet, nor even for the critic, if it were not simultaneously going on in the mind of the reader as well: in other words, if it were not a necessity of artistic communication in general. Much more essential to modern art than the answers or the lack of answers, or answers that lead to endless disputes, is this continuous interrogation of the "reasons why a work is admirable," which is to say, the act of enquiring into its supposed poetics.

Poetics, in the very specific meaning that the word acquired in the twentieth century, is the program that guides individual artistic practice, that is, that set of reasons that motivates an author or a group of authors to choose a certain form of expression rather than another. These reasons often touch on the most crucial problems: the relations between language and reality, between art and society, between art and artistic institutions. Let us take, for example, the definition that Umberto Eco once provided, which can be of immediate use to us here (although we will have to reexamine it shortly). For Eco, "poetics" meant "the operational program that the artist proposes from one time to the next, the project of the work to be done as the artist explicitly or implicitly intends it." According to Eco, poetics can be implicit or explicit. An example of an explicit poetics is that exhibited by the avant-garde movements in their manifestoes, or in the "declarations expressed by artists (e.g., Verlaine's *L'Art poétique* or Maupassant's preface to *Pierre et Jean*)." In contrast, those that critics and readers squeeze out of closely read texts are im-

---

3. A contemporary trend of Italian fiction marked by innovative techniques and a narrative voice that often cynically or naively records the brutalities of daily life.

4. For example, Cesare Segre reviews Aldo Nove's *Puerto Plata Market* in this way: "The abuse of foul language (which ends up deprived of any effect due to its mechanical repetition), the abolition of subjunctives, the juxtaposition of sentences without apparent logic, are all charged to the account of its youthful style. And yet, a style is exactly what it is, and one is in fact able to catch even more refined aspects of it. . . . And I would above all mention the knowing use of the short paragraph, with its effect of suspension and surprise, and always of expansion" (*Corriere della Sera*, January 20, 1999).

plicit, just like the poetics of the open work, which Umberto Eco reconstructed in his book on that subject, deriving it from "an analysis of the structures of the work, so that through examining the way in which the work was made, one might deduce how it was intended to be made."[5]

But what the manuals do not mention is that poetics has by now become the indispensable mediation to the act of enjoying a work of art. It constitutes that complex of "reasons why the poetry is admirable," as the result of that "secondary labor" that develops around the texts, and which, like an unknown in an algebraic equation, we must calculate in order to be able to "admire" the work. So it should come as no surprise that critical essays and treatises as well as book reviews and debates on literature increasingly concern the poetics that a work embodies. Endless examples of this phenomenon could be provided. I will only mention here the debate that took place from the end of the 1980s to the early 1990s over Gruppo 93, a gathering of writers, mostly poets, who identified themselves, or were identified by others, through their adherence to a common poetics. Their chosen name itself proposed such a poetics; it suggested, no matter how problematically, a continuity with the early-twentieth-century avant-garde, from which, one generation before, Gruppo 63 had claimed its own descent.[6]

The debate took the form of a long series of inquiries into this supposed continuity. Granting such a continuity existed, how was the poetics of Gruppo 93 to be appropriately modified in order to fit in with what

5. Eco 1962, p. 18. [The English translation does not include the preface by Eco, from which the citations are drawn.] It is worth recalling that within the sphere of Italian literary criticism, the notion of "poetics," which had been effectively liquidated by Croce, was brought back into vogue by Walter Binni (1947) in order to account for a "heroic Leopardi," different from the "idyllic" figure proposed as the sole line of interpretation by criticism until that time. Crocean criticism, just like that inspired by romanticism, was capable of understanding the unity of a poetic production only as the expression of personality, which could not be doubled or tripled. Thanks to the notion of poetics, however, Binni was able to maintain that one and the same personality "can realize itself at different moments in different expressions of poetics." The critical and theoretical utility of the notion was discussed by Binni in a subsequent essay (1963), with a brief reference to Riegl's *Kunstwollen* and the line of thought that runs from Poe to Valéry. In addition, there was Luigi Pareyson, who in the early fifties spoke of poetics as the "idea of art" which can be "implicit in the style of the author or in the taste of the reader, or laid out in a concrete and specific artistic program, expressed in manifestoes or treatises or normative codes" (Pareyson 1954, p. 310). See also Anceschi 1962.

6. Gruppo 63 was a movement of writers, poets and academics including Elio Pagliarani, Alfredo Giuliani, Edoardo Sanguineti, Nanni Balestrini, Antonio Porta, Luciano Anceschi, Umberto Eco, Angelo and Guido Guglielmi, Renato Barilli, and Enrico Filippini, who shared a critical stance vis-à-vis the dominant literary tradition of the 1950s. It is viewed as the birth of the Italian "neo–avant garde."

the poets and narrators had been doing thirty years earlier? Were they to
be satisfied with the (by then) classic "poetics of rupture," of the type
that breaks linguistic codes, involves the mixture of heterogeneous languages, and so produces a kind of expressionism (the perfectly golden
expressionism endorsed by Gianfranco Contini and well received by the
academy!); or were they to stick with the mere reference to Benjamin and
allegory, or to Bakhtin and polyphony? Some Gruppo 93 writers, and
critics involved with them, mourned the exhaustion of those earlier poetics. And then the main question became how to respond to new technologies, to the commodification of art and to the aestheticization of
commodities, which have profoundly changed social languages. Was it
preferable to continue down the path trod by the previous avant-gardes
(transgression, the mixing together of heterogeneous forms, compulsion
for the new), even if at the risk of being mere followers? Or was it better
to change direction, break out, if possible, from the dialectic of modernity, in order to head toward a "critical postmodernism" that acknowledges the impossibility of proposing anything genuinely new, while
maintaining a responsible critical attitude in regard to the existing state
of reality?[7] In any case, it is clear that whoever declares the road of the
avant-garde to be impracticable cannot help summoning up the role of
poetics. And herein lies the catch, since that entire debate was really an
exaltation of the role of poetics, and in no way an abandonment of it.

The Artist and the Label Pusher

Following the current debates one also notices another phenomenon:
poetics not only legitimizes a literary production by making the act of
enjoying the work possible, but has also now become a means of promoting that production.[8] In contemporary artistic communication there
is a great demand for pigeonholing "categorizations," the framing of the
writer within (or against) a particular personal or historical trend. And
where there is demand, there must also be supply. Thus we find the appearance of a new figure, one which we might call the vendor, or pusher

7. The lines of this debate, which were developed through conferences and maga-
zines (among which were *Baldus, Altri luoghi, Campo, L'immaginazione, L'anello che non
tiene, Le voci della poesia*), can be retraced in D'Oria 1992.

8. Thus, for example, the poets of Gruppo 93 took a stand against the work of poets
such as Giuseppe Conte and others close to him, and the latter, in turn, continued to oppose the Gruppo 93 line. Out of the *querelle* each side drew its own "differential advantage," which is to say, self-legitimation and promotion.

of poetics. It is not so much the writers who are doing the pushing as it is the critics and theoreticians. They are selling a particular product that serves to valorize and to promote artistic products. This phenomenon is not new in the visual arts (Bonito Oliva and his invention of the "trans-avant-garde" comes to mind). In the more modest market of poetry there are those who have tried their luck at cooking up labels and anthologies for promotional purposes, such as "poets in love," "poets of the contra-diction," "poets of the third wave," right up to the more recent and suc-cessful "cannibal youth," launched by a division of Einaudi, as well as through an anthology bearing the same title.[9]

But what is to be said about poets and narrators who allow them-selves to be categorized by others? At a conference in Reggio Emilia ("63/93: Thirty Years of Literary Research") in April 1993, Nanni Balestrini touched a sore spot with his reprimand aimed at the younger writers; it went something like this: "We in Gruppo 63 worked out our theory on our own. You, on the other hand, depend on the support of critics and theoreticians who do not belong to your generation." What has brought about this new division of labor, this recourse to outside the-oreticians? Surely one explanation for the phenomenon has to do with the need for promotion. But there is also something else involved here. Recent literary production has argued its way into a curious impasse: on one side it has need of a poetics in order to be recognized and accepted; on the other, however, it is unable to produce its own proper manifesto without thereby falling back into the worn-out dialectic of modernity. That is why it cannot do what Balestrini would like it to do: create a the-ory that legitimizes itself. It is precisely in the rejection of a strong poet-ics, one that is encompassing and self-proposed, that many contempo-rary writers indirectly express their strong unease in the face of the mechanisms of modern art. Thus, for example, Tommaso Ottonieri, a poet and narrator who was initially, though not so easily, "categorized" as belonging to Gruppo 93, criticized the logic of "positioning" that ani-mated even his own literary companions and proposed instead a "per-spective of nonmembership."[10]

Outside of Italy too there are innumerable examples of allergic reac-tions to being categorized and labeled. Raymond Carver, considered by some to be the leader of American minimalist writing, stubbornly re-

---

9. Cf. for example the anthologies *Terza ondata* (Bettini and Di Marco 1993) and *Gioventù cannibale* (Brolli 1996).
10. Cf. Ottonieri 1994.

fused such a label; and so have David Leavitt, Jay McInerney, Bret Easton Ellis. Artists don't like being categorized or defined. In their relations with critics, who are typically the dispensers of labels, writers seem to have developed an ambivalent attitude, made up of dependence on one side and intolerance on the other. At times the mixture ends up in outright belligerence, as was the case at Brown University in 1988, during a conference that brought the greatest representatives of American postmodernism face-to-face with various critics who were "specialists" in the work of those authors. At that meeting William Gass bitterly attacked the deconstructionists; Stanley Elkin declared in a spirit of provocation that he wrote only for Faulkner; and Robert Coover, the organizer of the event, concluded by remarking that while novelists hope critics will read their work, they never bother to read the work of the critics.[11]

I cannot think of similar confrontations having occurred among Italian writers (who are perhaps somewhat more docile toward label-pushing critics), not even at the conferences in Reggio Emilia, where it was (and still is) common practice to put critics face-to-face with writers, for direct, rapid-fire exchanges. However, there have been some individual expressions of impatience in Italy as well, both among visual artists[12] and writers, some of which have even taken the form of short stories or poems.[13]

This kind of rejection of poetics on the part of artists is, nevertheless, inevitably impotent and paradoxical since even a "nonpoetics" can be

11. This episode is described in Couturier 1995, p. 18.

12. For example, Gino De Dominicis, who won first prize for painting at the Bisannuel de Paris in 1985, refused to exhibit some of his works at the XLVI Biennale di Venezia in 1995 (directed by Jean Clair) because he was annoyed by the "mediations" and by the "protagonism" of the critics who organized the Big Exhibits "as if they were the product of their own work" ("Signori critici accomodetevi fuori," interview given to La Repubblica, April 12, 1995).

13. For example, Silvia Ballestra's story Gli orsi (63–93) (1994) ridicules some of the critics and organizers of the Reggio Emilia conference. As insulting as they may be, these expressions remain, nonetheless, at the surface of the phenomenon. There is no comparison between them and the radicalism of Antonio Moresco's Lettere a nessuno (1997), in which the author, an anomalous and uncategorizable writer, has succeeded in making visible the graveyard role played by critics and mediators, as the guardians of what already exists. He refers to this literary establishment (critics, publishers, et al.) as a "bloc of editorial-literary-publicity powers, the custodian of horizontality and irrelevance" (p. 251). A book both tragic and regenerative, Lettere a nessuno has opened up a breach in the ideologies that dominate contemporary culture. Even though Moresco's writing is not discussed in these pages, the fissure cut by him in the late-modern labyrinth (through which he has pushed himself far beyond the phenomena described here) has stimulated my thinking on several things I have written about.

received as a poetics. Take Celati's case: in strongly criticizing every "strategic" aspect of writing, he ended up proposing, centered on the notion of reserve[14] (which is poles apart from every programmatic practice), a true and proper poetics of the short story. Though less noisy than others, it is still consistent and purposeful, as is apparent in the number of writers who recognized themselves in it.[15] In contemporary literary and artistic production, then, more and more often we are witnessing a curious circle, one of the many double binds that ensnare late modernity: on one hand, poetics is rejected, while on the other, one can never really do without it.

Then there are the writers who religiously dedicate themselves to "nonpoetics," though with a comic self-contradictory gesture (which is not always deliberate), they end up espousing this choice in programmatic declarations, exactly as if it were a question of poetics. One example of this is the so-called "return to narrative," of which Vittorio Tondelli has doubtlessly been the most representative figure, especially given his editorial initiatives (the "Under 25" project, several anthologies compiled by him, and the founding of the review *Panta*). This phenomenon never had as its unifying moment a poetics in the true sense of the word. What brought together and identified those writers sufficiently for them to be perceived as a "group" was not an operational program (how to write, which formula to use to express what kind of intentions), but the mere fact of belonging to the same generation. Thus was born the category of "young writers." That writers and artists of a similar age should form themselves into a group is nothing new; attributing a special value to this bare fact certainly is. Both the futurists and the writers of Gruppo 63 identified with a common program, not a common date of birth. Now, however, after the collapse of poetics, it turns out that the "new" is sought for in a bit of census data. The generational fact, in short, is displayed *in place of* poetics, as the artists' strong identifying trait.

14. *Narratori delle riserve* or "Narrators of the reserves" is the formula used by writer Gianni Celati to refer to his poetics. In Italian, the word *riserva* can suggest a variety of meanings, similar to those associated with the words "reserve" or "reservation" in English, and Celati plays with this multiplicity of possibilities. [trans.]

15. Celati first explicitly sketched the lines of that poetics in his column entitled *Narratori delle riserve* in the daily newspaper *il manifesto* from 1988 to 1989. That title was then used for the anthology which Celati edited for Feltrinelli (Celati 1992). Although he furnished the book with a short introductory note, there were few traces of the ideas on fiction that he had laid out in his column. His poetics, which had been a prominent feature in the newspaper writings, was now tellingly reduced to the level of the implicit.

Yet there is also something paradoxical about such a substitution since if it is true that in this way one can avoid the irremediably ideological component of every poetics (which late modernity now perceives as something bothersome and paralyzing),[16] it is also true that the idea of "generation," to the degree that it legitimates a literary operation, functions exactly like a poetics. After decades of the antinovel, after the ostracism of the neo-avant-garde, fiction had to be relegitimized in some manner, and it was accomplished by calling on the generational voice,[17] the supposed bearer of a particular experience, which has value in and of itself. Back in the 1960s, writers such as Calvino and Pier Paolo Pasolini, even though they had been formed under the banner of a "strong," ideologized poetics, found their own voices through the process of settling accounts with the unsustainability of poetics, understood as an individuating stylistic formula capable of giving meaning and legitimacy to their activity of writing. But if in Calvino and Pasolini (and again in Celati) the collapse of poetics is the consequence of a tragic "apprenticeship," which at the same time expresses a criticism in the face of modern artistic logic, in the narrators of the 1980s, this fact has already become an undisputed given, which itself can even be exploited just like a true and proper poetics.

The rejection of poetics on the part of writers and artists is therefore not enough to cancel out the strong role of mediation implicit in the processes of valorizing art. Literary communication these days is a second-level communication. Not only artistic practice but the act of enjoyment itself contains an implicit reflection on literature. And it will not be so easy to remove it from this position by mere declarations of principle, by exalting the sensible, immediately enjoyable aspects of texts, or pure narration, as many authors and critics do today.

Reflectivity of Art

The triumph of poetics has a long history. One might go so far as to call poetics the emblematic sign of modernity. However, in this regard it should not be the avant-garde manifestoes that come to mind first. These

16. "There is no traditional ideology, nor a specific notion of commitment or militancy, that underlies the project of *Panta*" reads the editorial that introduces the first issue of the review (1990, p. 5).

17. "*Panta* is put together by a group of authors whose belonging to the same generation is expressed in their refound faith in fiction" (ibid.).

played less of a role than is often imagined. Romantic art was already, as Benjamin observed, completely penetrated by the *medium* of reflection to such a degree that for the romantics the consciousness of poetry is itself poetry.[18] It is this reflectiveness, which, moreover, had already been noted by Schiller and Hegel, wherein lies the caesura that cleanly separates modern from ancient and classical art. What comes after this break is what I call *reflective art* or *second-level art*. In this type of art, poetics acquires the strong role that I have been describing, and, along with it, the author-function.

From the nineteenth century up to our own times a proliferation of poetics and artistic ideologies has invaded the sphere of literature and art. From time to time there are those who start to worry about and decry it: might not poetics kill off poetry? Benedetto Croce instigated this pattern of behavior with his condemnation of the "most miserable manifestation of literary life, which are the programs . . . of [literary] schools and circles."[19] Today's proponents of the humanistic values of art continue the lament with equal apprehension. For them, poetics is a kind of extraneous body, growing out of the fabric of art like a cancer. What their point of view misses is that poetics, on the contrary, has really turned into a true and proper organ of art, with its own vital function. It is now the mediation required for conferring artistic value on the products of modern art. Nor has Croce's call for the "good rule," according to which, the important thing to search for is not what the poet may have wanted to do or claimed to be doing, but what he or she poetically does,[20] proved to be of much value. As the subsequent history of art has demonstrated, it is precisely that "wanted to do," which the reader presumes to have guided the artist, that is most often sought for in literature. It is sought for to such a degree that the theory of art has even coined the notion of "implicit poetics," extending the "wanted to do" to the point of comprising a kind of unconscious or nonreflective intention. Thus, where manifestoes and proclamations are absent, it is the critics and readers who reconstruct (or better, attribute to the author) the idea of art which they suppose has guided an artistic production.

We can still derive some useful observations from those anxieties, old and new. The reason for so many condemnatory words is that poetics has truly placed a certain idea of art in a state of crisis, the idea that

18. Benjamin 1920.
19. Croce 1952, p. 256.
20. Croce 1936, p. 306. English translation, p. 187.

eighteenth-century aesthetics has accustomed us to considering the only one possible. What poetics destroys is the idea of poetry based on the sensible values (i.e., those related to the five senses) of the artistic text, those values that could become the object of *aesthetic* experience (in the sense of *aisthesis*), those on which the judgment of taste was formerly based. In modern times, the importance accorded to programmatic practice, and to the idea of poetry that poetry embodies, comes into competition with those earlier sensible values, nearly claiming to supplant them altogether. With his attack on poetics, Croce was merely defending an idea of poetry that was already worn-out, if not altogether dead. Thus the anxieties over the presumed death of art speak of the triumph of poetics, long perceived as a threat. Since the early nineteenth century, when Hegel prophesied an end of art, the formula has been repeated in various ways by more than a few mournful souls.[21] And yet art has never died, and perhaps, never will. Which leads us to inverting the perspective from which these phenomena are usually viewed: the triumph of poetics is not the death of art, but rather the manner in which art in the modern era has reacted to the risk of dying. Threatened in its sensible aspect, art turned toward a more sophisticated game, one played out on the second level, based on the search for the new, the rotation of poetics, and the ascendancy of the concept.

Moreover, if one takes the trouble to examine Hegel's arguments a bit more closely, it turns out that he did not declare the death of art in general, as is sometimes believed, but only the passing of a certain form of art that has "the vocation of revealing the truth in the form of sensuous artistic shape," the form given full expression in classical art.[22] Modern art is no longer an art in which truth can "come to light in sensuousness." Something else has been superimposed on the "immediate enjoyment" of the sensuous appearance of art, which was the prerogative of classicism. The impression that works of art give us nowadays, Hegel wrote, "is of a more considered kind." It is precisely this more meditative quality that was to profoundly change art, separating the modern from the classical.

21. For literature, the last death certificate was issued by Ferroni 1996 (*Dopo la fine*). Cf. also Danto 1992, which in the French translation bears an analogous title (*Après la fin de l'art*), but which unlike Ferroni, offers observations on the Hegelian theme of the end of art that are less melancholy and more theoretically useful.

22. Hegel 1836; Italian translation, p. 66 (from which also come the following citations, pp. 15 and 16). Partial English translation by Bernard Bosanquet in Hegel 1970, pp. 87, 32, 33, 34.

What is the nature of that deeper consideration active in modern art? Hegel describes it as a thought and a reflection that come to mediate both creation and the act of enjoyment:

> Thought and reflection have taken their flight above fine art. Those who delight in grumbling and censure may set down this phenomenon for a corruption. . . . However all this may be, it certainly is the case that art no longer affords that satisfaction of spiritual wants which earlier epochs and peoples have sought therein, and have found therein only; a satisfaction which, at all events on the religious side, was most intimately and profoundly connected with art. The beautiful days of Greek art and the golden time of the later Middle Ages are gone by. The reflective culture of our life of today makes it a necessity for us, in respect of our will no less than of our judgment, to adhere to general points of view and to regulate particular matters according to them.[23]

In the execution of art, the artist is thus led to "putting more abstract thought into his works" in response to "the reflection which finds utterance all round him and the universal habit of having an opinion and passing judgment on art." Meanwhile, on the side of enjoyment, the way in which we approach works of art has changed: "We subject the content and the means of representation of the work of art and the suitability or unsuitability of the two to our intellectual consideration," so that art no longer arouses our pure immediate enjoyment, but also our judgment. Hegel concludes that "the science of art" is therefore a much more pressing need in our times than it was in previous epochs. Art invites us to meditation.[24]

What I call the "mediation of poetics" is nothing more than the radicalization of the phenomenon described by Hegel. Poetics is an idea of literature "incorporated" into the work, in the light of which, the work demands to be enjoyed and evaluated. Poetics is the conceptual mediation that allows the reader to approach the text as something endowed with artistic value. And it is not merely a matter of a reflection on art that orients our judgment, but a reflection of art on itself, a self-reflection required of every work in order to be able to justify its own artistic claim. It is a self-reflection of which the author becomes the perspectival center. An approach to texts is no longer possible without a reference to poetics,

23. Hegel 1970, pp. 32–33.
24. Ibid., pp. 33–34.

implicit or explicit, conscious or unconscious, which renders the single work artistically meaningful, and consequently, it is no longer possible without a reference to the author, who is presumed to be the subject of such a poetics.

Over and Over Again

The term *poetics* originally had a rather different meaning from that which it has acquired in modernity: neither Aristotle's *Poetics,* nor Horace's *Ars poetica* contemplated the projective aspect of the individual artist or group of artists. Such semantic slippage with respect to the classical denotation is already significant in itself, an indication of the advent of new processes in the universe of artistic communication. It will therefore be worthwhile to briefly examine this point.

In his *Course in Poetics: First Lesson,* Valéry wrote that "poetics" concerns artistic practice, the *poiein* that is realized in certain works.[25] From this point of view, one might be led to believe that the term has not changed meaning over the centuries. All considered, Aristotle, in explaining how a tragedy was made, what its style and subject were, what effect (catharsis) it produced on the spectator, was also furnishing an "operational program" for the construction of tragedies. The same can be said of Umberto Eco, who, in the pages where he defines poetics as an "operational program," maintains that he is using the concept in a sense closely "tied to the classical denotation." Theory, which is often inclined to the metahistorical use of notions, does not seem to take into account the abyss that separates today's meaning of poetics with that of antiquity. Aristotle had before him a literary genre with its own specific constraints: the "operational program" that he set down for tragedy thus remained a common program, a shared program. In contrast, modern poetics defines the operational program of the single artist (or of a group of artists, or even of a particular phase in the work of an artist), in its specificity and difference with respect to other artists (or groups or phases). When we speak today of "neo-realist poetics," of a "neo-Leopardian poetics," or of a "poetics of the open work," what we are doing really is valorizing the individuating and differential aspect of each single operation, with an implicit or explicit reference to the relative posi-

25. Valéry 1952.

tion that it assumes with respect to other *poiein,* to other embodiments of artistic practice, past or present.

This change is not insignificant. Above all, it presupposes other concomitant mutations having occurred in the modern artistic system. In a literature bound by the laws of genre, it would not be possible to conceive "poetics" in this individuating and differentiating sense. Moreover, that type of literature would not even have needed to valorize individual poetics to such a degree. Modern poetics, however, presupposes the possibility of choosing one form of expression in preference to another, which is to say that it enjoys relative freedom from the common grammar (as formerly constituted by genre, see chapter 4); it implies that a common grammar no longer even exists. Each individual poetics substitutes for what the common grammar used to be, and that is what makes poetics indispensable to modern artistic communication. Every modern work always re-poses the same question: what makes this text a work of art? And it is a question that each successive text must answer again and again. Every text is obliged to furnish the elements with which to justify its artistic claim. Or better, every text, in order to be appreciated, is interrogated reflectively, so as to draw from it that "concept of itself" which justifies it and renders it enjoyable as literature. The "meditation" that Hegel talked about, which was imposed over immediate enjoyment, is concentrated in the question that the modern reader can no longer do without asking in the act of reading a piece of literature: "What project has guided the artist in the act of composing this text?" or better, "What idea of literature justifies this text's claim to be considered a work of art?" In a literature where there no longer exists a strong and binding common grammar, approaching the texts is no longer possible without a reference to the individual poetics, implicit or explicit, conscious or unconscious, that renders the single work artistically meaningful.

Anticipatory Poetics

So far the common denotation of poetics has been useful for the purpose of posing the problem, but beyond this point of our analysis it reveals its limitations and imprecision. Poetics is not only the "operational program that time after time the artist proposes to himself," and which he has followed consciously (or not). It is also a supposed program, a project that the reader assumes to be at the origin of the work, and that he or she goes in search of at the moment of reading, picking it up through the traces that it has left in the text. Unlike the way it is usually understood, poetics is for us the product of an attribution on the part of the person experiencing the work of art. Whether or not it is really operative on the part of the artist or whether the artist has or has not made it explicit, poetics is above all else a necessity of reading, inherent in the mechanisms of modern enjoyment. It is the conceptual mediation that inevitably interposes itself between the modern reader and the work.

A bizarre corollary can be drawn from the above: even though they are more visible and showy, so-called explicit poetics are a secondary phenomenon. The primary phenomenon, that which leads us to speak of poetics as the indispensable mediation to modern art, does not reside in the declarations made by artists, nor in the programmatic manifestoes that were widespread mostly among early-twentieth-century avant-gardes. While it is probable that art theory began to use the notion in the modern acceptation in response to these more macroscopic phenomena, the role of poetics (that special act of reflection which characterizes all modern art and is consubstantial to it) precedes the advent of such phenomena and can actually be considered completely separate from it.

If an explicit poetics is not the primary phenomenon, there were nonetheless reasons for its appearance in the artistic communication of the twentieth century. It is a phenomenon loaded with meanings that have perhaps not been sufficiently brought to light as of yet. Today it seems normal to us to come across programmatic declarations; with our bifocal lenses, we have learned to look at the work and its program at the same time. But in the years when the avant-garde manifestoes first began to circulate, the phenomenon (as Croce's condemnation of those manifestoes demonstrates) had to have been quite upsetting. The avant-garde artist, in a showy and provocational manner, displayed for all to see the existence of a poetics within artistic practice. Above all, he displayed it in advance, paradoxically setting down the artistic project before the work. Usually it takes some time to grasp the "meaning" of innovative works and to be able to define their poetics; more than anything else, it requires the "secondary labor" of readers (or viewers) and critics.[26] With the avant-garde, however, it is the artist himself or herself who preannounces the reasons why the work is admirable. Thus, "prospection" takes the place of "retrospection." Poetics, in the form of a

26. For Shklovsky, the formulation of a poetics concludes the process of creation (see chapter 5).

manifesto, no longer concludes but rather precedes the poetic construction. In the act of providing the "recipe for the work," there is already a polemical attitude toward the modern artistic logic that had demolished the concept of genius. Whereas previously the author's choices and his or her supposed intentionality were attributed to the artist by the reader/viewer (as the mode for approaching and understanding the meaning of the work), now the artist reacts in advance of those attributions, with a kind of counter-attribution provocatively launched against the act of enjoyment (and criticism). Whereas a work's poetics once might have been attributed to the author as something semiconscious, or in any case unreflected, now those choices are displayed by the artist in their quality of being conscious, reflective choices, ones which have even been elaborated verbally, as a true and proper strategy for the work. There could not have been any stronger denunciation of the obsolescence of the concept of genius, nor of the demise of a certain kind of enjoyment of literature based on the sensual and "corporeal" aspects of works. With the appearance of the avant-gardes, the war of poetics is no longer fought out within the corpus of the artist's works, but on the field of poetics itself. Like certain science fiction stories, the battle has become symbolic rather than physical, fought out by means of robotic weaponry. And, perhaps, as often happens amidst such provocational gestures, genius has succeeded in engineering its comeback in the guise of a negative epic, even in an epoch in which everything was aimed at destroying it.

Thus, contrary to what the manuals of literary criticism might say, it does matter whether poetics is implicit or explicit. Between the two modalities there is an essential difference, both in terms of history and in terms of the attitude toward the institution of art. The poetics displayed in declarations or manifestos implies thereby a critical and desecrating attitude toward the mechanisms of modern art: it already implies that deutero-learning which is characteristic of the late-modern period.

Aisthesis and Noesis

Late modernity is in many ways the reign of antiphrasis and of elaborations that attempt to compensate for the loss of "genius" and the sense that creation is no longer possible. Even as artistic communication is placing so much emphasis on poetics, voices are being raised in all quarters that sing the praises of the sensual aspects of poetry, of an aesthetic experience based on the values of beauty, and on identity and catharsis.[27] Yet no matter how much is said and done to defend the immediate enjoyment of texts, modern enjoyment is inevitably marked by a conceptual type of mediation. The literature that to all appearance places its trust in the "eternal regions" of the senses has itself undergone a process of conceptualization brought about by the very mechanisms of modern art. The enjoyment of art no longer descends immediately from aesthetic pleasure, from the enjoyment of the harmony of form, or of the harmonization of form and content, or from the other sensual qualities of texts. Furthermore, most modern works have abandoned this ideal of beauty. The ugly, the discordant, the slipshod, the casual can just as well aspire to being valorized artistically *as long as there is a poetics* capable of giving them an artistic meaning, as, for example, a certain idea of realism, or of expressionism, or of alienation, or of experimentation.

However, there is an even more striking phenomenon in which one can more accurately measure the import of the process of conceptualization. Harmony and beauty are far from having been banished once and for all. Even these can aspire to an artistic value as long as they are inserted into an idea of literature that justifies them, that is, into a poetics that renders them *once again* necessary, such as, for example, a revalorization of the classical after a dominant tendency has long devalued it. All of which goes to show that every artistic practice, even that which in appearance appeals solely to the suggestiveness of the form, can only be appreciated in reflection.

The process of conceptualization involved in modern literature thus renders inadequate any valuation based exclusively on the sensual values of texts. For this reason I prefer to speak of *artistic* value rather than of *aesthetic* value. These two adjectives, often used as synonyms, are here instead considered as distinct. The first is for me more general because it indicates that which pertains to art independent of the modality with

---

27. A systematic attempt to "refound" the esthetic experience, weakened both by the tendencies of modern art and so-called negative aesthetics (like Adorno's), was made by Jauss, who articulates it in the three categories of *poiesis*, *aisthesis*, and *katharsis*. In particular, the moment of *katharsis* and identification, which Adorno had liquidated as a "crude" relation with the work (exploited by the culture industry), instead returns as fundamental for the aesthetics of reception insofar as it makes an "experience of the world through the eyes of others" possible to the reader (cf. Jauss 1982, p. 95 passim). But see also Jauss 1972, Bubner 1989, and Marquard 1989.

which it is valorized and recognized; in contrast, "aesthetic" indicates a particular modality of valorization based on *aisthesis*, and codified by eighteenth-century aesthetics through philosophical reflection on the beautiful. This latter modality (modeled on classical art, or rather on that which eighteenth-century aesthetics identified as typical of classical art), no matter how universal it was thought to be, cannot exhaust all the modalities of existence of modern art.[28] Therefore, both to indicate reflection on art in general, and the sphere of problems it deals with, we shall speak of the *theory of art* rather than *aesthetics*, reserving the latter term only for that particular theory of art that founds itself on aesthetic value and which, since the eighteenth century, has surreptitiously posed as valid in general.

The process of conceptualization of modern art is somewhat more evident in the visual arts, where the physical and visual qualities of a painting, or the visual rendering of certain forms and colors, are no longer what artistic value is exclusively based on. I am not referring so much to what is properly called conceptual art, which developed in the 1960s as a movement or space on the edge of artistic research. Nor am I only speaking of avant-garde art. It is obvious that one would not have been able to appreciate the artistic value of a cubist painting without reference to the idea of art that it embodied. But the same is true for a painting by Carrà, or other artists who, after the avant-garde movements, called for a return to "plastic values." No matter how much more immediately enjoyable, even these values could not be appreciated artistically except if grasped through the mediation of their (implicit) poetics, which valorized and legitimized them insofar as they represented a "call to order," thus making them stand out as differential values, "restored" after the destruction of the avant-gardes. As Kosuth wrote in 1969, "All art (after Duchamp) is conceptual (in nature) because art exists only con-

---

28. While remaining faithful to the scheme of eighteenth-century aesthetics, Genette maintains that the aesthetic is more general than the artistic: the "artistic function" of a work is for him only a particular case (specific to art) of the "aesthetic relation," and the latter can obtain with respect to any object, even those of nature (cf. Genette 1994 and 1997). But this is not the only reason why, at least for the purposes of our inquiry, Genette's conceptual framework is unusable. Though defining "artistic function" as "intentional aesthetic function," and thus encapsulating intentionality in the very definition of art, Genette interrogates neither the historicity of the phenomenon (which for us is tied to modern art), nor what his own definition implies: which is to say, the attribution of that intention to a subject. Thus, the problem of the author continues to be dismissed even in his theory.

ceptually."[29] The specificity of what we call conceptual art at most consists in its having attained an awareness of this phenomenon, and in
having critically demonstrated the conceptual nature of all modern art.

Contemporary literature, even if in a less deafening way, has not es-
caped this process of conceptualization. Here, too, there have been practices analogous to what the conceptual movement in the visual arts was,
which is to say practices of writing that display and exploit the conceptual nature inherent in modern literature while giving the lie to the
melancholic museum custodians who bewail the now "posthumous"
state of art.

Conceptual Literature

Borges's first short story was a kind of book review or critical essay on a
nonexistent novel, attributed to the likewise nonexistent lawyer, Mir Ba-
hadur Alì of Bombay. The story's Spanish title is "El acercamiento a Al-
motásim," which is also the title of the English language novel ("The Approach to Al-Mu'tasim") on which Borges pretends to comment. This
novel was supposed to have been published in 1932, that is, three years
before the short story, which was published in 1935. As Borges recalls in
a foreword to *Ficciones*, the text (published originally by the review *Sur*
in 1940) was taken for a real essay. And, indeed, similar to many critical
essays, it starts off by reporting the opinion of another critic; it then
weighs the possibility of considering the novel at hand as a combination
of allegorical poem and detective mystery; it goes on to describe the protagonist, gradually allowing an outline of the plot to emerge; finally, it
even discusses the possible sources used by the author. Borges would return to the formula of a story presenting itself as an academic treatment
of a nonexistent work (for example, "An Examination of the Work of
Herbert Quain," or "Pierre Menard, Author of Don Quijote," which are
also included in *Ficciones*) so often that it became the Borgesian formula
par excellence. He provides a rather telling justification of it:

> The composition of vast books is a laborious and impoverishing extrava-
> gance. To go on for five hundred pages developing an idea whose perfect
> oral exposition is possible in a few minutes! A better course of procedure

29. Kosuth 1996/1990, p. 18.

is to pretend that these books already exist, and offer a resumé of them, a commentary.[30]

It is out of the work of Borges that John Barth came up with his idea of "the literature of exhaustion": a literature that has almost completely exhausted the possibilities for innovation. The "fictions" of Borges are, according to Barth, not only footnotes on the pages of imaginary texts, but also "postscripts to the true corpus of literature," which is already over and done with.[31] In other words, it is a way of representing the death of literature, an event which is assumed to have already taken place. This is not the only instance in which someone has wanted to deduce an irreversible "destiny" from the work of the Argentine writer (whose work incorporates, like few others, the magic tricks of late modernity; see chapter 8). But if we look more closely into Borges's work, we realize that what others read as the death of literature can just as well be viewed as its rebirth: one particular way of telling a story is simply substituted by another.

"The Approach to Al-Mu'tasim" can actually be considered the emblem of second-level literature. It is not simply a text that comments on a text that is not there: it is the comment on a work that takes the place of the work, the comment on a work that can also only exist in thought, and whose "factuality" is unnecessary. Or rather, it is the concept of a work that takes the place of the work, a work that also can only be imagined. In his compositional idea Borges has grasped, or better, has availed himself of and exploited artistically, a fundamental aspect of modern literature: the concreteness of the work, its factuality, its sensuous beauty, all those things from which aesthetic pleasure was traditionally derived (as even the word *aesthetic* reveals in its etymology), may remain inactive. In their place there is a sort of intellectualized extract of the work, on which artistic enjoyment is based. The meaning of the work that the commentary provides constitutes the work; or rather, the meaning of the work that the imagination projects is the work. From whichever side we take it, that of artistic projection or that of commentary, which is to say, that of creation or that of enjoyment, what stands out is in any case the role accorded to the *meaning* of the work, that meaning which can be extracted from literary works as an essence, and which can be created or appreci-

---

30. Introduction to *Ficciones* (1941); English version by Norman di Giovanni in Borges 1993, p. 3.
31. Barth 1967.

ated in place of the work itself. Almost as if, once the meaning of a text has been broached, it is no longer worth the trouble either of constructing it or of appreciating it in its concrete textuality. This "intellectualized meaning," separated (or separable) from the sensual concreteness of literary works, is what mediates modern reflective enjoyment,[32] and what can even, in the extreme, with a provocational gesture, take the place of the work.

Here then is the phenomenon that Borges indirectly "denounces" in this story: *noesis* has taken the place of *aisthesis*. This substitution, in its unreflected aspect, is what characterizes all postromantic literature; it also amounts to what can be described as the triumph of poetics. However, the Borges story is also the emblem of other things. For example, it speaks to the paralysis that can block literary creation in the era of the reflectivity of art. It is not by chance that Calvino, who is very sensitive to this kind of uneasiness, grasps immediately the "authorial reasons" for such a practice of writing. According to Calvino, it was precisely by pretending "that the book he wanted to write had already been written by someone else, some unknown hypothetical author" that Borges was able to overcome the block that had held him back (up to his forties) from moving beyond essays into fiction.[33] Borges himself cultivated such a reading, not without a bit of *coquetterie*, as Gérard Genette, who considers it overly "psychological," recalls. Genette's treatment of the Borges text is, nonetheless, no more illuminating than that of Calvino. Genette classifies it as a "pseudosummary, or fictive summary," and therefore as an instance of "fictitious hypertextuality": "hypertextuality" insofar as it relates to an anterior text, and "fictitious" insofar as that anterior text does not exist.[34] Thus Borges is located in a simple specification within the vast class of hypertextual practices. But the fact that the anterior text is nonexistent is a detail that is too significant to be easily kept in such a pigeon hole. Obviously, from an abstractly semiotic point of view, Genette's classification works; nevertheless, it makes the Borgesian anomaly disappear behind a metahistorical category. What gets occluded is the late-modern specificity of the phenomenon: Borges's formula (the summary instead of the work itself, the intellectualization in

---

32. The tendency to lose interest in the linguistic and stylistic aspects, in order to gaze directly at the "meaning" of the text, is what Cesare Segre deplores in today's literary criticism (1993, pp. 7 passim). However, what he reads as a sign of crisis in the discipline may be no more than a peculiar trait of modern enjoyment.

33. Calvino 1988, p. 50.

34. Genette 1982, pp. 251–254.

lieu of the fully realized narrative) could only have been thought up in our epoch, which is to say, in an epoch in which the process of the conceptualization of literature has become reflective, to such a degree that it can be exploited for artistic purposes.

From the Borges "formula," then, one cannot simply draw the idea of a literature in exhaustion, already dead or irremediably left behind, a literature thought of as a labyrinth of things already written, where the creative act is reduced to a kind of comment, or a refined metaliterary game, more or less ironic, and cut off by a poorly concealed sense of the players being mere epigones. Such an idea of literature reverberates in many of the writers influenced by Borges, as, for example, in the already-mentioned John Barth and in Calvino. Yet in Borges the supposed death of literature is inseparable from the idea of a rebirth under another form, and this places his story-commentaries on a completely different level from that of his melancholic epigones, who often borrowed "recipes" from Borges in order to cook up their own aesthetically enjoyable auraed objects. (That is what Calvino did in *If on a winter's night a traveler,* where he transforms into a concretely realized text a work of Herbert Qwain, which Borges had only "described" in the story "An Examination of the Work of Herbert Quain.") In short, conceptual literature is not the death of literature, except for those who look forward to a "re-enchanted" and enjoyable literature, its aura and its sensual values having been artifically restored, as on the cosmetically embellished face of a corpse.

The exploitation of the conceptual nature of literature can, moreover, give way to "experiments" quite unlike those of Borges, and not deprived of their own kind of sensual and symbolic impact, in which *noesis* is there, so to speak, in order to support *aisthesis,* as in the late works of Pasolini, whether literary or cinematic (*La Divina Mimesis, Petrolio, Appunti per un film sull'India, Appunti per un'Orestiade africana*), where the project-form is adopted as a way of composing the work.[35] Of course, we are in an altogether different universe from that of Borges. Just the same, here too the artist considers doing without the concrete realization of that which he has dreamt about doing, refusing to pass from the project to the object: "Why bother going to the trouble of realizing a work when it is so beautiful merely to dream it up?"[36]

35. For a definition of the "project-form" in the late works of Pasolini, cf. Benedetti 1998, pp. 158–170.

36. The sentence is expressed by Pasolini in the role of Giotto at the end of the *Decameron* (cf. Pasolini 1975, p. 68). There is an analogous expression in Bachelard 1960,

Even in this longing for a work in the potential state, one can read a refusal, analogous to that of Borges, to construct the aesthetic object, the work-object "which functions on its own in the mind of the reader."[37] However, in Pasolini the concept enters into the work altogether unburdened with that melancholy which sometimes accompanies the commentary-work of Borges, and which many late-modern writers have stressed even more. The commentator-writer is one who observes the entire world, its entire history, its entire literary past as from an Aleph, or from a library, or even from a sepulcher. His attitude is that of the epigone, who believes that an act of creation *ex novo* is no longer possible. In contrast, for Pasolini the concept turns into a project, and the gaiety of the project designer takes the place of the melancholy of the commentator. Despite the differences, though, it can be said that both Borges and Pasolini reflect in their works the process of conceptualization that all late-modern literature involves (including literature that appears to rely only on the modalities of *aisthesis* or beauty of form) to such a degree that we can even consider their artistic formulas as two instances of "adaptation" to the changed conditions of art. In both Borges and Pasolini, the process of conceptualization is thus reflected in artistic practice. And far from reacting to this fact with a funereal lament for what has been lost, or wanting to resurrect it artificially, both exploit the conceptualization of art as a means of expression.

The Strategic Author

The reflective interrogation to which each modern work is subjected has so widely diffused a projective idea of literature as to make the question of "what the author intended to do by selecting that compositional form in relation to that given theme" inextricable from the mind of any reader. The result is that there no longer remains any margin for an idea of creation performed in a state of semiconsciousness. Today's author, unlike the model preached by Enlightenment thinkers and later by the romantics, is someone who is supposed to know. Nothing like what the ancients referred to as "poetic 'inspiration,'" and what was later called "genius," survives in the late-modern idea of literature. The reasons behind

---

p. 66: "Writing a book is always a hard job. One is always tempted to limit himself to dreaming it."

37. Pasolini 1992, p. 544.

this change have to do not only with how effectively the artist produces, but also with how works are appreciated. Consequently, even when genius reappears (for example, when an artist declares that she knows nothing about the way she produced a work nor what she intended it to mean), it seems like a vice or a vestigial belief, which really has no bearing on our enjoyment of the works, an act which is fundamentally guided by reflective judgment.

Under the idea of genius, Enlightenment thinkers contemplated a nature which, in the words of Kant, provides the rule for art:

> But the concept of beautiful art does not permit the judgment upon the beauty of a product to be derived from any rule which has a *concept* as its determining ground, and therefore has at its basis a concept of the way in which the product is possible. Therefore beautiful art cannot itself devise the rule according to which it can bring about its product. . . . nature in the subject must (by the harmony of its faculties) give the rule to art; i.e. beautiful art is only possible as a product of genius.[38]

Thanks to the subject's "internal guide," which is not dominated by the intellect, artistic results can have the appearance of nature, that is, "without there being any visible trace that the artist had the rule in sight." However, the supposition of a nature that "provides the rules for art" can only exist in relation to a nonreflective enjoyment of works of art, and this is exactly what has been done away with. Today's author is supposed to hold strategic control over the work; it is that control that allows the reader/viewer to consider the forms selected by the author as expressive of a certain poetics, whether explicitly or implicitly proposed. Yet this is exactly what causes trouble. Can creation exist where there is only cogitated choice? Can art exist without a margin of nonreflectivity, a moment that is spontaneous and not conceptually controlled? And if the idea of the work is more important than the work itself, and the projective moment more important than the final product, can art or literature continue to exist? The obscure premonition that authorialism provokes an end to art inhabits late-modern artistic practice like a recurring nightmare that one keeps trying to forget. Thus it is precisely such authorial control over the work that many artists have tried to negate, or at least to oppose, by (1) reinventing arbitrary bonds or constraints capable

38. Kant 1790, p. 166; for the following citation, see p. 165. English translation by J. H. Bernard in Kant 1951, p. 150.

of limiting the freedom of the artist (bound writings); or by (2) restoring a semivoluntary condition to creation (the search for grace). But writers are not the only ones to have sought remedies against the strategic author. Theory, too, has provided its contribution by way of the myth of the author's death. In drawing up the death certificate for that hypertrophic figure that devoured genius, poststructuralist theory perhaps intended to save art from its presumed doom.

Whereas the theme of genius, which is by now obsolete, fails to keep our idea of art within the limits of an activity that is only half-reflective, the myth of the author's death seems in effect to reestablish that minimum of "desubjectivization" necessary to reconcile the exasperatedly subjective traits of modern art with the classical requirement of nonreflectivity. No matter how weighed down by an excess of strategy, today's author will still keep getting knocked over or thrown off balance, no longer by his own nature, but by the blind and impersonal laws of writing, by the desubjectivizing mechanisms of language and by the autonomy of the texts, which are now capable of signifying and "dialoguing" without regard to the author's intentions.

A similar substitution that puts "being played by language" in the place of what once would have been called genius, is even more explicit in the hermeneutics of Gadamer, where it is openly posed as a thought capable of taking the place of the romantic aesthetics of unconscious creation: "But how can the nature of artistic pleasure and the difference between what a craftsman makes and what an artist creates be understood without the concept of genius?"[39]

That said, the numerous analogies that one detects between Gadamer's thought and the myth of the author's death are not surprising. Both make language into something that undermines subjective control over the work. Nor is it surprising to find Gadamer using the very same metaphor used by Barthes in defining the "intransitive" character of writing. In order to explain the fact that "we are played by language," Gadamer too has recourse to the middle voice of the verb: "The primordial sense of playing is the medial one. Thus we say that something is 'playing' (spielt) somewhere or at some time, that something is going on (im Spiele ist) or that something is happening (sich abspielt)."[40]

---

39. Gadamer 1995, p. 94; pp. 103–104 for the following citation.

40. In certain Indo-European languages, such as ancient Greek, in addition to active and passive, there is a middle voice of verb inflection, in which the subject is represented as acting on or for itself.

If asked how it is possible that the myth of the author's death arose precisely in a period during which the author-function has grown so powerful, our first answer is this: the idea of the author's death is in reality a kind of *wishful thinking*. It is the wish for such a death, expressed in a formula anticipating its ratification and fulfillment. To desire someone's death, it is first necessary for this person to exist; second, the person must play some important role, since it makes no sense to dream about killing someone who exists, but counts for nothing; third, this person's role must be perceived as threatening, since it is pointless to seek the death of someone who is harmless. All three of these circumstances lie behind the myth of the author's death. Never would it have arisen in a culture in which works were transmitted anonymously; above all, it would never have arisen if the author's function had not been accentuated to the point of being seen as posing a danger to the very constitution of art. The myth of the author's death is therefore to be read as one of the many indications of the strong investment in the strategic author, of his being the "evil" of the epoch, or at least of his being experienced as such by writers and theoreticians. The myth of the author's death is euphoric. In reality, however, as happens with myths, this too constitutes a sort of magic spell aimed at warding off a danger or removing a source of anxiety. That anxiety is not only over the fate of art. Authorialism has another agonizing face, of which we have yet to speak.

Author-Image

According to the myth, the author dies because he or she is revealed to be an empty instance, without psychological referent, like the linguistic "I" according to Benveniste: a mere function of writing or reading that frees literary communication from the belief in a subjectivity antecedent to the text. As Barthes writes:

> Linguistics furnishes the destruction of the Author with a precious analytical instrument, showing that the speech-act in its entirety is an "empty" process, which functions perfectly without there being any need to fill it with the person of the interlocutors: linguistically, the author is nothing but the one who writes, just as *I* is nothing but the one who says *I*: language knows a "subject," not a "person," and this subject,

empty outside of the very speech-act which defines it, suffices to "hold" language, i.e., to exhaust it.[41]

Barthes clearly alludes to the well-known formulations of Benveniste, according to which the linguistic *I* is an "empty sign, without referent," which has no other meaning except "the person who is uttering the present instance of the discourse containing *I*."[42] But in an earlier essay, Barthes had already discussed Benveniste's theory, hailing it as one that would allow the author of the piece of writing to be defined in an apsychological manner: "A weapon against the general bad faith of a discourse which makes or would make the literary form into merely the expression of an interiority that is constructed on this side or on the outside of language."[43]

Naturally there is a portion of truth in what Barthes asserts here. For modern artistic logic the author is really a function of the writing and of the reading, or as I would say, of the act of artistic enjoyment (*fruizione artistica*). The author is a phantom, or a doorknob fixed to the top of a rod, to which the reader can append supposed intentions and purposefulness. From this point of view, the author as full subjectivity is truly dead. What is not true, however, is that this fact brings about a cathartic dispersion of authorial identity. And it is exactly here that the myth is not to be taken literally, but as a denial. The yearned-for catharsis never arrived. The author-function can still be something terribly oppressive and highly identifying.

From the moment in which the author is supposed by the reader to be the subject of a choice, dispersion ceases; on the contrary, the author endures as an image constructed from outside. His or her place does not remain empty, but is filled with data (psychological, cultural, or biographical) that are attributed to the author by the reader, until an identity is constructed. Thus the full subjectivity of the creator "I" does not give way to some nebulous, bodiless haze, but to an instance that is corpulent

41. Barthes 1968, p. 51.
42. Benveniste 1956; English translation in Benveniste 1971, p. 218.
43. Barthes 1966, p. 17. Despite their limited linguistic importance, Benveniste's reflections on the "I" as "empty sign" made a great impression at the time because they seemed to open the possibility of defining the subject in nonpsychological terms. Lacan, for example, writes: "We can try, with methodological rigour, to set out from the strictly linguistic definition of the I as signifier, in which there is nothing but the 'shifter' or indicative, which, in the subject of the statement, designates the subject in the sense that he is now speaking" ("The Subversion of the Subject and the Dialectic of Desire in the Freudian Unconscious," in Lacan 1977, p. 298).

and heavy (the heavier, the more fantastic), which is the product of an external attribution. Whoever is doing the writing can well claim not to be the source from which the writing gushes, not to be the identity out of which spring the unity and singularity of the work. That is not because the writer's identity is no longer relevant; indeed, it is a highly relevant identity, but one that does not correspond to the person of the writer. The act of enjoyment gives the author back a fictitious identity, constructed by the reader and by critics in their operations of artistic valorization of the text. And it is often a botched identity, one without nuance, like that of a puppet in a farce, a simple signpost in the *querelle* of poetics: "in the tradition of such an author," "altogether different from that other one," or "neorealist and fairy-tale-like," "neo-avant-gardist," "experimental," and the like. Something quite different from the ineffable singularity that was once supposed to be at the origin of every style! The identity of an author attributed by the processes of modern literary communication is something confining and reductive, something in which the writer really does experience his own death, but it is a death of alienated survival rather than of liberating dispersion. Like a person who has been photographed and who is hard put to recognize himself in what the camera or the eye of the photographer has captured (to such a degree that the print seems to bear the likeness of someone else altogether), so writers sometimes anxiously live with this identity that is pinned to them. The "authorial experience" of Calvino, and his anxiety over being defined, even being watched by the reader, is a good example: "Readers are my vampires. I feel a throng of readers looking over my shoulder and seizing the words as they are set down on paper. I am unable to write if there is someone watching me."[44]

If on a winter's night a traveler is usually defined as the reader's novel; we ought instead to define it as the author's novel, by an author condemned to remain under the gaze of the reader. Barthes's essay on the death of the author ended with this apotheosis of the reader:

> Classical criticism has never been concerned with the reader; for that criticism, there is no other man in literature than the one who writes. . . . We know that in order to restore writing in its future, we must reverse the myth: the birth of the reader must be requited by the death of the Author.[45]

44. Calvino 1993, p. 166.
45. Barthes 1968, p. 55.

Through an irony of fate, however, it is precisely this reader, placed on the throne in lieu of the author, who freezes the author into an image. The "birth of the reader" is not simply the positive phenomenon hailed by Barthes. The reader's gaze paralyzes and petrifies, like that of Medusa, as Calvino recalled in the lesson on lightness. "We are seeing because we are visible," Merleau-Ponty wrote. We are readers because we are readable, Calvino might have said: readable, visible, indentifiable.

Empty Cage

Even in Barthes's reflections, however, one can trace beneath the euphoria over the author's dispersion the anxiety of being watched, the uneasiness over an identity constructed by the readers, which comes back to haunt the writing subject, trapping him in an unwanted image, heavy and tiresome. In *Camera Lucida*, he writes:

> What I see is that I have become Total-Image, which is to say, Death in person; others—the Other—do not dispossess me of myself, they turn me, ferociously, into an object, they put me at their mercy, at their disposal, classified in a file.[46]

Barthes is speaking here of being photographed in reality, not metaphorically. But in that uneasiness he describes ("that faint uneasiness which seizes me when I look at 'myself' on a piece of paper") we have no difficulty in recognizing the same malaise felt by many contemporary writers: the embarrassment of a person who feels herself photographed in her own text (another piece of paper), and thus expropriated from herself, transformed into an image for the use of the readers and their card files, and perpetually exposed to their judgment.

   In Barthes's essay, photography can also be interpreted as a metaphor of modern writing and reading, a metaphor that he was perhaps not altogether unaware of, as the following passage suggests:

46. Barthes 1981, p. 14. But see too the following passage from *Roland Barthes by Roland Barthes*: "He is troubled by any *image* of himself, suffers when he is named. He finds the perfection of a human relationship in this vacancy of the image: to abolish in oneself, between oneself and others, *adjectives*; a relationship which adjectivizes is on the side of the image, on the side of domination, of death." Barthes 1975, p. 43 (italics are Barthes's).

What I want, in short, is that my (mobile) image, buffeted among a thousand shifting photographs, altering with situation and age, should always coincide with my (profound) "self"; but it is the contrary that must be said: "myself" never coincides with my image; for it is the image which is heavy, motionless, stubborn (which is why society sustains it), and "myself" which is light, divided, dispersed; like a bottle-imp, "myself" doesn't hold still, giggling in my jar: if only Photography could give me a neutral, anatomic body which signifies nothing! Alas, I am doomed by (well-meaning) Photography always to have an expression: my body never finds its *zero degree*.[47]

Here we find the short circuit between an expression which for Barthes is tied by a double strand to writing (*zero degree*), and the sphere of photography. It is certainly not enough to prove that Barthes was thinking about writing while he was speaking of photography, but it surely can be said that this linkage was in some ways active in his imagination and in his experience. It also reveals how the myth of the author's death was fundamentally ambiguous for him: on one side, he hails the author's demise as liberating; on the other, he describes its distressing permanence as image, felt in its turn as a death, which is no longer liberating but disquieting. The image is constructed precisely by the act of reading. In *The Pleasure of the Text*, moreover, Barthes quite clearly states that the author returns as a "figure" constructed by the reader. Like "the joker," like "the dummy in the bridge game: necessary to the meaning (the battle), but himself deprived of fixed meaning," the figure of the author is necessary to the reader for the latter's enjoyment of the text. Even if dead as a "biographical, passional, civil person," even if dispossessed of every right of paternity over the work, and therefore altogether at the mercy of a play of images, the author reappears in the text as the reader's object of desire.[48] What then is the true meaning of the author's death? Cathartic dispersion or alienating persistence in image?

Modern writing is not the locus of the dispersion of authorial identity; on the contrary, it is the locus of the author's identification in image through the act of enjoyment. This is surely the point at which the artistic phenomena that we are describing reveal their affinity with the epoch. The image that others stick on us is what mediates identity and

47. Barthes 1981, p. 12 (italics added).
48. Barthes 1973, pp. 27 and 34.

reduces the subject to a complex "game of faces" (in Goffman's sense of the term) constructed through interaction. And the uneasiness that the author-image produces in the writer is not very different from the one produced in social interactions by the narcissistic nature of identity.

"What matter who's speaking, someone said what matter who's speaking," Beckett wrote.[49] And yet this irrelevance of the "true" speaking subject, and of his psychological depth, does not prevent the formation of the authorial image projected by the act of enjoyment, nor reduce its weight. The author, who today has such a high profile in the processes of artistic attribution, is therefore not the "full" subjectivity, antecedent to the text, with which nineteenth-century criticism was concerned. The "author" is instead precisely that empty subject, that mere function of the writing that the myth of the author's death ambiguously hailed as a liberation, though it has become so powerful and oppressive as to be anything but. What really happened in the twentieth century is not the cathartic disappearance of the author (cathartic for art, but ultimately also for the subject, whose only tragedy is that of not being able to really disperse herself, in an effective "what matter who's speaking"); what happens instead is the persistence of an imposed identity that holds the writer in an empty authorial cage. Thus an idea of literature that cancels out the author to the advantage of the texts and the reader, that is, a literature with neither work nor creation, gets back in return an author-image, which itself is perceived by many contemporary writers as the "evil" of the epoch.

49. Foucault uses Beckett's phrase as a point of departure in "What is an Author?" in Foucault 1969, p. 115.

CHAPTER 3

The Author as Condition of the Work

In the twentieth century the notion of author was subjected to an array of increasingly subtle distinctions. Proust began by separating the *deep self* of the artist from his or her *worldly self*; discourse theory distinguished the *implied author* from the *real author*; semiotics created the *ideal author* in opposition to the *empirical author*. Thus it can be said that twentieth-century reflection on this subject has been a long series of distinctions as well as the negation and denial of what for so long had simply been called "the author." Perhaps some day, in a hypothetical future, all these distinctions will appear as byzantine as a disquisition on the sex of the angels. Nonetheless, the reason why they interest us here is that they are an indication of a phenomenon unique in itself: the notion of author, obvious and familiar for centuries, began at a certain point to cause trouble, so much so that it could be employed only in conjunction with reassuring adjectives. Beyond that, although the concept of "implied author" (as it is commonly used) is of scarce theoretical utility for our analysis, a discussion of its insufficiency will permit us to determine our own notion of author with greater precision and to take another look at the work of Wayne Booth, whose reflections today appear richer, as well as more problematic, with respect to the amputations performed by succeeding theories of narration based on structuralism and semiotics.

Useless Precautions

For some time now the word *author* has had a suspicious ring to it. To some it calls up the "obsolete realm" of the subject, made up of states of mind, intentions, goals, responsibilities. But for most it evokes the specter of a literary criticism dedicated to searching for the meaning of works in relation to the person who produced them, inquiring into that person's supposed peculiarities of thought and style, or worse, into the supposed peculiarities of his or her psychological profile and biographical data. Literary criticism of a formalist or structuralist stamp had to struggle long and hard against such practices in order to affirm its view of the autonomy of the texts. It is sometimes said that this battle was the continuation of that undertaken by Proust in his *Contre Sainte-Beuve;* however, there is a substantial hiatus between the two. When Proust wrote that "a book is the product of a different self from the self we manifest in our habits, in our social life, in our vices,"[1] he was not simply referring to an intratextual instance as opposed to an extratextual one. It is not only the criterion of immanence to the text that distinguishes the artist's deep self from the worldly self, but more importantly the deep self's involvement in an act of creation, with its obscure and tortuous labor, with its itinerary of sufferings and disappointments, things that succeeding criticism and theory have altogether excluded from their discourse. The thematics of reception have replaced those of creation. Besides, as Mariolina Bertini notes,[2] if for Proust the critic was supposed to ignore the worldly self, and so give up every approach based on biographical facts, it was because Proust considered the critic's task that of grasping the deep self as it reveals itself in the work, that is, in flashes and through fragments, by means of those "singular traits" that make up a style;[3] and if the first part of such a theoretical pronouncement could also converge with the positions of the *nouvelle critique,* the second was unacceptable to it. Thus, today, whoever wants to invoke the author is forced to make clear not only that she is not referring to the author in the biographical sense, but also that she is not even referring to a creating subject, which, though acceptable at the time when Proust was writing, has since turned into a true and proper taboo. The fear of naming the au-

---

1. Proust 1971, p. 221; English translation by Sylvia Townsend Werner in Proust 1958, pp. 99–100.
2. Preface to the Italian edition of *Contre Sainte-Beuve*, in Proust 1974., p. XLII.
3. Proust 1974, p. 131.

thor, or the habit of naming the author modified by some mitigating term, is also the product of this act of exclusion (which drove the creativity, style, and individuality of the artist out of the realm of phenomena deemed meaningful to literature) and not only the result of the triumph of an immanent, that is, text-centered, perspective.

But let us now consider the apparently more reasonable aspect of such terminological caution: the fact that the creative author ought to be kept distinct from the biographical author, from the artist's historical and psychological person. Such a distinction is of no greater necessity in literature and art than it is in many other fields. Even the president of the republic, who addresses the Italian people every year, is a function that does not entirely coincide with the person who fulfills it for each seven-year term. And yet nobody feels obliged to speak of an implied president! Such a caution, then, risks nourishing a prejudice that is no better than the one it was intended to do away with: to believe that similar distinctions between person and role are pertinent only to literary texts (or only written texts), when instead we must always take them into account, in all social interactions, as Goffman's studies on the ceremonial nature of identity and the construction of the self have amply demonstrated.[4]

The writer of the preface to the Italian edition of *Forms of Talk* lamented that sociolinguistic analyses were not, before Goffman's studies, as subtle as literary analyses in distinguishing the multiple roles stratified in the speaker.[5] And as proof, a passage taken from Calvino's "Cybernetics and Ghosts," of 1967, is cited: "The person "I," whether explicit or implicit, splits into various figures: into an I that is writing and into an I that is written, into an empirical I that is standing behind the I that is writing and into a mythical I that serves as model for the I that is written."[6]

It is certainly true that discourse analysis and the study of fictional language have produced subtle distinctions between author, narrator, character, narrator-character, and author-character, which sociolinguistics might well take as a model. For our part, however, we would lament a certain crudeness in literary theory in its ongoing assumption of the opposite pole of the distinction. For what is this real author, on whom is founded, through opposition, the notion of implied author, if not the

4. The division of the speaker into multiple identities, projected in the very act of speaking, is a cornerstone of Goffman's sociological theory, cf. 1959 and 1981.

5. P. P. Giglioli, "Introduzione all'edizione italiana" in Goffman 1981, p. xviii.

6. Calvino 1980, p. 15.

crude hypostasis of a subjectivity founded on internal states, of a personal identity preexistent to the interaction (in our case, preexistent to artistic communication)? True, theory names the real author only to exclude his or her importance to theoretical consideration, but by continuing to found the notion of author merely in opposition to the person who has written the text, instead of defining one *ex novo*, the theoretical concept will always remain bound to the real person by way of the negation.

Finally, it must be said that all distinctions aimed at separating the author in the historical and biographical sense from an instance immanent to the text, captured in its intratextual "purity," amount to no more than footprints in water. The act of enjoyment consists in processes of *attribution to an author*, necessary for the valorization of a text as work of art. It is just those attributions that decide time after time what is relevant for the artistic valorization of this or that text. If, for example, in order to appreciate the treatment of homosexuality that Proust presents in *Remembrance of Things Past*, a reader can't do without recalling, if only in a tiny corner of her mind, that the writer was homosexual, who will be able to prevent her from doing so? Or who can prohibit her from thinking that the author of *Illuminations* ended his life as a merchant in Abyssinia, while Emily Dickinson almost never left her house? Or that the author of *Petrolio* was killed by a *ragazzo di vita*, or young male "hustler"?[7] Though the author whom contemporary enjoyment finds interesting is rather different from the one that Sainte-Beuve's method was intended to examine, the notorious "empirical author" (censured by the formalists, structuralists, and practitioners of semiotics) can always offer hints to the processes of artistic valorization, and no matter what is said or legislated, no theoretician will ever be able to prevent this from happening. For these reasons and those mentioned above, we shall not use the terms *implied author* or *ideal author*, but simply *author* in order to name that instance that nonetheless remains, for us, too, only a function.[8]

But a function of what? This is the real question. The differences between what I mean here by "author" and the conceptualizations in common use arise precisely when it comes to defining the type of function. As I have already said, I mean a *function of artistic communication*, required by the literary text, and by every work of art in general, insofar as

7. *Ragazzi di vita* is the title of a Pasolini novel that depicts youths of the urban lumpen-proletariat who live by their wits. [See photo insert.]

8. Genette too considers the notion of implied author to be useless, and speaks only of "author," but for different reasons from ours, based on a demand for economy (Genette 1983, pp. 135–149).

these works are invested with artistic value. In contrast, what is usually understood with the term "author-function" is exclusively a *function of the text* as strategy of signification. Whether it is the implied author of discourse theory or the ideal author of semiotics, or the intending author of hermeneutics, all are functions of the text, required either by the mechanisms of narrative invention or by those of creating meaning and constructing a coherent text. Moreover, such a conceptualization corresponds to a theoretical choice opposed to our own: a tendency to subordinate issues of art (and creation) to those of meaning and signification. The author that we are concerned with is instead something specifically artistic, a phenomenon that goes beyond the problems of signification, something inscribed in the text not as "textual machinery" but as work of art.

For this kind of function those "facts" that literary theory has long excluded from its sphere of interest become relevant: that a subject is involved in an act of writing literature, or of creating art, with all the consequences and risks that such an act of "formal birth" implies.[9] Even though today's "Western tribe" of literary critics has become unaccustomed to considering such matters, they are serious enough to lead to criminal liability, even loss of life or liberty, as Ayatollah Khomeini's *fatwah* against Salman Rushdie demonstrated. Though there has been some recent debate over the responsibility of the artist within the visual arts in response to an essay by Jean Clair,[10] it always has to do with a responsibility totally internal to "aesthetic values." Not unlike Calvino (who celebrated the ethical value of literary qualities like visibility or lightness) or Celati (who invests the craftsmanship of narration with an analogous value), the French critic attributes to design, color, and painting technique in general, understood as craftsmanship and as "exercise of the senses" (as a *Kunstkönnen* distinct and opposed to the *Kunstwollen* of the avant-gardes), a "salvational value" in opposition to the distraction and technology that are devouring life all around us. Thus, for a culture habituated to the idea that the artist's responsibility is exclusively of an aesthetic kind, that is, totally limited to the confines of art, which shelters artists from risky contact with the outside world, the Rushdie case was an alarming wake-up call, a sort of resurfacing of the repressed. Yet it

9. The creation of an artistic form is a kind of passage into action, a kind of birth which, as such, exposes us to death. It is exactly this birth that, according to Antonio Moresco, many contemporary artists reject (cf. "La forma e la morte," in Moresco 1999, pp. 31–46).

10. Clair 1997. For the related debate, cf. also Clair and Fumaroli 1997.

was not that long ago when those very same artists to whom we owe the claim of the autonomy of art (I am referring to Baudelaire and Flaubert)[11] were themselves subjected to criminal proceedings "just" for having written some poems and a novel. Which goes to show that "autonomy" is not a quality inherent to art, one that is ontologically bound to it, as most today assert. Nor is the autonomy of art a "conquest" made once and for all. On the contrary, it is something that must always be fought for, that must be wrested time and again from the "world of ends" and the powers that be, whether those of the state or of the culture industry (which itself is nothing other than a network of micropowers). It is in such conflicts that the author, by which of course I mean the real author, at times runs risks.

Wayne Booth's Implied Author

The notion of implied author (*autore implicito*) was used by Wayne Booth to deal with specific narrative issues related to the "rhetoric of *fiction.*" The notion was of course intended to signify an entity that is always distinct from the real man or woman, something like "the author's second self," "built up in our minds from our experience with all the elements of the presented story,"[12] an effect created at the start of every narrative text. It must, however, be made clear that "implied author" has been translated into Italian as "autore implicito" and into French as "l'auteur implicite." As noted by Genette, the adjective (implicit) tends to "harden" and hypostasize what in English was only a participial modifier,[13] a fact not unrelated to the reductive use that the notion has been put to since, which diverges from Booth's own.

But let us attempt to bring into focus the reasons why Booth, in constructing his discourse on "distance,"[14] might have needed to call on an author, even if only an implied one. Examined in this way, Booth's notion

11. Bourdieu 1992, in particular the section (Part I) entitled "The Conquest of Autonomy," pp. 47–166.

12. Booth 1967, p. 93.

13. Genette 1983, pp. 138–140.

14. Distance between narrator and implied author, between narrator and characters, between narrator and the reader's own norms, between implied author and reader, between implied author and characters, as they are listed in Booth 1983a, pp. 155–159). According to Genette 1972, Booth confused problems of "voice" (who speaks in a story) with those of "mode" (who sees). Booth in turn criticizes Genette's method in the afterword of Booth 1983a (pp. 439–441) and in Booth 1983b.

turns out to be more intricate than its apparent simplicity would have us suppose. Here, implied author is a servant of more than one master, a notion called forth to fulfill at least two or three different tasks.

The first question to which Booth addresses himself is generically narrational. The voice that speaks in a story is always a fictitious instance, which like a character, the author creates. However, this fact is usually recognized only when the narrator is "dramatized," when, that is, the novel makes him or her into a vivid character.[15] In other cases (undramatized narrators), though, the narrator tends to be confused with the author: "One of the most frequent reading faults," writes Booth, "comes from a naive identification of such narrators with the author who creates them." The best way of avoiding this confusion was therefore to assert once and for all, in the form of a principle, that between the narrator and author there is always a distinction. The notion of implied author is thus introduced in a negative way, in order to sustain the author/narrator distinction (the very same one that Bakhtin's notion of "indirect discourse" secures with greater economy and explanatory capacity).[16]

Next in his inquiry, Booth tries to account for a more specifically narrational phenomenon. What provokes his reflections above all else is a particular kind of story: that in which the narrator is not only represented but also "unreliable," which is to say, not worthy of the reader's trust insofar as the narrator's "moral and intellectual qualities" are not in accordance with the norms of the work, which is to say, with the norms of the implied author.[17] An extreme example is provided by those narrators who exhibit faulty reasoning, who lie or who hide something. The reader becomes aware of the existence of another instance beyond that of the narrator: a mute instance (because it is not incarnated in a narrating voice), which is, nonetheless, indicating something. This instance is the implied author. The distance created between an unreliable narrator and the implied author is, moreover, the one variety that Booth considers most important since it is the implied author "who carries the reader with him in judging the narrator." Here the reader not only realizes that

15. Booth 1967, p. 93.

16. For Bakhtin, fictional discourse is always "indirect" in the sense that it does not directly express the author's intentions, but refracts them through other subjects: a conventional author, a represented narrator, a character, or even subjects who are not personified in the fiction, but whose languages echo through the polyphony of the text as belonging to others (Bakhtin 1975). Bakhtin thus (perhaps because he comes out of a different tradition) feels no need to differentiate between a real author and an author internal to the text.

17. Booth 1983a, pp. 158–159, from which is also taken the following citation.

the narrator is not identical to the author, but is even obliged to distrust the narrator. It is as if the reader is being guided by someone else, who from behind the curtains indirectly provides cues for reading, inducing the reader to mistrust the narrator who is speaking on stage. This other instance, "superior" to that of the narrator, on whom falls the responsibility of the text, is, in the true sense of the word, an "implied author" (*autore implicato*). The participle here is made doubly necessary as it no longer indicates merely that abstract entity, to be named by way of negation alone (to indicate, that is, that the narrator is not the author). Much more, even if mute, this instance also constitutes a presence within the work, one not only implicit to but also *implicated* (*implicata*) by the work and crucial for its comprehension and valuation.

And it is here that we are confronted by a parting of the ways with respect to latter-day discourse theory. Booth deals with the complex rhetoric of fiction from an angle different from that which Genette would try a decade later. In Genette's "grammar" (where problems of "distance" are replaced by those of relations between history (*histoire*), discourse (*récit*), and narration (*narration*), just as in succeeding discourse studies, the author has disappeared: Genette speaks only of narrators, homodiegetic or heterodiegetic, first, second, or third level. Paradoxically, the consequence of the greater rigor that Genette and narratology seem to have brought is nevertheless based on a simplification. Eliminated is the entire field of phenomena regarding the distance between the author and other instances of the story, which, since Flaubert, had occupied many writers and theoreticians (from the reflections of Henry James to the studies of Lubbock, up to, within an entirely different tradition, those of Bakhtin on fictional discourse). Booth continued to take these phenomena into consideration, so his thinking might appear more "confused" than that of Genette, but in reality it is richer and more open. What Booth tries to account for is the construction of the fictional work in its entirety, as a "product of choices and of valuations" for which the implied author (*autore implicito*) is really responsible. His approach to the narrative text, then, begins (as Calvino would say) from the "I am writing" that stands behind the "I am narrating," and not only from the "I am narrating," as do most of the subsequent studies on narration.[18]

18. Couturier makes an interesting attempt to take up the research on fictional texts exactly where Booth left off, rightly asserting that "it is now clear, a decade later, that the inquiry cannot go much further if we insist on excluding the author from the discursive field: no matter how much we multiply its instances in the text, we end up sooner or later at an impasse" (Couturier 1995, p. 9). I think, however, that the problem of the author is not posed exclusively by the fictional text; it must be considered in regard to the work of

A Second Self

In regard to Booth, one last thing should be brought out. There is a slight discrepancy between the role the notion of implied author serves in the economy of his investigation and the way in which it is defined. On one side, indeed, it serves to explain specifically narrational phenomena, on the other, however, it is described with such generality as to be applicable to every literary text (not only narrative texts) insofar as they are works of art. But let us follow the course of its definition. First of all, for Booth the implied author is an *image of the author* that the reader creates for herself based on the work. And what allows its formation is not only the distance between the unreliable narrator and the implied author, but that vast array of elements that constitute the work insofar as it is a "completed artistic whole":

> Our sense of the implied author includes not only the extractable meanings but also the moral and emotional content of each bit of action and suffering of all of the characters. It includes, in short, the intuitive apprehension of a completed artistic whole; the chief value to which *this* implied author is committed, regardless of what party his creator belongs to in real life, is that which is expressed by the total form.[19]

Thus even the form of the work contributes to the projection of that authorial personality. Indeed, Booth considers the possibility of naming that "core of norms and choices which I am calling the implied author" *style* since "style is one of our main sources of insight into the author's norms." Though he rejects it, it is only because style places too much emphasis on the merely verbal experience, whereas the reader constructs an image of the author based on other aspects of the work as well, such as "skill in his choice of character and episode and scene and idea." But still more significant is the fact that, regardless of the number of textual aspects involved, Booth brings them all together under the concept of *choice*: if every literary text projects a personality of the author, it is because the author is considered as the "sum of his own choices": "The 'implied author' chooses, consciously or unconsciously, what we read;

---

art in general. My inquiry therefore follows a different path from that pursued by Couturier, whose importance, nonetheless, I recognize, above all for having reopened the discourse on the author.

19. Booth 1983a, pp. 73–74; see also pp. 74–75 for subsequent citations.

we infer him as an ideal, literary, created version of the real man; he is the sum of his own choices."

Thus Booth does not hesitate to consider the image created in the reader's mind, that is, the implied author, as "one of the author's most important effects." At this point, it becomes very difficult to fit Booth's notion within the bounds of the typical questions posed by today's discourse theory, or within those of textuality understood as machinery that produces meaning. Booth is concerned with phenomena that subsequent literary theory has to a great extent cleared away: the so-called "personality" of the writer, that individual trace that the writer supposedly leaves in the work; and finally, that phenomenon which in the past would have been called "the style," which was long the grand manner of alluding to the author. With his notion of implied author, Booth in a certain sense also provides for the recuperation of that earlier problematic, giving it a sounder basis than that which stylistic criticism (with its search for the writer's "spiritual etymon") had had in its own time. Booth does seem to admit that there is something like a personality of the author captured in the text, but it is a personality reactively constructed through the eye of the reader who evaluates the choices of the artist. In short, Booth is asserting something analogous to what Calvino was to write a few years afterward:

> Sitting down to write each time presupposes the choice of a psychological attitude, a relationship with the world, a pitching of the voice, a homogeneous gathering of linguistic methods and experiential data and figments of the imagination, in short, a style. The author is author in so far as he assumes a part, like an actor, and identifies himself with that projection of himself in the moment in which he writes.[20]

Calvino, too, we see, talks about choice. The projection of an author's image occurs because the writer, at the moment in which he writes, chooses: he chooses a psychological attitude, a relationship with the

---

20. Calvino 1980, p. 111. Booth cites the following passage from Jessamyn West in a footnote: "Writing is a way of playing parts, of trying on masks, of assuming roles" (Booth 1983a, p. 71. The passage is extracted from "The Slave Cast Out," in *The Living Novel*, ed. G. Hicks, New York 1957, p. 202). However, the most clamorous example of authorial *construction of a personality* through writing, or rather of a *multitude* of personalities, is the work of Pessoa. His system of heteronyms (much more complex than Kierkegaard's) contemplates the "projection" of multiple authorial images, each of which is constructed on the basis of different "choices" of style, psychological attitude, relationship with the world and even poetics (see Pessoa 1979).

world, and a vocal pitch, among other things. Calvino, however, expresses this truth from the side opposite to that of Booth, that is, from the side of someone who has already experienced the intolerability of that projection. Thus, in *If on a winter's night a traveler,* he even arrives at imagining that impossible catharsis anticipated by the myth of the author's death:

> How well I would write if I were not here! If between the white page and the writing of words and stories that take shape and disappear without anyone's ever writing them were not interposed that uncomfortable partition which is my person! Style, taste, individual philosophy, subjectivity, cultural background, real experience, psychology, talent, tricks of the trade: all the elements that made what I write recognizable as mine.[21]

This "second self" of the author, of which Booth speaks, this authorial identity projected by the work, this image constructed by the reader, is then, among the various conceptualizations of the author, the one that comes closest to the themes that we are concerned with here. It is also the one that subsequent theory has dropped from its purview. For all literary criticism influenced by structuralism, the author, just like style, has been buried beneath the architecture of texts, crushed by the iron laws of textuality, which allow very little margin for the artist's selections. The only thing that counts is the text conceived as textual machinery. And if a machine produces an image of its author, it will still always be an "engineering" image, someone who instructs us on how to make the device work, not the image that we as readers can construct for ourselves on the basis of what kind of device it is, or what ideology supports it. Even if they were dealing with an antipersonnel weapon that kills only people of color, structuralist theoreticians would never be able to say that the device projects the image of a racist author!

Guardian of Meaning

The *ideal author* of semiotics, in effect, is nothing more than the source responsible for providing "reading instructions" for the reader, who, of course, is also implied rather than real. No matter how far beyond narrative texts its sphere of application can be extended, the ideal author al-

21. Calvino 1993, p. 167.

ways maintains the characteristic of being a function required by semantic and interpretive processes: the need to make reference to an author is tied to the problem of the correct understanding of the text's meaning. The author is nothing more than an interpretive hypothesis that the reader formulates based on the facts of textual strategy. The author, having been stripped of anything that might be considered "personal" (in the sense of a "personality" projected by the work itself), thus becomes the personification of the *intentio operis,* subject of the textual strategy that the reader hypothesizes in order to be able to correctly understand the text.[22] In short, the reference point is "how to interpret the text," not "what image of the author does the text provide," and even less "why is this text accepted as a literary work," and so the very notion of text is deformed: "a text," Eco writes, "is a machine conceived for the purpose of eliciting interpretations."[23]

Hermeneutics, too, is focused on interpretation, both when it abandons the idea of the author's intention in favor of the *intentio operis,* and when it is forced to put the author back into play so as to avoid the interpretational drift that legitimizes anything and everything. Hirsch's resuscitation of the author's intention is worth recalling in this regard, for it contravenes the ban which New Criticism in its heyday had lodged against the "fallacious" notion of the author.[24] Having abolished what for nineteenth-century criticism used to be an obvious and basic concept of literary communication (i.e., the author), theory has ever since been in constant turmoil, seeking shelter from a storm it itself created. Hirsch dusted off the author's intention in order to wall off the dangerous relativism that lies lurking in Gadamer's hermeneutics. The author's intention did indeed constitute a limit to the possible meanings of a text, and so provided a criterion of validation to which interpretations could be subjected, and it is with this function in mind that Hirsch brings it back.[25]

22. All these notions (from that of the author-model to that of the *intentio operis*) can be found in the essays of Umberto Eco (cf. for example Eco 1979 and 1990). The author-model is conceived there as an interpretive hypothesis that the reader constructs in order to settle certain types of questions: to discern the parodic use of a style or an expression from its serious usage; to understand whether or not the author is aware of a source that the reader discovers within the text; to determine whether certain semantic associations advanced by the reader are acceptable or not, etc. (Eco 1990, pp. 110–111)

23. Ibid., p. 122.

24. Cf. Hirsch 1967. A critique of Hirsch can be found in Hoy 1978, chapter 1, "Validity and the Author's Intention."

25. Nevertheless, with his distinction between "meaning," toward which interpretation aims, and "significance," toward which evaluation aims, Hirsch still leaves open the possibility that the second might change over time, according to the context of reception.

The terror of interpretive babble, however, has descended not only on the camp of hermeneutics. In the ranks of semiotics, too, the demand to find a criterion with which to keep interpretations within the bounds of the legitimate has become ever more pressing, as is shown by the very title of Umberto Eco's *I limiti dell'interpretazione* (*The Limits of Interpretation*). The specter of relativism periodically haunts all theories of textuality, with the result that their practitioners may at times go running for the hills, calling the author back to life! As remedy to the excessive interpretive liberties taken by *"reader-oriented"* critics and deconstructionists, the author is invoked as a way of restoring a criterion for philological accuracy. Even Cesare Segre has recently expressed a similar concern and here, again, the anchor is the same: the author as guarantor of the "semiotic value" of the text, the author as guardian of its meaning:

> A communicative conception of literature invokes the author (the sender) in defense of his message. It is through his message that the author communicates, *dissolving then as a historically identifiable person*. . . . It may happen that we understand the text only a little or not at all, that we distort it, etc., but we know that the text is not a *res nullius*, and that actually it is our duty to respond in kind to whoever has delivered it, trying to understand it in an exact way.[26]

And so, dead or alive, the author is being called back, even if prudently (notice the longer phrase in italics), since the "empirical" author is still almost as alarming as the blather of interpretational relativism. Like a replicant created for a specific purpose and with limited vital functions, the author is called on to fulfill the role of defender of the correct use of the text. The definition remains the same as before: the author is someone who has "left a series of 'instructions' in the work which can reduce the danger of misinterpretation on the part of the receiver." In short, this definition remains the classic engineering image of a builder of machines (texts). The focus is on what the text means or signifies: it is a matter of its *interpretation*, not of its *artistic valorization*. The same can be said for Antoine Compagnon's recent proposal in opposition to the theme of the author's death and the various anti-intentionalist positions. Compagnon introduces his own concept of the author's intention; for him it is pre-

---

26. Segre 1993, p. 12; in the first italicized expression the italics are mine. The citation which follows comes from the same source.

supposed in every interpretive act as the text's underlying "hypothesis of coherence."[27]

Having an Author

Semiotics has as its guiding image the textual machine, that is, a device whose mode of operation it is necessary for us to understand. However, any written text can be viewed as a textual machine that poses the same kinds of problems that semiotics anticipates with respect to literary texts. The interpretive processes described by semiotics and the mode in which they evoke an ideal author can be activated just as well by nonliterary texts: for example, by the letters of Aldo Moro, which Umberto Eco analyzed on the basis of those very principles.[28] The same may be said about the other notions considered above (the implicit author [*autore implicito*] of discourse studies, the author as hypothesis of coherence, the author as guarantor of meaning): in each case, reference to the author comes into play for the interpretation of something that might not even be a literary text. The author-function to which I refer is instead activated solely by literary texts. The author-function is what institutes that particular status enjoyed by literary texts, making them not merely texts, but *works* (*opera*).[29] As Foucault writes:

> The author's name characterizes a particular manner of existence of discourse. Discourse that possesses an author's name is not to be immediately consumed and forgotten; neither is it accorded the momentary attention given to ordinary, fleeting words. Rather, its status and its manner of reception are regulated by the culture in which it circulates.[30]

Foucault was aiming at a typology of discourses based on their specifically discursive properties, those irreducible to the rules of grammar and logic, or to the laws of content, those which instead concern their modal-

27. Compagnon 1998, pp. 77 passim. Compagnon explicitly makes reference to Hirsch.
28. Cf. Eco 1979, p. 75.
29. Consequently, from this point on, we will no longer speak of *texts* but of *works*, by which we mean any text to which an artistic value is attributed. Brioschi 1983, Di Girolamo 1978, and Di Girolamo, Berardinelli and Brioschi 1986 have shown the importance for such a distinction, but from "conventionalist" perspective, similar to that of Fish 1980 (see the section on "Fish's experiment" in chapter 6 of this book).
30. Foucault 1969, p. 123; see also Foucault 1971.

ities of existence: the modalities of circulation, valorization, attribution, and appropriation. Among these purely discursive properties, the relationship (or the nonrelationship) with an author's name holds a position of first rank. Foucault attributes three functions to the author's name. The first is classificatory: the author's name allows a certain number of texts to be grouped together; it allows us to exclude others from it; and it allows us to oppose those thus grouped to other groups. The second function is that of *instituting relationships between the texts* that are so classified: the fact that various texts are placed under a single author's name indicates that some of them can be used to establish relationships of homogeneity, filiation, authenticity, or reciprocal explanation with others.[31] For example, we might explain Gadda's *La cognizione del dolore* by considering what he wrote in *Meditazione milanese*. Finally, the third function, and the most important for us, is that the author's name serves to *give a certain status* to a specific group of discourses, in other words, a particular mode of existence, of circulation, and operation, which, within a culture, renders these discourses different from others:

> The author's name is not a function of a man's civil status, nor is it fictional; it is situated in the breach, among the discontinuities, which gives rise to new groups of discourse and their singular mode of existence. Consequently, we can say that in our culture, the name of an author is a variable that accompanies only certain texts to the exclusion of others: a private letter may have a signatory, but it does not have an author; a contract can have an underwriter, but not an author; and, similarly, an anonymous poster attached to a wall may have a writer, but he cannot be an author. In this sense, the function of an author is to characterize the existence, circulation, and operation of certain discourses within a society.[32]

But if these discourses receive their own particular status from the fact of having an author, a reading or use of them in conformity with such status will imply an activation of the author-function. In other words, I can't help referring to the fact that the discourse has an author since the way I look at it is determined by the fact that I presuppose it to be endowed with an author. When we are confronted by this group of discourses, the reference to the author is inscribed, even before its inscription by the processes of textual interpretation, in the very attitude we

31. Ibid.
32. Ibid., pp. 123–124.

assume toward them. It is inscribed in the fact that these texts require understanding, interpretation, commentary, respect, and care (including, in the philological sense, scholarly editorial preparation). The implied author, the ideal author, and all those other notions that make the author a function of comprehension or of interpretation of the text thus presuppose as already given and as nonproblematic those unities that are literary texts. For this reason those notions do not prove useful when it comes to explaining that fundamental reference to the author implied in the very status of the literary text.[33]

Modern literary theories have almost always avoided questioning the conditions of possibility of the object of their discourses. Their problematic is chiefly one of describing or interpreting something that is assumed as already constituted, regardless of how that may come about. In an essay that has become a classic of literary semiotics, Maria Corti twists Foucault's author-function concept in a curious way, providing an eloquent illustration of what I am arguing here. Distinguishing "artistic writing" from the "instrumental" writing of everyday usage, Corti writes that the former is "such as would presuppose the author-function."[34] But the essay never goes on to explain what that function involves. Following in the path of a long tradition originating in the Russian formalists and in Roman Jakobson, Corti does furnish us with some indications regarding what would distinguish "a literary text from all other texts." (Having discarded as insufficient Jakobson's poetic function, here she proposes "hypersemanticity" as the characteristic of literary texts.) However, these indications deal with aspects of the text that contemplate no reference to the author-function. In compensation, when she returns to speaking about the author-function, she immediately falls back on the implied author (or illusion constructed by the reader) of discourse studies:

> In the reflections of the text such an omnipresent illusion becomes the author-function, to which Foucault ties the very typology of discourses. . . . Into such a typology, then, will re-enter the variable relation, which has been the object of innumerable studies (Todorov, Kristeva, Chatman, Rousset), between the "I" of the narrator and the "I" or "he" of the explicit character or characters, the subjects of utterances.[35]

33. This does not mean that they are useless when confronting texts from the point of view of the semantic processes activated by the texts.

34. Corti 1976, p. 37.

35. Ibid., pp. 41–42. A citation from Foucault has been cut out of this passage.

Once again, then, everything goes back to a specifically narrational textual problematic. What is surprising, though, is how even Foucault's typology gets led back to the same place along with the rest. This despite the fact that Foucault's typology belongs to an altogether different problematic, one directed toward not what is internal but rather what is external to the text, in other words, toward those elements that constitute the conditions of its possibility.[36] And that provides a measure of just how refractory to this view of literature semiotics really is, so much so that it fails to discern it even where it is explicitly stated.

Modern literary theories, the descendants of the Russian formalists, have almost always avoided the problem of the conditions of possibility of the object of their discourses. This, obviously, does not mean that for them a literary text is equal to any other text. On the contrary, the specificity of literature is their first postulate. What makes a text a literary work is, from Jakobson on, the most difficult question that literary theory ever posed (see chapter 6). But its difficulty arises from its being poorly formulated. Instead of interrogating, to use Foucault's words, that "rupture which gives life to a certain group of discourses," the usual approach has been to interrogate the textual properties (formal, structural, or semiotic) of those same discourses. That is equivalent to opening up an insoluble problem, because such properties (which are drawn from the poetic function of the language or from its "hypersemanticity") come to light only by virtue of the fact that the texts are treated as works of art. Thus the answers that have been given are among the most fantastically tautological things ever thought up by literary theory. Even the "hypersemanticity" described by Lotman, that is, the fact that, as Corti says, "everything is meaningful" in a literary text, can be viewed as the consequence of the fact that the text is approached as a literary work, rather than as an objective characteristic of the text itself.

Literary theory inquires into the characteristics of that which it already supposes to be a work of art. The formal description of a text, its critical interpretation, just like all the philological operations performed on it, already presuppose its status as a literary work. But it is precisely

36. That is why Foucault's essay has more than once been misunderstood by theoreticians of literature, who are always ready to censure everything that steps outside of the "law of the text." Compagnon, for example, even scolds Foucault for having confused "the author in the biographical or sociological sense" with "the author in the hermeneutic sense" (i.e., the author as "criterion of interpretation," which is precisely what Compagnon is interested in renewing); he concludes that Foucault's author-function is the perfect example of such a reduction" (Compagnon 1998, p. 155).

the concept of "work" which presupposes the author. There is then in modern literary theory a kind of hypocrisy that consists in denying the role of the author-function beyond the narrative, interpretive, or in general semantic problems of the text, and at the same time, "benefiting from it" tacitly insofar as the author-function is implied in the very constitution of literary theory's object of inquiry. In short, theory continues to repress not so much the importance of the author-function in general, but that particular nexus introduced in modern art between the author-function and artistic value.

Being Authored

Foucault's indications are thus extremely useful for posing the problem of the author in our culture; still, they too are aimed at covering many types of discourses, including those of philosophy.[37] We, however, are interested only in a particular modality of reference to the author, one which is valid solely for literary discourses, and which allows them to be accepted, circulated, and treated differently from other discourses, even if those others too have an author. In other words, literary texts, though endowed with an author-function (like philosophical texts and, formerly, scientific discourses), are also subject to a phenomenon beyond that treated by Foucault. In literary texts, reference to the author is indissolubly tied to the processes of artistic valuation, which, moreover, is a characteristic common to all works of art in the modern age.

Let's begin with a very simple observation. A literary text, if it is not anonymous, *has an author,* which makes it similar to many other kinds of texts, such as essays and treatises. Nonetheless, only a literary text, insofar as it is a work of art, *is authored.* What I mean by this expression is merely what is usually meant when a person says in Italian that an object (a painting, a film or a photograph, though not a philosophical essay) is "authored." "Being authored" (*essere d'autore*) is used in this case as equivalent to "endowed with artistic value." This expression is in itself an interesting phenomenon. A special nexus exists between author-function and artistic value, one which is so close and obvious as to have actually precipitated out into the common Italian expression. The em-

37. Nonetheless, this does not produce in Foucault's discourse the same vicious circle that arises in literary theory, which surreptitiously presupposes as already given the constitutive distinction on which its object of inquiry is based. Foucault treats the author-function in general and does not take any definition of his own object of inquiry for granted.

blem of modernity is inscribed in this nexus: the special feature of a culture that establishes a conditional relationship between the possibility of attributing artistic value to an object and the fact of supposing that object to have been produced out of an artistic intention.

Formerly, as everyone knows, texts that we call "literary" nowadays (narratives, stories, epics, tragedies) used to be received, circulated, and valorized without the question of their authorship being posed. The anonymity of those texts raised no difficulty. As Foucault recalls, "Their real or supposed age was a sufficient guarantee of their authenticity."[38] Today, people want to know where every poem or piece of fiction comes from, who wrote it, when, in what circumstances, and why. And if that piece of writing should reach us anonymously, either through happenstance or the author's explicit will, the game immediately becomes that of discovering who wrote it. "Literary anonymity [is] of interest only as a puzzle to be solved as, in our day, literary works are totally dominated by the sovereignty of the author." The inevitability of the author-function is measured by the reader's very need to pose such questions, and not by whether the answers are found or not.

Several years back a Milanese publisher (Gitti) tried to start up a collection of anonymous novels. The enterprise was pursued under the slogan: "We are looking for writers, not chickens for the henhouse." This was evidently an allusion to the commercial side of authorialism, to the fact that publishing houses "construct" the author's image as a brand name to be attached to the merchandise (books) they sell. Anonymity, however, can also be fruitfully exploited for promotional purposes. Gitti's startup did not meet with much success, but it is significant that someone came up with the idea to begin with. Perhaps the publisher's intention was to provoke curiosity by leaving out exactly that function that our epoch demands must be filled. In contrast, the novel published by Einaudi under the pseudonym of Luther Blisset did much better: it "unleashed" a facile and short-lived hunt for the author, which soon climaxed with a routine press interview and photos of the four no-longer-anonymous writers.[39]

In the case of anonymous works (whether genuine or fake), the questions that we normally pose implicitly become explicit. These questions are, however, not limited to those set down by Foucault. In order to be able to attribute an artistic value to a text we certainly must ask our-

38. Foucault 1969, p. 125; the following citation is from the same source, p. 126.
39. See chapter 1, notes 7 and 9.

selves who wrote it, when, in what circumstances, and for what purpose. Nevertheless, we must also ask ourselves something more; we must also pose certain questions that are specific to artistic communication. Why, for example, did the author create that particular form? Out of what need? Or through which choice? And what does such a selection signify? How, and from what, is it different? What place within literature does the author thereby take? Every literary text, therefore, is "authored" not only in the sense that we suppose it to have been produced by someone, but also in the sense that we suppose it to have been produced by a subject *that has an artistic intention.* The author of a work of art is that person to whom we can attribute the responsibility for how the text is made, and conceive it as his or her necessity, or as his or her choice, motivated by particular artistic intentions; the responsibility, therefore, is not merely for what the text means, that is, the "instructions" for reading, as semiotics or hermeneutics would have it. The verb "suppose," which I have used over and over, is meant to indicate, as has already been mentioned, that "being authored" is not a quality that belongs to the works themselves, on account of measurable textual facts like the presence of a signature, or certain stylistic or linguistic particularities that are objectively observable.[40] Textual qualities cannot explain anything, since such qualities must first be valorized, and that valorization immediately implies processes of attribution to an author. Being authored is in short a *quality attributed* by the processes of artistic communication, which, as we have seen, can also exploit, among other things, extratextual facts, such as historical and biographical information.

The type of reference to the author specific to modern literary texts is inextricable from their being authored: it is inextricable from the attribution of artistic value to the text. Problems of paternity (the attribution of a text, which philology deals with), literary property, and criminal liability, or even the understanding of the textual machinery, are instead tied to the author-function when it is considered under the specification of "having an author." Such problems obviously concern literary texts as well as objects of art in general, but in a nonspecific way. Until now, literary theory has almost always been dedicated to problems tied to "having an author." That, however, does not mean that in these cases one can ignore taking into consideration those problems which are tied to "being authored," given that they are obviously activated by the object of study

40. In this regard, stylistic criticism is paradoxically quite close to literary criticism of a structuralist or formalist stamp, even though methodologically at opposite poles: according to the former, there are textual marks of the writer's individuality; for the latter, there are textual marks of the work's literary quality.

itself. Thus, if one studies the differences between our epoch and preceding epochs in respect to the paternity of literary works (anonymous or signed, presence or absence of the author's name), however deeply one inquires into questions tied to having an author, it will be difficult to evaluate them correctly without keeping in mind the different constraints of artistic valorization to which modern works are subjected, precisely insofar as they are literary in nature.[41]

Authored (*d'autore*) versus Generic (*di genere*)

But what exactly does "being authored" signify? Digging a bit deeper into the common usage, it is not difficult to discover the oppositional origins of the expression. It was intended to separate the class of objects endowed with artistic value from that which was merely run-of-the-mill. What is worthy of note is that, beyond all those transparently nonartistic objects (as are, to limit our examples to verbal productions, documents, letters, scientific treatises, and newspaper articles), modernity also refuses to relegate to the category of "authored" certain "quasi-literary" texts, for which the borderline with literature becomes, one might say, more hotly disputed. Consider, for example, all those forms of entertainment which used to be classified under the category of "lowbrow" literature: serial novels, gothic tales, mysteries, adventures, sentimental romances, vaudeville farces and melodrama, occasional poetry, as well as more recent forms like science fiction and New Age writing. Judged according to certain parameters of genre (e.g., the fact of being narrative fiction, drama, or poetry) all these texts ought to be included under the heading of literature; yet, by virtue of some further parameter, they are not. The expression "authored" has to do with this second line of demarcation much more than with the first. None of these texts, even though they are fiction, drama, or poetry, are considered works of art.

This second line of demarcation is typical of the modern era. A literary text has always been distinguished from other nonartistic genres of discourse, such as a philosophical treatise or a newspaper article. (Contamination, i.e., the radical mixing of heterogeneous literary forms practiced in the modern epoch, can complicate the distinction; it can make it

41. The study that Genette dedicated to this subject (Genette 1987) does not take into account the specificity of the modern processes of artistic valorization; these processes, however, make the modern phenomena related to the author's name (e.g. anonymous, pseudonymous, apocryphal, uncertain, etc.) incommensurable with such phenomena in other epochs. Genette's approach puts everything on the same plane.

intentionally problematic; even so, that does not prevent such a distinction from being made.) It is only in modernity that the distinction between a novel of "high" literary value and a piece of pulp fiction has been drawn, ever since the occurrence of that typically modern divergence separating the conventions of genre from artistic value. According to modern artistic logic, not everything that belongs to a literary genre is necessarily granted artistic value; not all novels are literature, not all dramas, not all poems. It is necessary to make further distinctions. It is precisely this later distinction, one which is subtle and byzantine, that the expression "being authored" has come to signalize in the modern period.

There are other interesting things that we can observe on the flip side of the opposition: that which is not "authored" is indeed, according to common speech, "generic" (*di genere*). The broad category of literature for mass consumption, or entertainment, which the Germans call *Trivialliterateur*, is also sometimes referred to as "genre writing." This is another linguistic sign of the romantic concept of literature, where artistic value is based on originality, and everything that stays too close to the norm or to a stylistic-thematic convention, is looked down on. Before the rise of such an idea of literature, no one would ever have used the term "genre writing" (*letteratura di genere*) with a deprecatory connotation. Nor until that time would anyone have used "authored" in the sense that it is used today. It can therefore be supposed that between the two phenomena (investment in the author-function and devaluation of genre-bound production) there is a certain relation, in their genesis, if in nothing more. Not even the late-modern tendency to contaminate authored literature, that is, mix serious writing of artistic ambition with elements of genre writing, has completely subverted this relation. To the extent that this trend continues to be perceived as a kind of sensationalism, a kind of giddiness, a perverse pleasure taken by art as it rubs shoulders with its opposite, the distinction between serious writing and cheap fiction is not emptied of meaning, but rather valorized, since it is exploited to achieve a particular artistic effect.

Film and the Birth of the *Auteur*

We find indirect proof of the same phenomena in cinema. Today the French expression *film d'auteur* (in Italian, *film d'autore*; in English, "art film" is also used) appears obvious to us; nonetheless, it is a concept that arose relatively recently compared to the birth of cinema. It is a concept that had to be fought for along with the demand that film be considered a true and proper art, and not merely a low-brow entertainment, or craft. In an article of 1949, Alexandre Astruc wrote:

> The cinema is quite simply becoming a means of expression, just as all the other arts before it, and in particular, painting and the novel. After having been successively a fairground attraction, an amusement analogous to boulevard theatre, or a means of preserving the images of an era, it is gradually becoming a language. By language, I mean a form in which and by which an artist can express his thoughts, however abstract they may be, or translate his own obsessions exactly as he does in a contemporary essay or novel. That is why I would like to call this new age of cinema the age of the *caméra-stylo*.[42]

The image of the motion picture camera as stylographic pen (and as *stylus* and style) is really a way to claim for cinema the prerogative of every art: that of expressing the "individuality" of the artist, in this case that of the director, with his or her obsessions, recurring themes, and particular view of the world. "Directing is no longer a means to illustrate or present a scene, but a true form of writing," Astruc adds. For this reason, there is something individual and induplicable about it. The cinematic author writes with the movie camera just as the writer does with the fountain pen, adopting a certain form and expressing a certain outlook on the world: "Can we imagine a Faulkner novel written by anyone other than Faulkner? And would *Citizen Kane* be acceptable in any form other than the one Orson Welles gave it?"

The young art of cinema, which had in a short space of time passed through modernity's stages of artistic evolution (and remains, for this reason, quite revelatory), thus began to use the formula *film d'auteur* in the early fifties, when it gained consciousness of its own artistic status. It is further proof that in our culture it is impossible to separate the artistic nature of a product from the fact of supposing it to be authored. Most important, however, this notion arises just when the problem of producing films unencumbered by the dictates of the movie industry is first posed. André Bazin and the critics of *Cahiers du Cinéma* put it into circulation with their so-called "politique des auteurs":

> The *politique des auteurs* consists, in short, of choosing the personal in artistic creation as a standard of reference, and then of assuming that it

42. Astruc 1948, p. 5, from which the following citations are also drawn.

continues and even progresses from one film to the next. It is recognized that there do exist certain important films of quality that escape this test, but these will systematically be considered inferior to those in which the personal stamp of the *auteur,* however run-of-the-mill the scenario, can be perceived even minutely.[43]

The concept of *auteur,* therefore, gets introduced at the moment when cinema acquires the awareness (which literature had gained more than a century earlier) that there was a commodified, industrial form of production from which it was necessary to distinguish itself. From then on, cinema too begins to use the category of "authored film" (*film d'auteur*) not in opposition to documentary or educational films or to its other nonartistic uses (an opposition analogous to that between an essay and a literary text), but rather in opposition to entertainment films made for the broadest audiences possible and degraded to objects of consumption (an opposition analogous to that between a serious novel (*romanzo d'autore*) and a cheap novel (*romanzo d'appendice*).

What were the commercial films of those years? By and large they were "genre" films (*film di genere*) though it must be pointed out that neither the distinction between *auteur* films and commercial films, nor the negative connotation associated with genre films, then existed. Prior to the fifties, the cinema, somewhat like classical literature, was entirely, but happily, a production of genres. Lubitsch, Lang, and Hawks made comedies, gangster films, or westerns, that is, films that fit perfectly into a common grammar: cinematic genres that the broad public could recognize and appreciate and within which lower-quality products could also fit. Today, the cinematic "auteur" makes works that either go beyond the codified genres or revisits (with a greater or lesser degree of originality and/or necrophilia) an already established one.

But are not those great directors of the past, the authors of genre films that are still memorable, proof that there is no contradiction between a film's "being authored" and its "being generic"? Do we not say, ever since the "politique des auteurs," that the comedies and westerns of a Howard Hawks are "authored" films? This is a perfectly reasonable objection that can be raised against what I have been saying. Nonetheless, if one examines the matter more closely, it is one more example of how the distinction between authored films and genre films functions. Today, post–*Les Cahiers du Cinéma,* a Hawks film is perceived as "authored," yet it is a perception

43. Bazin 1957, p. 255.

altogether different from that which its contemporaries had of it. Moreover, we perceive it as "authored" *even though* it is a genre film. In the artistic enjoyment of a great western film, there enters today the subtle perception of its anomaly vis-à-vis the dominant artistic axiology, which tends to devalue everything that conforms to an established set of norms. (Cinema arrives at such an axiology, which for literature begins with romanticism, precisely at the moment in which the notion of "authored film" was coined.) But such "reacceptance" of the cinematic genre hardly nullifies that axiology: on the contrary, it makes use of it. It is somewhat similar to the snobbery of the duchess of Guermantes, who dares to associate with characters normally shunned according to the standard snobbishness of her class: it is in no way an abandonment of snobbishness, but a variation on it. Similarly, the *cult movie* transforms the crowd-pleasing "craftsman" who produces commercial films into an "auteur."

As to the genre film, there is no need to imagine it as a production that remains tied to the normative purity of a canon. The modern tendency toward the mixing and interpenetration of heterogeneous genres today includes commercial movies. A typical example is the "new horror" film, which from "B-movie" rapidly became a genre generating high box-office sales. From this position it has not only influenced all the other cinematic genres, contaminating them with its "show everything" poetics based on special effects, but has ended up parodying itself, stepping over into comedy, and the grotesque, while parading its own devices. The novel passed through a similar trajectory, though its course lasted more than three centuries rather than a few decades. As it became the dominant genre, the novel impacted the entire literary system, provoking what Bakhtin called "the novelization of literature," ultimately arriving at the point of exposing its own techniques and parodying its own varieties just as they were being canonized. The story of cinema, if properly read, could reveal all sorts of things concerning the "physiology" of genres, presenting us with a compressed version of the processes which literature took centuries to pass through. The "new horror" movie arrived, developed, exerted its influence on the other genres, incorporated them, and finally began to make fun of itself, all in a time lapse of less than twenty years, from George Romero's *Night of the Living Dead* (1968) to Sam Raimi's *The Evil Dead* (1983) and *Evil Dead 2* (1987), as compared to the two hundred or three hundred years it took for the novel to complete a similar cycle.

Even the so-called art film (*cinema d'auteur*) has a rather complex relationship with genres. The "revisiting" of conventional film genres is by now a standard practice. This too is reminiscent of the ironic use of literary genres, and the tendency to utilize for literary purposes forms that were long considered "lowbrow" (see chapter 4). But one would be mistaken to think that such phenomena signify the end of the distinction between "authored" and "generic" writing and film. On the contrary, this distinction has only begun to be exploited for artistic ends; it remains as the condition of possibility for all these subtle games of the mixing and interpenetration of heterogeneous art forms.[44]

Our first conclusion: in contemporary culture it is impossible to separate the artistic value of a product from the fact of supposing it to be authored. The author assumes the artistic function.

Our second conclusion: things have not always been this way. As long as artistic production could be serenely framed within the genres, that is, before their modern devaluation, the author did not fulfill this role, or at least fulfilled it in a much less marked manner. Whereas the current theories of the author-function aspire to a universal, metahistoric validity (the implied author, the ideal author, and the subject of intentions as guarantor of meaning are supposed to be valid for all epochs), ours, which bases itself on "being authored," is defined as something absolutely specific to modern art.

Third, if the author carries less weight where genres hold sway, one might suspect that the author has taken on a duty that was formerly handled by the genres. This, then, is the subject of the following chapter.

---

44. The notion of the author in cinema has been treated by Ropars and Sorlin 1990 from a perspective close to that presented here. They pointed out the strange contradiction between the way cinema multiplies the roles played in the creation of films (from the screenwriter, to the editor, to the sound technician) on one side, and the way film criticism, on the other, "re-invents the author in order to find in him or her the source and guarantee of a film's unity" (p. 24). Cinema requires the activity of a team. Nonetheless, there is something akin to a "hypostasis of the author" on the part of film criticism. It is supposed that there is an intentionality, a "tone," an identity, running through the separate spheres of expertise, and that the artistic quality of the finished work passes through the unifying action of a director. The paradox consists then in the fact that the multiplicity of talent can be understood and appreciated only if placed under the jurisdiction of a sole creator. That, write the two theoreticians, is perhaps due to "an esthetic requirement that demands unity in order to make the artistic quality of the work recognizable." I too believe that the hypostasis of the author is needed for the artistic valorization of the product: without the supposition of an author, the artistry of the work cannot be recognized. However, it is not necessary to accentuate the *unity of the sole creator* (from which derives the paradox of the film's being a collective product, even though considered as the achievement of a creative individuality). One might accentuate instead the *choice* that has been made: the fact, that is, that at the origin of the cinematic work there is a meaningful selection among what is artistically possible and such a choice can easily be considered collective without entering into contradiction with the hypostasis of the author.

CHAPTER 4

From Genres to Authors

Genres and authors are two points of reference indispensable to literary communication since each allows us to go beyond the single text, creating links, expectations, and therefore structures.[1] Together they provide the mediation that makes the enjoyment of a text possible. That genre can play this role is perhaps something unforeseen but easily intuited. In order to appreciate a chivilric poem such as *Orlando Furioso,* and even more so, in order to write it, some minimum experience of the genre will be required: that kind of experience or foreknowledge that memory of the characteristics common to several works of the same type furnishes us. The idea that the author can play an analogous role is something that might at first seem strange, yet that is what happens in modern literary communication. On the great chessboard of literature, authors (single or in groups) mark out "positions"; they incarnate choices of form and content that have "motives" and that are endowed with a differential value within the history of forms and the successive changing of poetics. Such motives and differences are precisely what create associations and expectations and generate the structures that orient the act of enjoyment.

1. The notion of structure is used here in the sense of Niklas Luhmann's theory of social systems, that is, as *structures of expectations* that orient communication, by reducing its complexity. Through the mediation of expectations, a system is in a position to determine relationships and therefore what is effectively possible. See Luhmann 1984.

However, genres and authors stand in a relationship of competition: where the mediation of the genre is strong, that of the author carries less weight; and vice versa, where the genre begins to weaken, the author-function gets stronger especially insofar as it is the bearer of the selection of poetics. Indeed, poetics became a mediation essential to literary communication when genres ceased being so. In other words, in modern literature, the author has assumed some of the functions that formerly belonged to genres. In discussing the author, then, we cannot do without a chapter dedicated to literary genres so as to explain the reasons and modalities for such a transfer of custody.

The Ancient Functions of Genres

Modern literary theory offers us a very extensive treatment of the ancient functions of genres, which it would be impossible, as well as useless, for us to survey here. We will limit ourselves to picking out the concepts that seem most important within the scope of our argument, scrutinizing each function to determine whether or not it is valid today. But we must also settle accounts with the lacunae of theory since among the generic functions described in innumerable treatises, the most important one for us is hardly ever mentioned. Having been for the most part overlooked, it has remained nameless; we will call it the *metacommunicative function,* and set aside its precise definition until later. Let's first consider those functions that the theory of genres has already treated, beginning with the one most commonly discussed.

The Classificatory and Normative Function

As is well known, classical theory gave great prominence to the classificatory and normative aspect of genres, which made demonstrating the uselessness of genres quite easy in the modern epoch. Thus, Crocean aesthetics, at the outset of the twentieth century, was able to dispense with genres in the name of the expressive singularity of every work of art. This act of liquidation was, moreover, the last stage of a critique of the normative universality of the canons, which had begun in the eighteenth century (starting from the question of imitating the classics, passing to the demand for artistic freedom in opposition to the rigid codifications of Aristotelian poetics in the classical and neoclassical eras, and right up to the revolt, first of the Enlightenment and then of romanticism, against every normative attitude).

However, the normative rules of the genres, in the restrictive sense of prescription and conformity to a canon to which neoclassical poetics had reduced them, may never have existed outside of the abstract world of theoreticians,[2] so it would hardly make sense to speak of their disappearance today. More subtly effective are the functions that literary genres exerted over the centuries, which we will have to look into in order to understand if they are still valid today.

The Selective and Orientative Function

If we abandon, as Hans Robert Jauss proposes, the normative (*ante rem*) and classificatory (*post rem*) points of view in favor of one that is historical (*in re*), the notion of genre regains all its theoretical and critical importance.[3] It becomes an indispensable category for investigating both the complex relations that single works maintain among each other and the manner in which they are received by readers. This is why, in the very same cultural climate out of which the studies on intertextuality would arise, a new historico-hermeneutic and structural-semiotic theory of genres strongly reasserted, against Croce, the necessity of the genre perspective in literature.

Jauss views genres as empirical groups or historical families that form the reader's horizons of expectation. Genre is the continuity of a structure common to a number of works that appear in a historical series. This "continuity that creates the genre" is not a canon to be reproduced, but a horizon of information and expectations that has been formed on the basis of a tradition, a horizon in which each new text inserts itself, thus making the text recognizable to a certain public.

> It is also unimaginable that a literary work set itself into an informational vacuum, without indicating a specific situation of understanding. To this

2. As Croce himself noted, it always turned out that "each true work of art has violated some established genre, thus throwing into disorder the ideas of the critics, who have then been obliged to broaden the genre, without however being able to prevent the broadened genre from proving too narrow as soon as new works of art arise, which are followed, naturally, by new scandals, new disorders, and new broadenings"(Croce 1902, p. 37 [modifications have been made to the translated version]).

3. Jauss 1970, p. 80.

extent, every work belongs to a genre—whereby I mean neither more nor less than that for each work a pre-constituted horizon of expectations must be ready at hand (this can also be understood as a relationship of "rules of the game" [*Zusammenhang von Spielregeln*] to orient the reader's (public's) understanding and to enable a qualifying reception.[4]

Not even the singularity of a work, which was the crucial issue for Croce, can possibly emerge except against the background of a generality. And even when the work seems to belie every expectation, there still remains an orientation of expectations on which its deviation and originality are measured. The manner in which the horizon is formed and the manner in which each individual work makes reference to it are really very different from what a normative canon might demand. The continuity that the genre creates is not simply a confirmation and reproduction of expectations, but also and above all a succession of variations, enlargements, and rectifications: "The relationship between the individual text with the series of texts formative of a genre presents itself as a process of the continual founding and altering of horizons."[5]

In the sphere of structuralism and semiotics, too, what spurred theoreticians to take up the old notion was the need for a concept vaster than that of the text as an instrument for tackling the processes of literary communication. Genre is no longer viewed here either as a normative canon or as a classificatory catalogue, but as a "location" in which every work ideally inserts itself through the relations that it enters into with others and, together, with the literary system as a whole. "The text," writes Maria Corti, "does not exist alone inside literature, but due to its very signifying function belongs with other signs to a whole, i.e. a genre, which takes shape as the site where the work enters into a complex network of relations with other works."[6] Genette considers the literary genre as a particular type of "textual transcendence" or "transtextuality," meaning by this term everything that brings a text into manifest or hidden relation with other texts. In the case of the literary genre, it has to do with a "relation of inclusion that links each text to the various types of discourse it belongs to," which Genette, still playing with the word *text*, calls "architextuality."[7]

4. Ibid., p. 79.
5. Ibid., p. 88.
6. Corti 1976, p. 151. Cf. also Segre 1979.
7. Genette 1979, pp. 81–83. Rather than on genres (mode + theme = historical process), Genette's attention is concentrated on the *modes* (dramatic, epic, mixed), which

Of course, such points of contact among the different theories are graspable only at a very high level of generalization, which sets aside the diversity of their approaches. In one case, the visual angle in which the theory is located is that of reception, and the recourse to a category that "transcends" the text explains the manner in which the reader's horizons of expectation are formed, the manner in which an individual text is received, interpreted, evaluated. In the other case, the visual angle is instead that of production and construction of the text, and of its levels of structuring. One then finds, even within structuralist and semiotic thinking, a notable diversity of approach: at times deductive and atemporal (Genette), at times inductive and diachronic (Lotman, Segre, Corti, who from this point of view, are closer to the reflections of Jauss than to those of Genette). However, providing a panorama of the different theories is of less interest here than laying out their common assumptions so that we may draw our own observations.

Turning from its function to its concrete definition, it can be said that the genre usually is seen as a relationship between two planes, the thematic and the formal. Typical of the literary genre is not so much the presence of particular themes or motives (which as such can be common to several genres), but rather the relationship between these themes and the plane of form. For example, the theme of love is not sufficient to characterize Petrarch's poetry because the same theme is found in many other genres; what characterizes it instead is the relationship between a certain mode of treating that theme and its formal and metric rendering in the sonnet or canzone. This relationship remains unvarying within a certain number of texts, and that is why we can recognize the genre as a sort of text (or architext), even if, as Lotman noted, it is impossible to make such a category the object of an artistic perception.[8] This unvarying relationship allows some theoreticians to consider genre as a code: certainly not a code of strong normative characteristics like that of language, but a code that presents itself instead as a "program constructed upon very general laws" that concern the dynamic relationship between themes and forms.[9] A genre, then, is a program for the construction of a

---

he considers as the a priori conditions of literary expression, deduced from rhetorical and linguistic structures, and which are defined as "the panorama in which the evolution of the literary fact is inscribed." Genette's approach is therefore not only transhistoric but also deductive, and ends up locking the literarily possible inside a paradigm (but see also the objections to him made by Derrida 1986, in the chapter *La Loi du genre*, pp. 256–261).

8. Lotman 1970.
9. Corti 1976, pp. 157–158.

work in which the writer finds it economical to guide his or her own creation, but with which the work never fully coincides.

Alongside of the codifications there are then the variations introduced by individual texts, among which is a dynamic relationship of noteworthy interest for theory: such variations can transform the codes from within, or corrode them to the point of destruction. The evolutive moment is always innate to the existence of genres: in the course of history, genres evolve, die, rise anew, and the literary system, as a whole, is subjected to continuous reorganizations.

For all these reasons, a purely normative function cannot be attributed to genres. Insofar as they are programs, they play what we might call a "selective" role. They operate as a kind of preselection of the literarily possible, indicating already-beaten paths to follow or to deviate from; in either case, however, there are certain restrictions such that the creative act does not begin ex nihilo. By selecting themes in relation to the form, a genre also imposes on those who make use of it the acceptance of an interpretive model of reality, though only as a simple frame of reference in which to locate its further selections. Of course, the genre plays not only a selective function for the author but also for the reader, orienting the reception of a text toward certain types of decoding rather than toward others. The genre is the "location" of the extratextual relations in which the very life of the text is inserted: that series of already known texts, on the basis of which is formed, on one side the competence of the author, and on the other the competence of the reader. It thus fulfills a function that we might call "orientative" since it guides both reception and production by selecting from among the possible thematic-formal possibilities; selecting, that is, both "what can be written," and "what one can expect to read there."

The Metacommunicative Function

However, the genres over the centuries have also fulfilled another extremely important function, one that modern theories have almost always left in the shadows. I call it the "metacommunicative function" because it is entrusted with a sort of metacommunication, or implicit communication, about how the communication underway should be taken. In this case, it concerns the manner in which the text should be approached and enjoyed. When a text is recognized as a chivilric poem, its artistic nature is implicitly recognized as well, and so it is approached as a literary work, and not, for example, as a treatise on theology. That may seem tautological, but such an impression dissolves as soon as we consider this simple fact: what we today call literature (and what formerly was called poetry), which is to say the entire set of verbal texts endowed with artistic value, constitutes a restricted region within a much vaster space, which is the entire set of verbal practices, not all of which are artistic. I call metacommunicative function the capacity that literary genres formerly possessed to immediately signal that a text belonged to this restricted region, thus requiring a certain type of approach and enjoyment. *Orlando Furioso* was received as a literary work by its contemporary readers not so much because it incarnated the aesthetic value of beauty, nor because it was written by Ariosto, but above all because it was a chivilric poem. At a time when belonging to a genre had not yet become a synonym for low artistic value (as it is in modern literature), the genre had an extremely important function in the processes of identifying literature. Between the individual text and the essentially indefinable sphere that is literature, stood the genre as a class recognizable and well defined. And it was precisely the recognizability of generic traits that implicitly communicated the "literariness" of a text.

Unlike many other theoreticians, Genette does not overlook this important function of genres; he describes it, however, as one of three possible universal "modes of literariness" (specifically, the "constitutive" mode based on a "rhematic" criterion), equally valid for antiquity and the modern period.[10] In contrast, I view the metacommunicative function of genres as noticeably weaker in modern literature as it gives way to other modalities of artistic valorization. The primary role is no longer played by the genre but by the author and his or her choices of poetics.

The Identity of Literature

The metacommunicative function may be less visible than the other functions of the genres because, as happens to all those operations on which others are premised, it is fulfilled in an implicit way. The function of any particular advertising campaign is not only to sell the product of a certain brand, but also to contribute, together with the totality of all advertising campaigns, to the reinforcement of consumption. Similarly, a literary genre has not only the function special to it within that certain sector of literature (i.e., that of selecting theme-form relations), but also,

10. Genette 1991, chapter 1.

implicitly, that of designating (and continually redesignating) together with the other genres the boundaries of the literary system of a particular epoch. Indeed, many theoreticians have emphasized that genres are to be considered in relation to each other: the ensemble of literary genres of a given epoch constitute a system. And for this very reason, the fact that a text belongs to a genre implicitly signifies its belonging to literature. Since a genre is defined and perceived in a relation different from or opposed to other genres that form the literary system of an epoch (for example: tragedy, epic, and comedy in the system described by Aristotle), belonging to a genre implicitly confers on a text, along with its position inside the system, the legitimacy of its being inscribed there, too. Such metacommunication, which was formerly entrusted to the generic markings of texts, had a crucial role: on it depended the very identity of the literary system, enabling it to differentiate between what was "inside" and "outside" it. Without this constitutive distinction there could not exist that set of verbal practices that we today call literature. Perhaps for this very reason, however, modern theory, reluctant to deal with constitutive problems, has almost always overlooked the existence of such a metacommunicative function.

For the art of words to exist in whatever epoch, there needs to be an active delimitation between it and the nonartistic use of language. No culture having the concept of verbal art (whether it is called poetry, as in the time of Aristotle, or literature, as we call it today) can do without this act of distinction, and without continually reproducing it through techniques that often remain implicit. The distinction between art and nonart is certainly necessary to every artistic system, not only to that of literature. Nonetheless, in the other arts, as for example, in painting and sculpture, the distinction has no need (at least it did not in the past, though things changed in this regard during the twentieth century) of being assigned in a manner so conspicuous as the thematic and formal conventions of literature, for it was in a certain sense already guaranteed by the *intrinsically artistic* nature of pictorial and sculptural practices. Of course, we can also recognize "genres" within the sphere of painting as well, but the metacommunication "this is art" does not principally depend on such a recognition. Sculpting marble or spreading colors on canvass are not easily confused with nonartistic activities, whereas using oral or written language to talk about facts, express a thought, or communicate an experience can fall into a variety of classes, very few of which are actually artistic. Literature, therefore, much more than other arts, has always needed to actively mark its own boundaries with respect to nonartistic verbal practices.

An indirect proof of that point is furnished by the theory of genres itself, which in no other artistic field has ever had the moment and consequence that literary theory has always accorded it. The reason why all the poetics of the past, starting from Aristotle's, gave so much importance to the description of genres, their classification, their mutual relations, does not simply depend on normative demands but also and above all on constitutive issues. Knowing what a literary genre is (which are the "true" literary genres, and their relations) is equivalent to knowing what literature is. And this is not only an issue of theory and definition. It is also a matter of the competence of the reader (knowing how to recognize the constant traits shared by several texts) and that of the writer (who makes use of certain models). The theoretical definitions of genres have always had some effect on the world of phenomena that they described. The Aristotelian definition of tragedy, for example, influenced the production and enjoyment of texts for almost two millennia. What the theory of genres has elaborated over the course of the centuries is not solely of theoretical importance, but in a circular way affects the very processes of literary communication, which is not constituted only by the moments of production and enjoyment, but also by those of theorization and evaluation. In each of these moments, which are linked to each other, the generic categories have succeeded in playing a major role in setting the limits between literature and nonartistic verbal practices. Strangely enough, in an essay on genres, Jean-Marie Schaeffer neatly expressed this "truth," not in order to explain it, but rather to censure it. He notes that the theory of genres "became the site where the fate of literature's range of extention and definition of intention is played out."[11] And that is supposed to be the underlying vice that has always spoiled the reflection on genres, from Aristotle to the moderns. It is a strange reproof to charge theory with such an "error" when, in reality, this function has been one of the principal modalities for the identification of literature for almost two millennia.

A New Perverse Function

But do those incorporeal entities called literary genres still exist in contemporary literature? And if so, do they still fulfill the same role they did in the past, or a different one, which has yet to be described? The first question may seem silly since for more than two decades literary pro-

11. Schaeffer 1989, French text, pp. 9–10.

duction in both prose and poetry has offered us numerous examples of "returns" to the genres, which have been serious rather than transgressive or parodic.[12] But for a long time the idea of a "dissolution" of the genres was rather widespread, and it may stick around for a good while longer. In the time of triumphant modernity, a work "of value" that did not corrode some codified genre, or explode the very possibility of a generic classification, was inconceivable. This made it seem that the genres had become a thing of the past. For example, Blanchot has asserted that "only the book matters, such as it is, far from genres, outside of categories—prose, poetry, novel, testimony—under which it refuses to be classed, and to which it denies the ability to assign its place and determine its form."[13] It seemed, in short, that genres were failing to furnish either criteria of classification or guidelines on the possible form of a text to such an extent as to look, where still visible, like mere vestiges. This opinion, for which Blanchot was the authoritative, though certainly not the sole, spokesman, was formerly, and in certain cases still is, almost a commonplace. It should, however, not be confused with that of Croce. Croce had declared the genres irrelevant in the name of the individuality of every work of art, whether past or present, while Blanchot did so in the name of the greater freedom from codification won by modern literature: his liquidation of the genres thus laid claim to a specifically modern, and especially twentieth-century, trait. Indeed, the theory of genres reacts differently to the two liquidations: while Croce's position was contested by all those who returned to the study of genres, the other has sometimes met with their approval, or at least an agnostic neutrality.

The second question (whether genres have the same role today as they had in the past) is, on the contrary, crucial for a theory of literature that wants to cross swords with the present, but it is also rather shapeless and hazy. There are no sufficiently far-reaching analyses to refer to; in compensation, there are opinions that have never been put to rigorous scrutiny. Moreover, it is useless to ask the modern theory of genres for illumination since on this point it has little or nothing to say. If it has made any contribution at all, it has only been to thicken the haze. Certainly the modern theory of genres has given birth to rigorous conceptualizations, but only by taking the literature of the past as its model, and avoiding, except in rare cases, dealing with contemporary works. That is a legiti-

12. Furthermore, there are those who define the postmodern as "an attempt to reclaim the genres," in opposition to that refutation of literary genres that held sway for so long in the modern period. Cf. for example Schulz-Buschhaus 1995, p. 6.
13. Blanchot 1959, p. 200.

mate choice, but one which poorly jibes with the pretension of universality to which such theory usually aspires. Jauss, for example, describes the function of the orientation of expectations played by the genres based on a corpus of medieval texts. That however did not keep him from claiming a more general validity: though modeled on premodern literature, his definition is formulated in such a way as to be extendible to all epochs, including our own. So even today the genres would still have the same role they always had, that of orienting the expectations of readers. Nevertheless, if one looks carefully, such an extension of the notion's validity is never thematized, and consequently neither argued out nor verified. It is instead an implicit opinion that Jauss and the theory of reception generally *authorize us* to have. Strictly speaking, one might not even be able to challenge him on it, seeing how it is never explicitly set down. When dealing with modern literature, Jauss rarely speaks of "genres," whereas all the emphasis is placed on the concept of "horizon of expectations."[14] Even so, the inference comes about because he elaborated that notion in relation to medieval genres. While no one can deny that a horizon of expectations is also at work in modern literary communication, that this horizon still coincides today with the genres (i.e., that the orientation of the act of enjoyment is still mediated by genres in the same manner in which it was in premodern literature), is something that would have to be demonstrated and verified. From my viewpoint, that is totally unfounded: what orients the act of enjoyment today is not the genres but altogether different processes.

If the theory of reception in its very prudent way authorizes the belief that the genres still conserve today the same function as always, others, even more prudently, completely suspend their judgment on contemporary phenomena. The majority of theoreticians (from Genette to Schaeffer) avoid saying whether the genres described by them are still or are no longer active today. And yet even in this case there is no renunciation of the claim to general validity. That renders the theory's position somewhat bizarre. If nothing can be said about contemporary literature, how can there be any aspiration to providing a universal definition of genres and of their functions? These treatises encompass dizzying expanses of literary history, from Aristotle up to the romantics, but they say nothing about the literature that came after. Why this silence? Is it perhaps be-

---

14. The concept, as is well known, is central to the theory of reception. It has many affinities with Husserl's *protention* (Cf. Husserl 1966), although Jauss states that he elaborated it before having read Husserl (cf. Jauss 1993, p. 64). Iser, on the other hand, goes directly back to Husserl (Iser 1978, pp. 111–112).

cause in the contemporary period the relationship between works and genres became more intricate and complex? Or is it perhaps that the last hundred years are a trifle compared to the centuries of literary history that theory has cared to account for? In either case, such reasons are hardly acceptable. The only plausible reason that we can imagine for this strange silence of theory, especially if considered in relation to its claim to generality, is that it takes for granted that the genres have today exhausted themselves to the point of disappearing. There would then be little to be described in the production of the twentieth century, except the late stages of a progressive crisis offering little material for theorization. As a result, the theory of genres ends up in certain cases by authorizing the opinion opposed to that of Jauss, that is, that of Blanchot. And sometimes it is not even necessary to search between the lines for such a stance. Maria Corti, for example, openly maintains that genres have radically lost their function because the literary system has entered into crisis.[15]

Thus, there are two opinions in the field: on one side, the "reassuring" one that the theory of reception seems to authorize (i.e., that genres still conserve today the same function as they always had); on the other, the "modernist" (that genres have by now lost their function). There is also a third: the "postmodern," according to which the genres long banished by modernist poetics, are making a strong comeback with their functions intact. Which of the three is true? I would say that the second is less inexact than the others, if for no other reason than that it brings out into the open the irreversible caesura of modernity. Basically, however, none of them hits the target. Still, it should be noted how all three differing opinions are in agreement on one point, and that is exactly what I would like to take up for discussion. The functions of genres would seem to be permanent insofar as they are universal and immutable; at their limit they may disappear, jump back, enter into crisis, leave the scene and return, but they never change their function. For theory, there exist only those "eternal functions" defined on the basis of a literature that may no longer exist, and these functions may suffer a momentary interruption or even die off, but they are immune to change. Theory thus fails to conceive that literary genres may have by now acquired a different role, unknown to the literature of the past; they may have, in short, modified, al-

15. "The entrance into ideological, therefore non-literary, crisis among the most informed writers, of the concept of the literary system coincided with the current loss of the genres' esthetic function; . . . the genres are in crisis because the codes that regulated the theme-form relationship have broken down" (Corti 1976, pp. 159–160).

tered, or converted their old function into something different, without having died off.

Here is my view of the matter: genres never disappeared, but their role has undergone a radical change in the modern literary system. More precisely, modern artistic logic modified the old functions of the genres, as also their forms of existence, from the moment in which it transformed them into a negative category, synonymous with conventionality. This profound transformation has led to a fundamental change in the relations between the work and the literary system (the mediation of which is no longer performed by the genres but by something else), one that not even the postmodern revalorization of genres has been able to annul. Even if the old genres are reclaimed, they come back not with the complete function of old, but as ironically reaccepted conventionality, under the banner of the notion that "the conventional is inevitable."[16]

The most telling sign of the transformation undergone by genres in the modern period is their slippage toward the margins of the literary system. I am referring to that vast portion of literary production that continues to be *peacefully* classifiable within well-defined generic categories (horror stories, mysteries, westerns, romance, science fiction, among others) and is for this reason even called "genre fiction." In English, such writing is variously referred to as "popular" or "lowbrow" literature, light reading, or pulp fiction; in French, as *paralittérature;* in German, as *Trivialliteratur.* This is a kind of writing that modern culture, especially in Europe, has long considered marginal, for mass consumption, devoid of literary merit, in opposition to a not-much-better-defined "highbrow" literature, or "serious" writing, which we might now call *authored literature.* Genre writing has been around for at least two centuries (if we choose to trace it back to the gothic novel), but has experienced a continual influx of new formations (from science fiction to the New Age novel), and it has gradually crystallized into a series of relatively stable generic codes. Such predictability is in contrast to the openness and rapid dynamism typical of authored literature, which instead prevents any of its varieties from stabilizing into a code.

In the modern epoch, then, genres have continued to function at full tilt only in popular literature. Here, they really still do maintain *all* the functions with which they were formerly invested: criterion for classification of the texts, "program" for their construction, and orientation of the reader's expectations. It is often said that popular literature is

16. Schulz-Buschhaus 1995, p. 14.

schematic and repetitive because it rigidly conforms to a canon. That opinion (perhaps even shared by Jauss) is superficial. Looking more closely, one realizes that in this parallel literary reality the canons of genre often go through fecund modifications and variations, owing to individual and original contributions. One need only think of the science fiction novel and the variations introduced to it by writers like Philip K. Dick or Stanislaw Lem. Just as in premodern literature, the path of the genre, in cases like these, continues to support creation, and the canons are transformed from within without being destroyed, exactly as Ariosto was able to do in respect to the chivilric romance. Based on this, one might also say that, in the modern epoch, the dynamic of reproposing and varying expectations (which for Jauss is a universal function of genres) now finds its paradoxical illustration solely in popular literature. But that dynamic really works only on the margins of the system, in a zone that merely constitutes the background of the class "authored literature." The possibility of associating a modern work with a generic label and reading it within the horizon of a genre (which, we will repeat, does not simply equate with rigid conformity to the norms of the genre, but also their innovative variation) goes hand in hand with the impossibility of attributing to it a full artistic value. Even an innovative work of this kind, which exemplifies how the genres were supposed to function in the literary system of the past, would not today be considered "literature." And the exclusion does not depend so much on the text's thematic-formal qualities, its structure or "poetics," which may be of high value, as in the case of the above-mentioned science fiction writers. Even before arriving at a true and proper critical evaluation, its banishment to popular literature is decreed by the genre label, by its being legible within the horizon of a genre. Here then is the phenomenon that the theory of reception seems to repress in toto: the value of genres has been inverted as their sign has changed from positive to negative. As a result, they now fulfill the function of orientation as described by Jauss, not *within* literature but *outside* of it.

What happens then on the side of authored literature? When Blanchot denied the genres the power to fix the position of a book or to determine its form, he was obviously referring to "high" literature, as viewed through the particular artistic logic of modernity. And here it would be hard to argue with him. In modern authored literature the genres no longer furnish a program for the construction of a text nor the horizon for its enjoyment. But it would be mistaken to deduce from this that they have no role to play at all. Genres do serve, if for no other purpose, as a way to negatively define "high" literature. "Serious writing" or authored literature is, by definition, that which is no longer subject to the "grammar" of the genres, and so cannot be labeled or enjoyed within their too limited horizons. A new function of genres is thus activated, and without our being aware of it, each time we have recourse to the distinction between "high" literature and "genre" writing, which was unknown to premodern literature. It is precisely the relation that the work is supposed to maintain with the codes of genre that functions as the gatekeeper for valuation, allowing us to distinguish between two types of literary production: on one side, we have "authored" ("high," serious) literature; on the other, we have "genre" literature (light reading, literature for mass consumption, pulp fiction, B-quality, or industrial writing).

And yet if we take a closer look at this function, although negative, there is nothing new about it: in it, the old metacommunicative function of genres lives on despite the change of sign. Even in its modern devaluation genre continues to metacommunicate something regarding the manner in which a work demands to be received, evaluated, and enjoyed, by furnishing a criterion for the identification of what is and what is not "literature." In the modern epoch, bearing a genre label signifies a text's lack of artistic quality and its banishment to the literature for mass consumption; exiting from the horizon of genres signifies its artistic nature and right to be received within the sphere of authored literature. The distinction between genre literature and authored literature has therefore become in modernity a criterion for artistic valorization, or better, a kind of regulative idea that guides the judgment of a work's value. Indeed, from a certain point of view, modern artistic logic is nothing other than this regulative idea, and postmodernism defines itself insofar as it simultaneously denies and exploits this logic. The postmodern reclamation of popular generic fiction reintroduces into authored literature not the genre in its old function, but the genre as a refusal of modernity, in other words, the genre decayed to mere convention.

In conclusion, genres continue to have a well-defined and important role in modern and late-modern literature, even in those artistic practices usually identified as postmodern. However, it is a negative and, I would say, subtly perverse role, one completely unknown to preceding epochs, and that fact, among others, gives the lie to the idea of a universal function of genres, valid for all literatures. On this role, which is in no way comparable to the ancient one, modern literary communication founds its own criteria of artistic valorization. In modern authored literature, genres are actually the normative "background" against which are measured both the breaking away from convention that the originality of every artistic work enacts, and the postmodern renunciation of originality (which is only a denial, not an abandonment, of originality).

The Cunning of Convention

In addition, this new perverse function presupposes that the genre is no longer what it was in the past, that is, a "full" category that describes the characteristics common to a number of texts within a tradition, which in its turn is inserted into a system of genres that provide each work its due place in literature. In acquiring a negative role, in other words, becoming synonymous with conventionality (that very conventionality that modern artistic logic has declared war on in all its possible forms and to which the postmodern, either in an ironic or melancholic way, reopens its doors),[17] the genre is transformed into an "open" and mobile category ascribable at different times to the most varied literary formulas, even to those that at first had seemed to be the most innovative. In brief, what at first was enjoyed as an authored practice can, if repeated, fall into "genre." That is a paradigmatic illustration of the fate to which modern poetics (which has replaced the genres), even the most innovative, is subject: poetics too become "generic" as a result of multiple new productions in a similar vein or even simply as a result of the sensitization of enjoyment, which learns how to spot poetics in the commonalities shared by different works and develops an allergy specific to them, the *allergic reaction to convention*.

This slide into convention of every "original" formula can not be described in terms of a "cunning of tradition," as Jauss would have it. In this expression, Jauss refers to the fact that tradition succeeds in making classic even what constituted, on its appearance, a deviation from the recognized canons. An original work defies preexisting expectations, but thereafter expectations are newly designed on the basis of the deviant work.[18] And so, *Orlando Furioso*, after having modified the horizons of expectation tied to the chivilric romance, became a classic. But the mod-

---

17. On the struggle against conventionality unleashed in modern literature, see Benedetti 1991.

18. In fact, for Jauss there are two changes to the horizon of expectation: the first occurs when the original work defies the preexistent expectations; the second neutralizes the negativity of the first change, redesigning the new expectations on the basis of the deviant work, which then rises to the rank of "classic" (Jauss 1982, p. 17).

ern deviant practice (for example, an avant-garde work), after new expectations have been redesigned on the basis of its initial deviation, is never absorbed into classicism; instead, it falls into convention.[19] Modernity never elevates its fruits to the serene heights of the classical; on the contrary, it causes them to fall into stereotype, into convention, in short, into "genre."

Modern artistic logic can only canonize the work of an author, withdrawing it momentarily from the dispute over its artistic value. This is nothing but a surrogate for what the classic used to be. The classic work could become a model for further artistic productions. Nothing like that happens in modern art. Samuel Beckett's work, for example, is today in the canon, whereas nothing that imitates or repeats it is. Modernity does not consecrate a thematic-expressive solution, but only the work of an author. Any specific solution that is repeated instead falls into formula, convention, genre (to be avoided or to be reclaimed ironically, which does not substantially change the phenomenon). Thus, where Jauss sees the classic as the cunning of tradition, it is necessary instead to see the genre as the cunning of convention.

The genre, then, as a mobile category, at different times refillable with new traits that enjoyment discovers to be common to several works, can be considered a category of reception. Reception, as Wolf-Dieter Stempel observed, is essentially a generic process.[20] And not even the reception of modern works, oriented toward differential values, can escape that inevitable process which is the forming of generic expectations. What Stempel, however, does not observe, and what the whole theory of reception seems to repress, is that such a process is intrinsically devaluing for modern artistic logic: the moment the genre is formed and is recognized as such it smacks of stereotype. The ongoing formation of generic expectations, which is always inseparable from enjoyment, can therefore nowadays occur only in conflict with the regulative idea of modernity and with its need for shock and "differential sensations" (those which Victor Shklovsky placed at the foundation of artistry, see chapter 5). And a text succeeds in producing differential sensations only insofar as it differentiates itself from a recognized code. As Jan Mukařovský wrote: "A living work of art always oscillates between the past and future state of an aesthetic norm. The present, from which we observe the work of art,

19. As the current widespread intolerance to anything that "smacks of the avant-garde" demonstrates.

20. Stempel 1979, p. 192.

is felt as a tension between a former norm and its violation, and the violation is intended to become a future norm."[21]

This tension between the past norm and the future violation, which will soon become norm itself, and will then require in its turn new violations, is the very essence of the dialectic of modernity. And the genre, as codification, plays an important role in it: as the background from which the individual work endowed with originality must break away. That not only condemns the genre to being a negative category but also (as a consequence) a *hidden category*. The postmodern return to genres, especially fiction genres, does not restore to them the right to a clear and untroubled existence (like the one they enjoyed in ancient literature) because this return is still subordinate to the cipher of quotation, the ironic distancing of the writer. Besides, no one can exclude the possibility that even this technique of reclaiming the genres of popular and pulp fiction (whether long defunct or barely alive) may itself come to be gradually perceived as a "generic" practice, that is, as something to be avoided.[22] Today everything that is repeated for a certain time, and has thus become recognizable, imitable, and available to parody, is generic. It may be that a true escape from the artistic criteria of modernity has never been pulled off.

The Surviving Genres

Modernity then has not made literary genres disappear; it has only substituted their old functions with other new ones, thereby modifying their forms of existence as well. We shall now try to summarize the various modalities of their present survival. In late-modern literature, we can still recognize the existence of genres under three different forms: (1) the genres of popular fiction; (2) the recycled genres; (3) the "industrial" genres.

The Genres of Popular Fiction

We have already talked about the genres of popular fiction, and there is little to add except that these genres survive in an overt form, one highly resembling that of their "classical" antecedents: they present more or

---

21. Mukařovský 1966, p. 36 (the English translation by Mark Suino has been modified).
22. Something that is now happening, for example, to so-called *pulp* fiction.

less rigid norms, certified by a tradition and a common grammar, thus amounting to a complete category that functions as a "program" for the construction of texts and for the orientation of readers' expectations. Except that the old metacommunicative function here has an opposite value: from positive it has gone to negative. A work belonging to such a genre has been and continues to be subjected to artistic devaluation. From the gothic novel to science fiction, from the mystery to the New Age novel, this kind of genre is consigned to the dull reverse side of the medallion whose obverse bears the shining and "glorious" effigy of authored literature. This type of generic survival is also easy to describe unlike the following types, which instead cropped up paradoxically on the very terrain of authored literature, that is, the kind of literary production that, by definition, is supposed to flourish beyond the horizons of genre.

The Recycled Genres

The literary production of the last decades, whether in prose or poetry, offers us numerous examples of the return to the codified genres, dusted off with a good dose of irony and playful distancing, yes, but definitely without any intention to disfigure or smash them, as modernist taste would have it. In Italian fiction, Calvino's *If on a winter's night a traveler* and Eco's *The Name of the Rose* were the first examples of this trend, with many others to follow. The former recycles the novel in its most openly conventional form, with amazing intrigues and a happy wedding ending. The latter revives a genre really considered as low, as a form of fiction fit for mass consumption, namely, the mystery. Following the success of these two novels, published between 1979 and 1980, there was a strong resurgence of fiction in Italy, much of which can be considered as a massive recycling of the genres. The devaluation of genres had already carried twentieth-century fiction toward antinovels, stories without plots, "open works" constructed in a way such as to frustrate the fictional expectations of the reader.[23] Such a high-profile and compelling resurgence of fiction, evident even in the marketing of books, as that which has taken place since the end of the 1970s, would be unthinkable without the ironic overturning of the modernist axiology of art brought about by the postmodern. Postmodernism made reopening the road of

---

23. Which can also serve to explode a rather idle argument that blames the "intimidating" theorizations of Gruppo 63 for the lack of fiction in Italy prior to the eighties (cf., among others, La Porta 1995, p. 9).

generic writing to authored literature possible. Consequently, even where it is not clearly postmodernist in its expressive choices, the so-called new fiction is nonetheless in debt to this change in taste. The "re-cycled genres" are substantially the product of the postmodern, even though the phenomenon goes well beyond postmodernism when the latter is understood as a specific poetics.

As is well known, one of the special traits of postmodernism is the refutation of the opposition (which is typically modern) between popu-lar (generic) literature and "high" (authored) literature. If modernity de-valued everything generic, the postmodern actively clashes against that devaluation. The new writing draws heavily on generic literature, whether the genres of popular fiction (mystery, romance, westerns, sci-ence fiction);[24] the nonliterary genres of pop culture (comic strips,[25] rap[26]); the moribund genres of the past (the sestina, the sonnet,[27] the mannerist treatise[28]); or the novel in its most conventional forms. Cer-tainly modern production has for many decades seen a mingling of high and low traditions, but it was almost always a matter of transgressive usage, at times openly parodic, based on the noisy clash of mismatches, which twisted the original intentions of the genre employed. The new production, to the contrary, makes use of nonliterary genres "seriously"; at least, their use, no matter how ironic and winking, is never parodic or inappropriate. If an author uses the narrative forms of a comic strip or the historical novel, for example, it is not to make them collide with some other "elevated" aspect of the text, but in order to appropriate the narra-tive powers of that genre. Nor is the reclamation of regular meters, or dead poetic genres like the sestina or sonnet, done for the purposes of parody; these have become widespread in contemporary Italian poetry (as in the work of Gabriele Frasca) in response to a need for "discipline." This discipline is understood as being both formal and moral, like a hedge that encloses, limits, and brakes the supposed anarchic effusive-

24. The most recent work of Tondelli (1985, 1989) could serve as the Italian example for many of these categories. Another literary use of the mystery conjoined to themes of so-cial commitment is that of Tabucchi 1997.

25. "I would advise young people who want to write that they should first study how a comic strip begins, how an advertising slogan is made; I would advise them to immerse themselves in sophisticated American comedy, to pass from Balzac to Kubrick, to learn the techniques of that infallible creator of stories: Hollywood films" (A. Baricco, in "La Repubblica," July 27, 1994, p. 27).

26. See, for example, Ardemagni 1992.

27. The reclamation of regular metric forms will be discussed in chapter 7.

28. See Manganelli 1969.

ness of the hypertrophic poetic ego. This will be discussed further in chapter 7, where bound writing is treated, which in some ways could also be considered as a late-modern surrogate for the genres, something like "artificial genres."

Like the genres of the literature for mass consumption (and like the industrial genres, of which we will presently speak), this second form of generic survival, contrary to what one might expect, continues to presuppose their transformation into a negative category. The genres have undoubtedly been taken up again, but in the form of a paradoxical recycling that exploits, rather than cancels, their devaluation.[29] For the purposes of an artistic practice, the postmodern exploits the very criterion of literary quality on which the "modern tradition" is founded, by overturning it in appearance only. Furthermore, the phenomenon is not exactly untainted by a certain "necrophilia": the taking up of what is already dead. As happens in cinema with the films of a Hawks or a Lubitsch, genre literature is esteemed and put back into practice *despite its being generic*, even though it bears (or just because it does) the "nonaesthetic" marking with which modernity has branded it.

The Industrial Genres

It is known that publishers follow criteria that often correspond to implicit genre classifications, and have recourse to them when making decisions on both what titles to carry and which collections to include them in, as well as what kind of promotion they will be given. Writers in search of a publisher are sometimes told that the book does not fit into the "genre" that the publishing house usually handles, or into one that they believe will sell. Moreover, publishers are highly skilled at identifying, especially on the terrain of authored literature, a "hot genre" and at exploiting it with further titles in the same area. Just think of "cannibal" fiction, which established itself in Italy as a true and proper narrative genre, with its own distinctive markings in regard to form and theme (a narrating voice that speaks in a naive or cynical tone about everyday brutalities). Or of the "Holocaust genre" most highly visible in the cinema (as shown by the success of Spielberg's *Schindler's List*, or of Cerami

---

29. This is somewhat analogous to what happens, according to Grice's theory of implicature in conversation, where many pragmatic inferences are produced through the *exploitation* of conversational rules or "maxims," that is, by means of their apparent violation (cf. Grice 1967).

and Benigni's *Life is Beautiful*) as well as in essay writing.[30] But the phenomenon has also extended to literature (from the publication of new novels such as Eraldo Affinati's *Campo del sangue* [Field of Blood] to the "literary" revival of Primo Levi).[31] An example in the field of visual arts might be the "mutant body" genre, promoted in catalogue books and exhibits.[32] At times, the publishing industry even succeeds in creating a genre. Take, for instance, the Italian publishing house Adelphi, whose literary catalogue sets itself apart by both its thematic and stylistic features (a tradition of popular, light scholarly works with a Central European focus and provacative style) to such a degree that one could speak of an Adelphian genre.[33]

However, the phenomenon is not limited to the "literary marketplace," to be investigated with exclusively sociological tools. It extends as well to artistic communication in general, which is ever more difficult to distinguish from the culture industry, as the latter has appropriated some mechanisms typical of modern artistic logic. Thus many of the recent industrial genres are presented as new poetics. The "cannibals," for example: do they belong to a commercial genre or a poetics? And the generational "new narrators" published during the 1980s: were they a promotional phenomenon or a poetics? The obvious answer is that they were both, and that is a sign of how the differential logic of poetics, typical of modern art, has by now become inextricably consubstantial with the culture industry.

Genres, then, continue to exist in authored literature precisely where they intersect with the culture industry, even though in a form less transparent and obnoxious than that of the recycled genres. I therefore call them "industrial genres," despite the fact that they have nothing to do with the standards of industrial production. On the contrary, as Adorno once observed, every product of the culture industry is offered to us as

30. Cf. for example Daniel J. Goldhagen, *Hitler's Willing Executioners: Ordinary Germans and the Holocaust* (New York: Knopf, 1966). The Italian translation, *I volenterosi carnefici di Hitler*, was published by Mondadori in 1997 and immediately reprinted in the Oscar collection.

31. The Italian-Jewish writer Primo Levi was captured in 1943 and deported to Auschwitz by the Nazis. One of the concentration camp's few survivors, his first book, *If This Is a Man* (1947), analytically records the atrocities he witnessed.

32. On which, see Macrì 1996 and Alfano Miglietti 1996.

33. Referring to this type of production, not only Adelphi's, La Porta speaks of "authored kitsch" (1995, p. 79). There are a number of interesting studies on the publishing industry and its promotional strategies (cf. Ferretti 1994), and on trends among publishers and readers (cf. Spinazzola 1999) that touch on the phenomenon of industrial genres, even though they do not thematize it as such.

individual, as if created by "presumably great personalities." That entails no rejection of the "aura" of the authored work. The intersection of the demands for profit and for the authenticity of art has produced absolutely new phenomena, both for art and for commerce. Artistic production comes to be manifestly stylized, channeled toward already tested formulas, and ultimately standardized; this is what authorizes us to speak of genres. On the other side, however, the industry too is constrained to embrace a principle that was initially foreign to it: the value of estrangement, of "differential sensations," and thus the very logic of modern art. That is what obliges it to continually go, as far as it can, beyond the conventionality of the genres that it itself produces. Industrial genres are quite different from those of popular literature. In any case, it would be naive to think that today's culture industry consists exclusively of phenomena analogous to that of the gothic novel, or that it is limited to exploiting only openly "genre" products such as detective stories or science fiction. Modern industrial literature does not coincide, except in small part, with genre fiction.

Industrial genres, unlike those of popular literature, are not codified by any tradition; indeed, by their very nature they are unstable, fleeting condensations of fashion, public tastes, commercial strategies, and trends among writers. One might hypothesize that even the horror story, the detective story, and science fiction were born out of an analogous intersection of literary production, public tastes, and the culture industry's capacity to exploit them. Nevertheless, it would be mistaken to view them as similar since they constitute two very different phenomena. The genres of popular literature are still today relatively stable, responding to recognizable canons and recognized as such, whereas industrial genres are in continuous flux. From this perspective, we can consider them as "open genres" (and I deliberately pick the expression Bakhtin used for the novel), characterized by an absence of stable canon and by an openness to the present and its evolution. Open not only to fashion, as is obvious, but also to what has been for some time the special characteristic of modern authored literature, the succession of poetics. Moreover, as Baudelaire well demonstrated, there is a substantial affinity between the phenomenon of fashion and the logic of modernity.[34] The industrial genres participate at full-tilt in that search for shock and differential sensa-

34. "Beauty is made up of an eternal, invariable element . . . and a relative, circumstantial element, which will be, if you like, whether severally or all at once, the age, its fashion, its morals, its emotions" (Baudelaire 1863, p. 280).

tions around which modernity revolves; they present themselves, in short, as we have already said, as new poetics. That is something that does not happen with "traditional" genre literature like detective stories or westerns, or that happens only to a very limited degree and as a secondary phenomenon.[35]

However, the most important difference is that the genres of "traditional" popular literature formed, and continue to form, a system, correlated in an oppositional manner to authored literature. The industrial genres, in contrast, are not opposed to authored literature, and draw on it, setting up an osmotic relationship with it. If it is rather improbable that an authored practice (for example a new poetics, endowed with a strong innovative value, such as "cannibal" fiction) should over time slip into popular literature, it is almost the rule that it becomes, in the event it achieves a certain level of success, a genre of the culture industry.

In this third modality of its existence, the genre continues to play, in part, some of its former roles: it is indeed a grammar, though hidden and of brief life, on the basis of which publishers can label, select, and promote; readers can develop expectations and a specific demand; and writers at times, though sub rosa,[36] allow themselves to be guided by it in the construction of texts. And it is to this extent that we can consider them genres. Nonetheless, industrial genres tend to conceal their own canonical nature, preferring to present themselves as new literary tendencies. And this is the third difference that distinguishes them from traditional genres of popular fiction. The latter are immediately recognizable, seeing as they let themselves be read according to canons that are relatively stable, fixed in a tradition (i.e., canons that remain full categories). The industrial genres, on the contrary, are not recognized right away. As long as the reader is not in a position to identify their code, that is, to discern the common aspects that one work shares with a number of others (and to recognize also herself as part of the game, with the specific expectations that she has developed toward that genre of literature, having be-

35. Cyberpunk, for example, can be seen as a poetics that has penetrated science fiction. However, it is a recent phenomenon, contemporary to the parallel postmodern tendency toward the recycling and "reclamation" of low genres, which will be discussed shortly; in that sense, it may even be viewed as a phenomenon of authored literature.

36. It often happens that a writer declares having taken as his model one of the "low" genres of popular culture (even comic strips and other pulp forms), but as for the industrial genres, no writer has ever openly declared having adopted one as his model (i.e., having written a book according to the dictates of the market). Despite the postmodern rehabilitation of genre fiction, these new "genres of consumption" go on flying, somewhat hypocritically, under the radar.

come its target), the work will not be perceived as "generic." This tendency to self-concealment is explained by the very values of modernity (the new, the original), with which the culture industry has entered into a symbiotic relationship (a fact that testifies, even in this third case, to the complete transformation of genre into a negative category). But the industrial genres do not stay hidden forever. From the moment in which a literary practice, presented initially as authored, in other words, as a new poetics or artistic trend, is recognized as a generic practice, further works conforming to it will be perceived as repetitive and tiresomely conventional. At this stage of its life, one can't say that the industrial genre dies; indeed, it often lives on for quite some time. Nevertheless, it is very probable that the editors at the publishing house will once again throw open their doors in search of "the new."

Literature as Genre

If, then, modernity requires each work "of value" to leave genre behind, that signifies that genre is no longer in a position to orient enjoyment. Leaving behind the horizon of genre does not actually mean, as is often thought, transgressing its norms; it means rather entering into a different and vaster horizon. In every epoch, there has been a consistent and noteworthy rate of innovation with respect to the rules of genre. However, it was the genre that formed the framework within which the variations could be appreciated.[37] In modern literature a new phenomenon occurs. The horizon in which a text is (and aspires to be) evaluated and praised is no longer the "local" one of genre, but that of literature as a whole. The strong variations that Ariosto brought to the chivilric romance could be evaluated within the horizon of that genre. But when, for example, Calvino, in *Marcovaldo*, adopted a short story form with the tone of a fable, his practice cannot be evaluated simply in reference to the fable or the short story. Instead, it must be seen in relation to the tendencies of

37. In discussing Adorno's category of "newness," Bürger writes: "Newness as an aesthetic category existed long before Modernism, even as a program. The courtly minnesinger presented himself with the claim that he was singing a 'new song'; the authors of the French tragicomedy state that they are meeting the public's need for *nouveauté*. Yet in both cases, we are dealing with something different from the claim to newness of modern art. . . . For here [i.e. Modernism], we have neither a variation within the narrow limits of a genre (the 'new' song) nor . . . the renewal of literary techniques in works of a given genre. We are dealing not with development but with a break with tradition." (Bürger 1984, p. 60)

literary practice as a whole (contemporaneous and immediately prece-
dent); which is to say, it must be viewed in relation to the forms that it is
experimenting with and to all those it has now discarded. What stands
out then is that Calvino has abandoned the genre of fictional realism in
order to embrace a form of expression unusual in the literature of the
time, and unusual also with respect to preceding authored production. It
is this reference to the class of literature and to its historical dynamic that
renders the choices of the modern artist understandable and capable of
being appreciated. Even when we find ourselves confronted by a contemporaneous work that recycles a literary genre (take, for example,
Eco's *The Name of the Rose,* or some new collection of sonnets) and that
accepts, contrary to the modernist tendency, being bound to its parochial
laws, the valuation does not take place within the horizon of that particular genre, but rather within the horizon of the history of poetics, for
which a literature that *at first* had rejected the genres of pulp fiction or
regular metric poetry, now paradoxically (or snobbishly) reopens its
doors to them.

The board on which the game is now played is no longer that of the
genre, with its rules to be confirmed or disregarded, but the much vaster
one of literature, which knows no laws of genre but has a dynamic of its
own, made up of successive poetics (innovations, transgressions, deviations from the norm, pseudo-returns, reclamations, and revivals), which
cut clear across the entire system of genres. This dynamic, which alone is
capable of giving meaning to the practices of the individual artist, making them understandable to us, can also be seen as a history of poetics
that follow one after another, as long as we keep in mind that it has nothing to do with that historicity intrinsic to artistic techniques through
which, for example, a text or painting of the fifteenth century differs
from one of the seventeenth. In modernity, the most diverse styles and
techniques, whether "new" or old, whether current or past, are all
equally available, and therefore ideally simultaneous. The artist can
freely draw on each one, without constraints of any kind. And it is exactly in virtue of this freedom that his or her selections from the artistically possible can stand out as meaningful choices.

In the modern epoch, then, there has been a profound change in the
relations between work, genre, and literary system. This change is already fully visible in romanticism, with its tendency toward command
of all historical experience, toward using the ancient in order to estrange
the present. Schematically, we can say that while formerly the reference
to genre, its laws, and its internal history mediated the enjoyment of the

individual text, as well as the relationship between the text and the literary system, now a text belongs directly to literature, and makes reference to the laws and dynamics of the same. From this viewpoint, we must ultimately agree with Blanchot when he writes that:

> A book no longer belongs to a genre; every book belongs to literature alone, as if literature possessed beforehand, in their generalities, the secret formulae that alone allow what is written to assume the reality of being a book. It seems as if genres have vanished and literature alone asserted itself, gleamed solitary in the mysterious clarity that it propagates and which each literary creation reflects by multiplying it.[38]

Except that Blanchot misses the correlated phenomenon, one which anyone might find disturbing. Authored literature has itself become a genre, though one that is mobile, unidentified by conventional markings, and open to processes of change. It is similar in this way to the genre of the novel, as Bakhtin had intuited when he spoke of the "novelization of literature" (see chapter 5). Certainly, it cannot be denied that, today as in the past, enjoyment has need of an orientation of expectations; it's just that unlike what the theory of reception seems to believe, this horizon today is not provided by genres, but by literature, which has itself become a kind of genre (or macrogenre) with its own general laws that aspire to be valid over all its domains. These laws are no longer codes to be varied or confirmed, but dynamics ordered into a history.

The loss of the function of orientation fulfilled by the genres is, however, not one of those local, inconsequential phenomena that leaves the rest unaltered. It provokes a complex readjustment of the processes of literary communication, profoundly mutating the mechanisms of enjoyment, especially with regard to the relations between the individual work and the literary system. Formerly, the genres mediated these relations, signaling the literary nature of a text and furnishing particular laws on the basis of which to approach and understand it; today, instead, a text reports directly to that vaster and substantially indefinable sphere: literature. But since the mediation of the genres, as long as it was functioning, was vital to enjoyment (it would be impossible to imagine, as Jauss observed, a work of literature located in a space devoid of information), its loss must be made up by something else. Out of this necessity of comprehension arise the phenomena that we are discussing: the

---

38. Blanchot 1959, pp. 200–201.

succession of poetics takes on itself the function of orientation, which the genres today can no longer fulfill. And the author holds a key post in all this. The positions of different authors on the immense chessboard of literature, the reasons for their *choices* of form and content, the *differential value* of their practices within the history of poetics, all form today the "great network" capable of orienting enjoyment. This grand game of chess, over whose squares the author moves as a kind of pawn, constitutes the new horizon of expectations that has replaced the one formerly constituted by the genres.

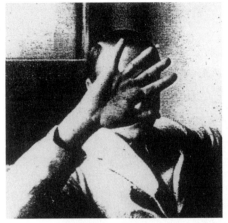

The author is there, but would rather not be. The Italian writer Tommaso Landolfi had his portrait printed on the reverse of the dust jacket for his novel, *La bière du pêcheur* (Vallechi, 1953). Along with the epigraph from Calvino at the front of this study, the image illustrates the ambiguous desire to disappear as expressed by numerous twentieth-century authors. Courtesy SIAE Sezione OLAF, Rome

In the Renaissance, on the contrary, the author faced the viewer. Masaccio, in this detail from "Saint Peter Enthroned," depicts himself among Brunelleschi, Alberti, and Masolino, the three points of reference for his style of painting. Beyond a "signature," this image is also a kind of manifesto, a declaration of his poetics. The author emerges as the subject of an artistic intention.

The author multiplies. Futurist painter Umberto Boccioni, (*Io noi Boccioni*, 1907–1910) multiplies himself into five simultaneous images, thus proclaiming one aspect of his poetics and of Futurist aesthetics.

Art always and only refers to the author . . . Marcel Duchamp (*Marcel Duchamp autour d'un table,* 1917) repeats Boccioni's technique but also transforms it into a nightmarish tautology: sitting around the table as if absorbed in a game of chess, there is no one but the author. © 2003 Artists Rights Society (ARS), New York/ADAGP, Paris/Estate of Marcel Duchamp

. . . or to the critic, who defines the author, and provides him with a label, a poetics. The artist Jan Wilson (left) and the critic Achille Bonito Oliva. Courtesy Achille Bonito Oliva.

The critic as author. Now it is the critic, Achille Bonito Oliva, who repeats Boccioni's technique. Courtesy Achille Bonito Oliva.

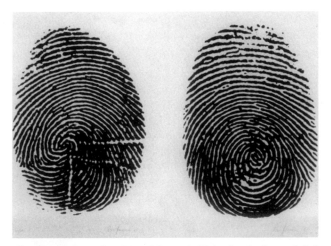

The sign of the author. Piero Manzoni, *Right thumbprint* and *Left thumbprint* (1960). It is said that the author leaves a mark, a signature, an unmistakable sign of himself in his work. Manzoni ironically streamlines the process, leaving only his thumbprint in place of the work. © 2002 Artists Rights Society (ARS), New York/SIAE, Rome

Fetishes of the author. Piero Manzoni, *Base magica* (1961). On the pedestal, the author himself becomes the work. Soon after, the paradox becomes a formula to be exploited, as in Gilbert and George, *Singing Sculpture,* 1976 (the two artists, standing on a table, make up the sculpture), or in a recent advertising campaign by Dolce and Gabbana (the two clothing designers appear in the photograph instead of their suits). © 2003 Artists Rights Society (ARS), New York/SIAE, Rome

The body of the author. Balzac, daguerreotype portrait. According to Balzac, a daguerreotype retains something of the photographed body: with every shot taken, the body would lose one of its "specters," that is, a fundamental part of its essence. The above daguerreotype was acquired by Nadar, who makes it the point of departure for his book, *Quand j'étais photographe.*

The author disguised as author. Marcel Duchamp dressed up as Rose Sélavy, in a photo by Man Ray, 1921. Rose Sélavy is a Duchamp character as well as the author of some of his works. This is a visual example of the "apocryphal effect." Calvino writes: "The author of any book is a fictional character whom the author invents for the purpose of being the author of his fictions." [See ch. 7, p. 184]

Sibilla Aleramo in a photo of 1917.

The artist empathetically revives the stereotyped images of film, television, and glamour maga-zines, to which she lends her body. Cindy Sherman, *Untitled film still, #16*, 1978. Courtesy Cindy Sherman and Metro Pictures.

Cindy Sherman, *Untitled* 1980–1983. "Did he wish to express himself, he ought at least to know that the inner 'thing' he thinks to 'translate' is itself only a ready-formed dictionary, its words explainable only through other words, and so on indefinitely." (Roland Barthes) Courtesy Cindy Sherman and Metro Pictures.

The aestheticization of politics. Benito Mussolini, an early "performance artist," in action at Sabaudia in 1934. Courtesy Farabolafoto, Milan

The conceptualization of art. Joseph Beuys, *Action Karl-Marx-Platz*, Berlin 1972. At the end of the May Day parade, Beuys uses a red broom to sweep up the litter left behind.

Alfonso Luigi Marra, advertising insert.

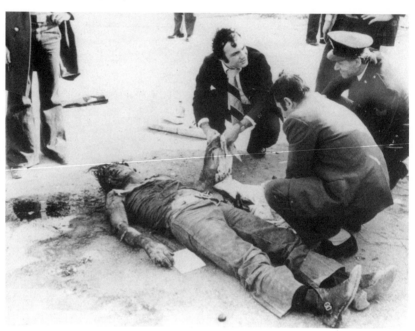

Death of the author. Pasolini's corpse at the Ostia seadrome. Courtesy Olycam, Milan.

CHAPTER 5

The Differential Logic of Modernity

Novels and Genre Criticism

The "crisis" of genres, or better, their transformation into a negative category synonymous with conventionality, is a long process that arose not in the twentieth century (as some claim), but with the dawn of modernity. And it was the novel that set off the crisis. As Bakhtin writes, the novel is a literary genre unlike any other. Whereas the old genres, such as epic and tragedy, had arisen and evolved out of oral traditions, the novel's process of formation and consolidation belong to an age in which the written word and printed book were already prevalent. Above all, however, the novel remains the sole "genre in progress" amidst others that are either fully matured or already moribund:

It is the only genre that was born and nourished in a new era of world history and therefore it is deeply akin to that era, whereas the other major genres entered that era as already fixed forms, as an inheritance, and only now they are adapting themselves—some better, some worse— to the new conditions of their existence. Compared with them, the novel appears to be a creature from an alien species. It gets on poorly with other genres. It fights for its own hegemony in literature; wherever it triumphs, the older genres go into decline.[1]

The oldest genres participate in that tendency to codification typical of premodern literature: every literary genre has its form, its thematic content, its style. The novel, on the contrary, has neither its own form, its own style, nor its own thematic content. From the chivalric to the picaresque, the epistolary, the Bildungsroman, the travel or seafaring adventure, the essay-novel, the psychological novel, and myriad other incarnations, the novel has never stabilized into a relatively constant form. Indeed, if it has one constant feature, it is that of continually changing its own themes and its own form. What then characterizes it as a genre? Precisely this mutability and absence of canon. The novel, as an open-ended genre, participates in the tendency typical of modern culture with respect to all previous cultures: its openness to the process of change, its *insertion in history*.

Bakhtin wrote down these observations in the 1930s. A contemporary writer breathing in the "terminal" atmosphere of the early twentieth-first century and in harmony with its millennial pulses, might counter that the "genre in progress" has already fully developed, having by now achieved its "golden age." Living or posthumous, though, the fact remains that the novel does not possess a canon like all the rest. It is a species of evolving organism, one that lives and reproduces by modifying itself, even by absorbing (and digesting) other literary genres. Precisely due to its lack of canon, it can introduce other literary genres into its own structure. Thus, in *Don Quixote*, Cervantes succeeded in bringing together disparate literary genres in a subversive mingling of codes without melting them down. While including elements of the chivalric romance, the pastoral, the adventure story, the novella, and even love poems, Cervantes's work loses none of its own identity. No other genre can do the same. Even nonliterary forms of discourse, such as travel journals, correspondence, diaries, autobiographies, and essay writing, can be incorporated without a novel's ceasing to be a novel.[2]

This capacity for inserting other genres of discourse into its own structure also means the ability to mutate their meanings and values, to

1. Bakhtin 1975, from which are drawn the citations that follow. English versions in M. M. Bakhtin, *The Dialogic Imagination, Four Essays*, ed. by M. Holquist (University of Texas Press, Austin, 1981), pp. 4 and 6.

2. There are innumerable examples, but take that of Goethe's *Elective Affinities*, which ends with Ottilie's diary, inserted into the text as a kind of document.

bend them to a purpose other than their original, to make them "sound in new ways," and to parody them. Like a parasite, *Don Quixote* feeds on the chivalric code, incorporates it into itself, and so parodies it. And the parody is aimed at the chivalric genre for the very reason that it is conventional, with its specific form and language and its particular ideology. Not having a rigid canon, the novel succeeds in unmasking the rigidity of other literary genres; or better, other genres appear for the first time as conventional, that is, ridiculous and ripe for parody, owing to the very fact that they are codified. The phenomenon is very important because it represents in a certain sense the emblem of modernity: the critique of conventionality, the idea that convention is something ridiculous. "The novel parodies the other genres (precisely in their role as genres); it unmasks the conventionality of their forms and of their language," writes Bakhtin, who calls this phenomenon "genre criticism."

The novel, then, does not insert itself peacefully into the literary system. Its relation to the other genres is by no means inoffensive, for it attacks the very principle on which they stand: the existence of a code. And as the novel becomes dominant (which, according to Bakhtin, starts to be evident around the middle of the eighteenth century), the criticism of genres is unleashed throughout the entire literary system.

> Those genres that stubbornly preserve their old canonic nature begin to appear stylized, a stylization taken to the point of parody, despite the artistic intent of the author. In an environment where the novel is the dominant genre, the conventional languages of strictly canonical genres begin to sound in new ways, which are quite different from the ways they sounded in those eras when the novel was not included in "high" literature.[3]

In short, the novel has no canon, and destroys through parody any of its own varieties that tend toward stabilization. Moreover, as soon as the novel becomes hegemonic, no other literary form can allow itself to stabilize into a canon either, since any form that does, contrary to what occurred in ancient literature, is now perceived as rigid, conventional, susceptible to being parodied (and implicitly devalued). This same process brought Friedrich Schlegel to say in 1797, "All the classical literary genres in their rigorous purity are today ridiculous."[4]

---

3. Bakhtin 1975, p. 6.
4. Schlegel, "Selected Aphorisms from 'Lyceum,' " in Wilson 1982, p. 60.

Literature Observes Itself

The literary forms in the modern epoch are thus in continual struggle not only with the already coded genres (in Benjamin's words, major works either establish a genre or liquidate one),[5] but also with the natural tendency of every new form to stabilize into a genre. Each "new genre," in its turn, becomes old for a subsequent "major work" that negates it. In the late-modern period, this process is exacerbated to the point of making everything that anyone has ever experimented with feel as if it were conventional. What has already been done before is now felt to be "conventional," not only when a form experimented with by one writer is repeated by another, but even when the same writer revisits an earlier phase in his or her own career. (Thus Calvino's continual changes of direction as he kept seeking different artistic solutions from those he had previously tried out.) Even if oriented toward differential values, the reception of works cannot escape the inevitable formation of generic expectations. Works of art, however, are required to counteract such a process. Every "work of value" must win its little war against conventions, old or new, already formed or in the process of formation, by attacking the expectations of its readers. And no matter how paradoxical it may appear, even postmodern poetics has declared war on one convention: that very rupture with conventions that the avant-garde has always devoted itself to, which now itself appears "conventional."

It is thus not true, though it is often said, that modern literature is free of the chains of codification. This idea, which runs through "modernist" literary theories,[6] is a highly partial representation of what really goes on in literary dynamics. No doubt there is greater artistic freedom in comparison to the constraints that used to be imposed by genres. What's more, this greater freedom, which is integral to modern art, carries with it the artist's responsibility for making choices, and with it, that powerful enhancement of the author-function, which is the subject of this book. But we need to understand what "greater freedom" means. There's a big difference between going for a walk in the countryside dressed as casually or unconventionally as we please and participating in a wedding, funeral, or graduation ceremony dressed in the same way. In the first case our freedom is total and not very significant. In the second it tears

5. Benjamin 1928, p. 27.
6. See Blanchot's observations cited in chapter 4 of this book.

away from what is expected, and it will inevitably have a value that is differential, transgressive, provocative, or simply ironic. The greater freedom that characterizes modern literature resembles this second case. In modern literature, conventions are not merely substituted. They are broken, parodied, or ironically recycled with an intention that may be provocative, playful, or purely "experimental," through a gamut of variation that ranges from desecration to "reenchantment" of the literary institution itself. In modern literature, then, there is no simple freeing of the artist from the bonds of codification, but a subtler playing with those constraints that renders them more problematic.

If we don't take account of that fact, if we limit ourselves to speaking of "freedom from every canon," or "total freedom" from manipulation by either genres or traditions, we run the risk of regarding the contemporary epoch as one of weak literary codes. On the contrary, the processes of codification have not at all faded away; they have accelerated. Just think about how quickly a certain literary solution is identified as a "genre" and immediately thereafter viewed as a stereotype. I call this phenomenon the "cunning of convention," and it is nothing other than the flip side of modern artistic logic and its compulsion for the new. The cunning of convention, which precipitates every innovative solution into "genre," is something that late-modern writers fear in an almost pathological way, to the point of complying ironically with it by knowingly adopting forms that have already been experienced as conventional.

The late-modern writer is continually struggling against the incumbent conventionality of whatever stylistic and formal choice he or she makes. And this condemns one not only to variation, but also to self-observation. In order to distance itself from the artistic techniques of the past, every artistic operation must be in a position to observe itself in relation to the literary system and its history. (The criticism of genre is a phenomenon that already presupposes a self-observation of the literary system as such.) The fulcrum of this struggle is lodged in the eye of the author, turned on her own work and its relation to literature in general. To innovate means to keep an eye on what is old, to perceive the process of exhaustion or of conventionalization that invests literary forms. This presupposes a great capacity, analogous and parallel to the one that readers have developed, to perceive the first signs of convention, to sniff out even its faintest whiff. It is a special "competence" added to the one that used to be the standard competence of genre: this typically modern sense of scent, exhibited today by writers and readers in equal measure, marks a kind of passage to a higher level of logic. It is no longer merely a question of knowing how an epic poem is composed, but of knowing how to write or read a text against the background of a code, of knowing how to evaluate the process of codification itself as realized through history and through the way in which texts are received. In other words, what is required is not only the skill to play the game, but also the ability to grasp its implicit rules, rules that, moreover, are no longer received, but are in the process of formation within the game itself. Thus, through its aversion to convention, literature can be said to observe itself and its own processes, generating in the late-modern writer that excess of awareness, and its menacing paralysis, of which Calvino can be considered the paradigmatic example. The compulsion to innovate, together with the self-observation that it involves, is what oppresses the protagonist of Italo Calvino's "A Sign in Space" (one of the stories collected in *Cosmicomics*). The notorious Kgwgk, inhabitant of another galaxy, who observes, imitates, and parodies the signs that the protagonist leaves in space, is the brilliant narrative incarnation of the phenomenon that we are describing. The fear of falling into convention, or of being judged "antiquated," oppresses Calvino's character in the form of the typical instrument of persecution—the observing eye—which ultimately, as in every persecution complex, is nothing other than an eye that observes itself.

What Is an Artistic Technique?

Insofar as I confer upon the vulgar a high significance, upon the common an enigmatic aspect, upon the already known the dignity of the unknown, upon the finite an infinite appearance, I render it romantic.
NOVALIS

Among the notions commonly invoked in the discussion of literature, that of artistic device or technique stands out as apparently neutral and nonproblematic.[7] No one feels obliged to define it, almost as if it were a "primitive" notion, self-evident like those of point and line in geometry.

---

7. The Italian expression *procedimento artistico* has here generally been rendered into English as "artistic technique," as in the following discussion of Shklovsky's concept of *priem*. It should be noted, however, that the Italian *procedimento*, like the French *procédé*, derives from the same Latin root as English words like "proceed," "procedure," and "process," in all of which the sense of change over time (history) is embedded. [trans.]

And yet as it came to be used in the twentieth century, it is not at all "primordial." Certainly the notion of rhetorical device has been around for ages, but that of technique, in its modern sense, is not exactly the same thing. Today it has acquired a connotation supplementary to that of the traditional devices discussed in treatises on poetics and rhetoric over the centuries. I am referring to a certain "elective" and projective character, as well as to its being understood in a self-referential circuit, which can only be tied to modern art. The shift is traceable to the studies of the Russian formalists, and in particular those of Shklovsky. The literary theory of this school is intimately connected to and based on values specific to modern art. Their concepts are embedded in the logic of modernity, and could never have arisen except through contact with the new processes of modern literature (and from this angle of vision, the formalist theory might even be considered a poetics, i.e., as the theorization of a particular form of art). Nonetheless, modernity permeates their concepts in a nonreflected manner. The logic of modernity is never described as such by the formalists; it is rather incorporated, and thus hidden, in general notions, formulated in order to describe supposed universal aspects of literature. As such, they would later be generalized (and rigidified) by Roman Jakobson and the structuralists.

In their studies, the formalists (from Shklovsky to Tomachevsky to Tynianov) talk a lot about artistic devices. The Russian term is *prïem*, which means "device" or "technique" (as it is variously translated into English). So, in appearance, there's nothing new with respect to the poet's traditional technical and rhetorical equipage. But looking a bit closer, one realizes that actually something has changed. When people begin to ponder *art as technique*,[8] there occurs a profound change in the way of conceiving and perceiving literary writing with respect to preceding epochs, a change that may never have been sufficiently examined.

What, then, is an artistic technique? If one thumbs through the formalists' studies, there seems to be no limit to what can be considered as such: it may refer to rhetorical figures, linguistic and lexical facts (such as the use of archaisms), phonetic or rhythmic elements, and methods of composition and plot construction, among other things. In short, anything regarding the formal aspects of the literary work and all of its "technical instruments" can be referred to as a device or technique. Up to this point there is still nothing special about the term *prïem* except its

8. Shklovsky 1929a.

strong generalization. What does distinguish it from traditional rhetorical devices, however, starts to emerge when one considers the fact that
the formalists also identify a particular class of techniques: that of "negative devices." In other words, not only can everything that has to do
with the form of a work be considered a technique, but even that which
is not there can be as well. The *absence* of certain devices can also be felt
as an artistic procedure. Thus, if the use of archaicisms in poetry is an
artistic technique, so is their elimination from a poem. When archaicisms
become the norm in the poetic style of an epoch, the use of a more collo-
quial, proselike language can turn out to be poetically significant and
constitute in itself an artistic technique. Artistic techniques, then, are not
so much rhetorical devices or methods of composition that can be described and classified once and for all; technique means *everything that
the artist uses with particular artistic intentions.* The specificity of the modern notion therefore does not reside in what the technique "consists of"
(trope, rhythm, verse, narrative style, etc.), but in what it "does." Its unifying characteristic in all the aspects and varieties mentioned above is, in
short, that of being a means to attain determinate effects, the principle
one of which, as Shklovsky clearly pointed out in explicating a trait already quite visible in romantic art, was that of "making it strange" or
"defamiliarization." But the effect of rendering the familiar strange is
produced on the reader in relation to his or her expectations, which are
modified as literature evolves. Here, then, is a relative and *historical* element that is inevitably inscribed in artistic techniques and in the evaluation of their efficacy, something that is never found in classical treatises
on poetry. From this point of view, it can be said that Shklovsky's theory
paradigmatically incorporates the logic of modernity. Let's take a closer
look at several of his most important passages.

Arguing against Potebnya and his idea of poetry ("art is thinking in
images"), Shklovsky writes:

> Images endure and last. From century to century, from country to coun-
> try, from poet to poet, these images march on without change. . . . The
> work of successive schools of poetry has consisted essentially in accumu-
> lating and making known new devices of verbal arrangement and orga-
> nization. In particular, these schools of poetry are far more concerned
> with the disposition than with the creation of imagery. . . . And it is not
> the changes in imagery that constitute the essential dynamics of poetry.[9]

9. Ibid., p. 2 (from which also come the following citations pp. 2, 6, 10).

It is clear that what most interests Shklovsky is something that neither Potebnya's theory, nor any other preceding poetics, had dealt with: the movement of poetry. Such movement consists not in the creation of new images, but in the sharpening of techniques for arranging verbal expressions in a new way. The notion of technique thus enters into an unusual constellation, no longer that of the poet's eternal bag of tricks, but that of change, of the new way of arranging the already given.

Shklovsky then recalls a curious phenomenon. We may perceive as poetic that which in its origin was not really intended as poetic: for example certain documents written in Old Slavic, even though not originally poetry (i.e., "never meant, originally, to serve as an object of aesthetic contemplation") can be enjoyed as literary works by virtue of the particular poetic quality that the old language holds for modern ears. One can say then that a work can be "created as prose and experienced as poetry" or vice versa, intended as poetry and received as prose. "This points out the fact that the artistic quality of something, its relationship to poetry, is a result of our mode of perception." Here then is the other fundamental point of Shklovsky's reflection: his interest in the way we perceive the artistic object. Rather than describing the intrinsic qualities of poetic language (falling into the ontological shackles of its supposed specificity), he insists on the perception that we have of it and its historical relativity. Change, technique, and perception thus form a single conceptual constellation: if any one of these elements has a value, it is due to the fact of its being tightly bound to the others.

The Exhaustion of Literary Forms

Perception obviously reminds us of the well-known theory of "making it strange," which Shklovsky set forth in those pages taking as his point of departure a general psychic law: the economy of mental energy, which is also applied to perceptual phenomena. In perception, too, the mind tends toward attention-saving mechanisms, making the recognition of objects "automatic." That is why we may cross the street we live on every day without "seeing it," or immediately recognize a familiar face without looking at the shape of that person's nose or mouth. Automatic perception substitutes the object with a symbol, a cipher, as in algebra. "And so, held accountable for nothing, life fades into nothingness. Automatization eats away at things, at clothes, at furniture, at our wives, and at our fear of war." The function of art according to Shklovsky is to impede automatic perception. "And so, in order to return sensation to our limbs, in order to make us feel objects, to make a stone feel stony, man has been given the tool of art." The aim of art is to transmit to us the impression of the object as "vision" rather than mere "recognition." Art makes the familiar seem "strange," obliging us to perceive it anew, as if we were seeing it for the first time.

The theory of "estrangement," "making it new" or "defamiliarization" (as the Russian *ostraneniye* has variously been translated into English) is too familiar to be recounted here in detail; we will limit ourselves to a few observations. In art the withdrawal of objects from the automatism of perception is accomplished in various ways. Quite often it is achieved through the use of unusual points of view, as in the case of Tolstoy's narrator-horse, which makes us "see anew," in their absurd arbitrariness, human institutions (private property among them), which for us have become almost a part of nature. In general, however, all poetic language and all the formal aspects of literature can contribute to the effect of rendering the familiar strange: metaplasms, the different spelling of words,[10] the type of lexicon (for example, the use of archaisms as mentioned above), the syntax, even the rhythm of poetry (viewed by Shklovsky as increasing the duration of perception) can each serve as a technique that "makes perception long and 'laborious.' "[11]

Up to here we have the standard version of the Russian formalist's theory. But for Shklovsky, beyond things, themes, and concepts, what was to be rendered strange was also the very means with which we communicate, i.e., language, as well as literary forms. In regard to language the matter is easy to explain. Typically, we do not "see" words, nor do we hear their sounds; only the meaning is perceived, and the words are like algebraic expressions, submitted to an automatic perception. Poetry would oppose this automatism by procuring for us a defamiliarized perception of language itself. Of course, that presupposes a certain idea of poetic language which today seems rather one-sided: the idea that poetic language is an end unto itself. But this is the idea that the formalists elaborated, having inherited it from German romanticism, and one that would later have considerable success in the popularized (and rigidified) version disseminated by Jakobson. An illustration of the

---

10. Thus, for example, Gadda (in speaking of the "cannibal wars, conducted by the very ferocity of the people, insofar as the people were unanimous with their leader: *ein Volk, ein Reich, ein Führer*") uses the etymological spelling *omicidiali* (literally "homocidal") in lieu of the more common (in standard Italian) *micidiali,* and thereby evokes its forgotten meaning ("Come lavoro" in Gadda 1991, vol. 1, p. 433).

11. Shklovsky 1929a, pp. 6–7, 12, 13.

idea is provided in this formula from Jakubinsky: "The practical goal becomes secondary (though it may not disappear completely) and the linguistic representations acquire an *autonomous value*."[12] And this, more than a theory of poetic language, turns out to be a poetics in disguise, since language does not necessarily acquire this "autotelic" weight in all forms of verbal art. What interests us here, however, is the manner in which Shklovsky's theory "incorporates" the logic of modernity, not so much its general theoretical validity. Shklovsky considers this capacity of poetic language to draw attention to itself as a particular case of the need to "make it strange," describing it in relation to the same perceptual phenomena that the objects described by language are subjected to. In poetry, language, itself an object, is to be rendered strange.

Tzvetan Todorov criticizes this passing from the object to the means, accusing it of being contradictory: how can one defamiliarize an object and along with it the means for expressing it?[13] And yet this is really the most interesting point of Shklovsky's theory, even more so inasmuch as the apparent vicious circle includes literary forms too, making them simultaneously the means and the object of "making it strange." What Todorov considers the inherent ambiguity of Shklovsky's theory, is in reality the central point of the logic of modernity, which Shklovsky, with brilliant intuition, incorporates into his theorization. The "circular relapse" of making strange the very means that makes that possible (i.e., artistic expression) leads theory for the first time ever to encompass the history of poetics, the change of forms and the reflective dynamics of literature within the very definition of the literary fact. For the first time, too, literature is perceived as a fundamentally *self-referential* circuit.

Beyond literary works themselves, how and why are literary forms able to be, or better, bound to be, defamiliarized? Because they too are subjected to the process of automatism. Let's take another look at the case of archaicisms. If poetry must block or impede automatic perception, and if poetic language must have the "character of the 'strange' and surprising," the presence of archaicisms inside poetic language will be perfectly justified. What could be better at rendering the language of a poem unusual and difficult? Nevertheless, it is well known that poetry is

12. Cited by Todorov 1984, p. 14.
13. Ibid. According to Todorov, Shklovsky's theory, based on defamiliarization, lies between the "standard theory of poetic language" (which the formalists derived from Kantian aesthetics and the German romantics) and another more original conception, which would later be developed by Tynianov, based not on the specificity of the literary (which, as Tynianov in fact asserts, does not exist) but on its historical relativity.

not always composed in a language so remote from everyday usage. At times it is instead created out of a plain language, approaching that of prose, and totally stripped of archaicisms, as in the case of Pushkin. Does Pushkin's language therefore contradict the just-explained law of poetry? Not at all. The language of poetry, Shklovsky asserts, is always a difficult, defamiliarizing language, even when it seems most simple, and Pushkin's case is an exemplary demonstration. When he was writing, the usual poetic language was the high style of Derzhavin, a language chock full of archaicisms, so that to his contemporaries, "the style of Pushkin, due to its banality (as was thought then), represented for them something unexpectedly difficult."[14]

It is clear then how the principle of "defamiliarization" introduces a criterion into Shklovsky's thought that is the very foundation of the differential logic of modernity: historical relativity. In order to judge a technique it is necessary to consider it in relation to the canon in a given epoch, and so in relation to what, in today's terms, we would call the readers' horizon of expectations. The effect of "estrangement" and the poetic value tied to it thus become *relative concepts,* relative to what is the norm in a given epoch. The criterion is then taken up by Jurij Tynianov, but deprived of the self-referential quality emphasized by Shklovsky. For Tynianov, literature is what falls within the tastes or conventions of the time; for Shklovsky, on the other hand, literature is what surpasses or denies such norms, and that makes a big difference. For Shklovsky, that which defamiliarizes is that which distances itself from the norm. The language of Pushkin is estranging because it breaks with the expectations of his contemporaries. For the same reason, it is a device ("Pushkin employed folk speech as a special technique for arresting the reader's attention") and, for that reason, too, it is poetic language.

Shklovsky then continues with a series of examples, analogies of which we will not take the trouble to search out in Italian or other languages. The use of dialects in Russian literature is estranging to the degree that, until that moment, literary language did not allow for them; the same is true about the leveling of literary language toward popular speech. Finally, however, when literary language and popular language seemed to have traded places, lo and behold, what turned out to be estranging anew was instead a kind of inversion of the trend, led by Khlebnikov with his "powerful new movement . . . making its debut with the creation of a new, specialized poetic language."

14. Shklovsky 1929a, p. 13, from which also come the succeeding citations.

The movement of poetry (innovation) thus has its origin in the necessity of withdrawing the literary forms from that process of automatism that consists in their becoming canonical. As Tynianov would say, every literary element (verse, meter, plot, etc.) is subject to "wearing out," to "fading," once having achieved a state of "automatism."[15] But the automatism of literary forms is nothing but their conventionalization: worn-out forms are those that have become usual, conforming to the expectations of the readers. An art that opposes this automatism can only be an art that continually supplants the forms of expression that gradually turn conventional; not so much or not always with new forms (since new can also be the old which comes back), but with unusual techniques that *for a while* will still be able to surprise, to produce that particular nonautomatized perception of the world rendered strange.

Differential Sensations

All that is generalized through the concept of "differential sensations," which Shklovsky picks up from S. V. Kristiansen, the author of *The Philosophy of Art,* from which the former relates a lengthy passage:

> Whenever we experience anything as a *deviation* from the ordinary, from the normal, from a certain guiding canon, we feel within us an emotion of a special nature, which is not distinguished in its kind from the emotions aroused in us by sensuous forms, while the single difference being that its "referent" may be said to be a perception of a discrepancy.[16]

The connection between this idea of Kristiansen and the value of formal innovation on which Shklovsky's theory is based is obvious; in the same pages the latter writes: "The new form makes its appearance not in order to express a new content, but rather, to replace an old form that has already outlived its artistic usefulness." In other words, we might say the new form arises in order to substitute the form that has by now lost its differential value in relation to the preceding forms, because it gradually has become conventional. Every process of deviation from a norm or from some kind of canon produces that particular emotional response,

15. Tynianov 1929a, p. 69.
16. S. V. Kristiansen, *The Philosophy of Art,* 1911, cited in Shklovsky 1929b; English version, pp. 20–21.

which is the differential sensation. Producing this type of sensation is the aim of those who generate literary evolution.

The process of automatization, or conventionalization, of literary forms is not solely destructive. In the same moment that repetition destroys the differential sensation borne by a certain form on its initial appearance, it also opens up the possibility for new differences: "Everything that can be a canon, Kristiansen writes, becomes the point of departure for differential sensations." If we think about Italian literary history, there is no lack of examples to illustrate this kind of "exploitation" of the convention for the purpose of producing new differential sensations. The innovation of free verse, as introduced toward the end of the nineteenth century by D'Annunzio or Pascoli, once it had lost its differential value, that is, once it had become canonical, ultimately made possible a new way of perceiving regular metrics, at which point metered verse came back into use. Thus, a certain restoration of metrics by subsequent poets, Montale, for example, could be poetically appreciated.[17] Even subtler possibilities of exploiting the canon are provided in all those cases where the very principle of deviating from the commonplace, once this principle has become the norm, becomes the point of departure for further deviations, so that now the return to the commonplace is received as if it were a deviation. Thus, while there is no limit to canonization, there is no limit to the production of new differential sensations either. (As I have stated before, eventually late-modern writers began to doubt this fact, working out that same logic in a "depressive" form, in other words, becoming aware of its impasses and setting a limit, so to speak, on the possibility of indefinitely producing the new, until they arrived at that paralyzing self-representation of a literature condemned to endless déjà vu.)

The differential sensation, however, is not produced with a simple *variation* on the appreciators' expectations, but with a transgressive *violation* of that which by now has become canonical, which means entering into a strong opposition to the preceding poetic forms. In the literary field something takes place analogous to what can happen in a marriage, when (according to Rozanov as reported by Shklovsky) the sense of difference disappears between husband and wife. Love is dead, and betrayal is love's last hope. Betrayal recreates difference between the lovers.

17. Cf. G. Contini, *Innovazioni metriche italiane fra Otto e Novecento,* in Contini 1970, pp. 587–600.

"The shifting movements represent just such a betrayal in literature."[18] The dialectic of modernity, with its need of differences, satisfied through the violation of expectations—it's all there. The movement that comes out of it is not a simple linear development, but a series of struggles and contrasts. From this derives the familiar metaphor about literary heredity, which does not go from father to son, but from uncle to nephew. Literary history, for Shklovsky, moves along a zigzag line. If the "saints" of literature, canonized from the seventeenth to the twenty-first century, were strung together, you would not have a continuous line, but a series of jumps, breaks, and backward-turning loops. The tradition begun by one writer almost never has a direct continuation (at least not one of equal value), so that it might be said that no great writer has ever produced his or her own offspring. Still, in every epoch there exists not just one but various literary schools (though we would call them poetics). While one gets canonized, the others stay in the background; they exist but remain in relative silence. And these are the traditions (the uncles) that will be taken up again by the next generation. At a certain point, one of these minor lineages, which has remained out of favor bursts forth to replace what until then had been occupying the throne. Which is not a simple reinstatement, but a complication of that lineage. The deautomatizing of literary forms is thus attained not with a simple variation on, but in direct challenge to, the preceding poetic forms. "In each literary epoch there exists not one but several literary schools. They exist in literature in a state of simultaneity." Perhaps this explains the array of warlike metaphors which the *querelle* of twentieth-century poetics gladly drew on, starting with the term *avant-garde*.

It is often said that formalist theory has been influenced by the avant-gardes, in particular by futurism. But the processes that we have been describing are fully active from romanticism forward (remember that even nineteenth-century realism was in many ways a reaction to romantic poetics). The early twentieth-century avant-gardes represent only a more radical and explicit form of the dialectic of modernity, which has always been founded on the binomial convention-transgression. The need of betrayal in literature is the sign of modernity, and it is an image that well expresses the struggle that every modern art employs against its own tendency to turn conventional. If a form is no longer able to produce defamiliarization, it is because it has decayed into a convention. In

18. Shklovsky 1929b; English version, p. 192. See also p. 190 for following citation.

order to revive the effect of defamiliarization, variation within the convention is not enough; it will take a kind of revolution that subverts that very convention. And that, in its turn, will fall again into convention, and the movement will begin all over again. The phenomenon described here is not, moreover, very far from that criticism of genre which, according to Bakhtin, the novel unleashes throughout literature; in both cases, no literary form is allowed to stabilize into a canon because every form that stabilizes is immediately felt as rigid, conventional, worn-out, automatic.

Variation, Transgression

In every epoch the genres have known transformations at the hand of single innovative personalities or epochal trends. So much so that one can say, along with Croce, that there is no work of art that has not violated the law of an established genre. But variation internal to the codes is one thing; something else altogether is their transgression, on which the differential logic of modernity is founded. That difference has to be heavily underlined; even theory does not always seem to be aware of it. Jauss, for example, traces all literary dynamics, past and present (including here the rupture with tradition typical of modern literature), back to the phenomenon of variation, to that "process of the continual founding and altering of horizons" that for centuries supposedly made literary evolution dynamic.[19] And yet, as Shklovsky had well intuited, and as many others have emphasized, beginning with Valéry, modernity takes shape not so much through variations internal to what had been valid before, but through radical breaks with everything that gradually becomes canonical, and is therefore conceived negatively as worn-out or conventional.[20]

In order to nail down this difference, it may be useful to consider the distinction that Maria Corti has drawn between two types of transformations of the code of genre; one is illustrated by *Orlando Furioso,* the other by *Don Quixote.* Ariosto's operation in respect to the genre of the chivalric epic, and particularly in respect to the model offered by Boiardo, is not one of violent rupture, but of a simple shifting of planes. The narration of heroic events is elevated to the same level of nobility as

19. Jauss 1970, p. 88. An analogous accent on the "positive" function of the disappointment of expectations can be found in Iser 1974 (pp. 58 passim) and Iser 1978.
20. See also Adorno 1967, Italian translation, p. 31.

lyric poetry; it abandons the paratactic structure (linear sequence of nar-ration and of inserts or subplots), and frees itself of regional linguistic traits (which in the Italian tradition were justified by the wide public to which the genre appealed). Both on the thematic and on the rhythmic, rhetorical, and linguistic plane, *Orlando Furioso*, in short, elevates the chivalric poem in the literary hierarchy, bringing it to the same level of nobility as that of lyric poetry, but without stepping outside the bound-aries of its genre. Ariosto thus transforms the genre *from within*, without putting its code into crisis, a code within which it continues to be read. Cervantes, on the contrary, radically offends the law of the chivalric genre, subverting its code to the point of demolishing it. Without any at-tempt at homogenization, he intentionally places the characteristics typ-ical of various literary genres side by side in a subversive mingling of codes.[21] The effect is a violent rupture with the chivalric tradition.

The dialectic of modernity, with its typical impulse toward the "su-persession" of codes, is much closer to the operation of Cervantes than to that of Ariosto. There are historical reasons for this similarity, as has already been shown: in literature, it is the novel that sets off the intoler-ance for genres. The difference between these two types of "transforma-tion" (variation and transgression) is therefore fundamental. For both *Don Quixote* and the dialectic of modernity, the relationships between the single work, the literary system, and codification appreciably change. The possibility of transgressively altering the codes of genre implies an overstepping of the bounds of their "local" horizons in favor of a vaster horizon constituted by literature as a whole. For Jauss, though, there is no difference between these two types of transformation, or if there is, it is merely one of a shade within the range of a single color. He is thus able to trace even the dialectic of modernity back to the eternal law of the dy-namism of genres, to that historicity that "is manifested in the process of the creation of structure, of its variations, of its expansion, and of its rec-tifications." But the consequence is a blindness to the facts that the genre in the modern epoch has been transformed into a negative category, that works of "high literature" are supposed to antagonistically oppose and not just vary vis-a-vis their predecessors. In his generalization, Jauss hides the specificity of modern phenomena. As he sees it, over the cen-turies there have been no ruptures in the evolution of the literary system, neither in regard to the functions fulfilled by the genres nor in the mech-anisms of enjoyment. The genre remains the horizon that orients expec-

21. Corti 1976, p. 162. See also Segre 1974, p. 192.

tations, which are perennially subject to the same type of dynamic: variations, modifications, rectifications, or else reconfirmation and reproduction (though in the case of the last, artistic value would be lost and replaced by use value). Just as it was in the past, so it remains today. But that view is a denial of all the phenomena that we are trying to describe in this book: not only the devaluation of genres and the birth of a new horizon of expectations, but also the reflectedness of literature and the conceptual type of mediation, which has by now become inseparable from the modern act of its enjoyment. In effect, Jauss's repression also serves another purpose: to deny what others have perceived as the death of art. Tracing every literary dynamic back to an eternal dialectic that has never known ruptures is the presupposition necessary for being able to stress the vitality of the aesthetic experience at a time when it has instead become noticeably weakened.[22]

Art and the Self-Referential

From the necessity of producing differential sensations derives, as has already been pointed out, another aspect of the logic of modernity: the self-referential aspect of artistic processes. The necessity of "deautomatizing" literary forms obliges every artistic operation to be circularly referred to preceding operations, setting up a typical self-referential circuit.[23] If literary forms are indeed subject to wearing out and the movement of literature is caused by the necessity of estranging anew that which has become the norm (and so, convention), then the principle factor of change in literature is internal to literature itself.

This self-referential circuit, intuited by Shklovsky (and which, in my opinion, falls by the wayside in the otherwise interesting thought of Tynianov), is essential for understanding the dynamics of contemporary artistic practices:

> A work of art is perceived against a background of and by association
> with other works of art. The form of a work of art is determined by its re-

22. See chapter 2, n. 27, in this book.

23. The term "self-referential" is used here in the sense of the theory of autopoeic systems, where it indicates those systems that refer to themselves through each of their operations, and not in the commonly used sense of a literature that has itself for its object, which would be more appropriately labeled "meta-literature." As it will gradually become more clear, even a poetics that aims at realism can be self-referential to the extent that its artistic valorization implies a reference (through difference or continuity) to the realist poetics that have preceded it.

lationship with other pre-existing forms. . . . All works of art, and not only parodies, are created either as a parallel or an antithesis to some model.[24]

Shklovsky here formulates a key principle, one which will become ever more central to the self-description of late-modern literature. When literature was regulated principally by the constraints of genre, the form of every work was determined above all by its object, in view of which certain forms or styles proved to be more adequate than others. Now, however, the form of a work is determined also *by something else:* by the differential relationship that every solution has with those that came before it, that is, by a historical relationship. This is the fundamental self-referential circuit in which modern literature is harnessed: writings that refer back, through difference, to preceding writings that are by now worn-out, languages that refer back to languages, techniques that refer back to techniques. The origin of change in literature resides not only in demands for the expressive rendering of the object, but also and especially, in the relationship with what has come before. Not even "realism," which quintessentially puts forward the demands for fidelity to the real, for adaptation to the object, for reflection of a reality external to the literary creation, escapes this fundamental self-referential circuit.

In an essay of 1962, while discussing the variety of manifestations of the term *realism,* Jakobson introduces one of considerable importance to our subject: "The tendency to deform the given artistic norms conceived as an approximation of reality."[25] Thus, realism becomes here not only a relative value, but also a self-referential value, which "measures" itself on the basis of the differential relationship that an artistic operation entertains with preceding operations, or with the canons of the time. Modernity, then, modifies traditional notions and "values," bending them to a kind of "second motivation," the demand of defamiliarization, the compulsion to innovate. On top of the reference to reality, forever implicit in the concept of realism, another is superimposed, the reference to how reality has been represented *until now,* the reference to the conventions being used in literature at that given moment in its history.

The self-referential relationship of literature to literature guides literary history, the evolution of its forms and the succession of poetics. Every poetics, furthermore, underlines the differential aspects of an artistic production, that which renders it different from another, that

24. Shklovsky 1929b, p. 20.
25. Jakobson 1921, p. 41.

which distances it from everything that has been written until now, or, on the contrary, that which renders it similar to what has already been done. In each case, in short, every poetics emphasizes its relationship to history. Not even postmodernist poetics, as has already been said, escapes from this relative, self-referential evaluation. The alternative between "do I make it the same or do I make it different" (to borrow again the words of Qfwfq, Calvino's protagonist of "A Sign in Space") is felt here too. And the fact that the positive values of difference and defamiliarization might now be ironically replaced by those of repetition and "return" does not eliminate the self-referential circuit involved in making that evaluation.

One could object that even in ancient literature every poet found himself, in some way, confronting what other poets had created before. As the Greek poet Bacchylides said, "One learns from the other; so it was in the past and so it is still. Surely it is no easy matter to find the doors to words yet unspoken." But such comparison was definitely not invested with the same significance it has in modern literature. More than anything else, it was the characteristics of genre that gave artistic value to the words of the poet, that enabled his or her verse to be received as poetry, and not the differential relationship with preceding solutions. It must also be remembered that in ancient literature, poetry was thought to come, by way of poetic frenzy, from a god or a muse, and that supposition provided both perception and enjoyment of artistic phenomena with a point of reference external to the "history of poetics." The modern self-referential circuit occurs instead in a world where literature is perceived as a system that is *differentiated* from the rest of experience (*autonomous*, and therefore *self-referential*), as a system that knows no other constraint but that produced by its own dynamics. It operates in a system devoid of divinity or muse, devoid too of such concepts as the *imitatio naturae*, which once exerted a heteroreferential constraint on premodern artistic practice and the act of enjoyment. Even the bond of reality, to which every realism refers, acquires in modernity, as has been said, a self-referential character. That which constrains modern literature is internal to literature itself: *estrange* that which is worn-out; or, in its latemodern "degeneration," *repeat* it ironically.

The self-referential circuit is therefore a fundamental trait of modern artistic logic, but as happens with other traits already described in latemodernity, it becomes a reflected characteristic as well. Artistic practice grows increasingly conscious of its self-referential aspect to the point of registering it as one of the "evils" of the epoch (due also to the self-observation connected to it, which has its center in the eye of the author), or trying to break out of its circle with radical gestures that call into question the very autonomy of literature (as happens in the late Pasolini), or finally elaborating it mournfully through the idea of the "impossibility of the new" (as in the epigonal idea of literature dominant today).

And like artistic practice, modern literary theory, too, is starting to perceive the self-referential aspect of artistic processes, encompassing them in the very definition of literature. To write, as Barthes says, is "a narcissistic activity" referring only to itself. Literature is a closed system vis-a-vis the world. It will be worth recalling that, in order to illustrate his famous thesis on the intransitivity of writing, he used the concept of homeostasis, which for the theory of systems was the first and fundamental intuition of a closed system. According to Barthes, "Literature is at bottom a tautological activity, like that of cybernetic machines constructed for themselves (Ashby's homeostat)."[26]

This way of perceiving literature pops up just about everywhere in late-modern literary theories, so much so that the growing awareness of the self-referential character of its processes can be said to spell out the stages of twentieth century reflection on literature. If defamiliarization and differential sensations are notions that already imply a self-reference of literature to itself, the notions elaborated by succeeding theory directly thematize it. Beyond Barthes's "intransitivity," we might also recall Bahktin's "dialogical" concept (literary discourse is fundamentally dialogical in that it "responds" to words already said by others); Harold Bloom's "anxiety of influence," in which the American theoretician really makes the self-referential coincide with his definition of poetry (every writer finds himself under the influence of some literary model, whom he must at the same time resist, and the history of poetry is the history of how some poets have outlived through their poetry, other poets). Finally, the notion of "intertextuality," a concept born in the sphere of poststructuralism (though it is worth mentioning that Kristeva coined it based on the work of Bakhtin), must be added to the list.

Even if named indirectly and with different formulas, the self-referential becomes the modality through which late-modern literature perceives itself. Literature describes itself increasingly as a set of operations that refer each to the other, as a set of texts caught in a network of infinite references, whose artistic value is defined in relation to preexist-

---

26. Barthes 1960, p. 122. However, see also Benedetti 1998, pp. 116–124.

ing literature. The phenomena that such notions describe today are thus not very different from those identified by Shklovsky; all that has changed is the tonality with which they are elaborated. Especially in the case of intertextuality, the axiology that implicitly supports the theoretician's gaze is no longer the valorization of differential qualities, but the accentuating of the impossibility of differentiation; the emphasis falls in short on the nonsustainability of the new, on the epigonism that has by now been absorbed and metabolized.

The Spiral of Self-Consciousness

The differential logic of modernity presupposes an artistic system relatively free of the constraints of genre. Thus a system of values like the modern one, based on defamiliarization and differential sensations, could never have developed had there been no phenomena such as to make it possible: the criticism of genre, the struggle against conventionality, the end of the mediating function of genres. What's more, a conception of literature like the one we have traced in Shklovsky's work could only have been formed in an epoch in which one could *freely* dispose of artistic means beyond the constraints that the genres formerly imposed. This sort of "liberalization of techniques"[27] permits thinking of the creative process as a choice between different techniques, made with a view to obtaining the desired effect. (It is from this choice, conscious or unconscious, real or supposed, that the figure of the author, as has been said, takes shape.) The values of modernity thus inevitably introduce into the idea of creation a certain degree of purposefulness, or "rationality oriented toward a goal." If the technique is indeed seen as a means to attain a certain effect of perception, that is, a rendering of the familiar strange, it means that the creative process is conceived as a choice of the *most efficacious* means. Recalling a famous passage in *War and Peace,* in which the description of a theatre is conducted wholly from the point of view of a provincial girl, Shklovsky immediately asks himself, "What is the artistic purpose of this descriptive method?" Obviously, the answer is defamiliarization. But what is important for us to note is the type of question; the fact that he asks himself here about the *purpose* of a technique. Today a similar question has become inevitable for every modern work. It is precisely this questioning oneself about the purpose of tech-

27. Cf. Bürger 1974, p. 23.

niques that constructs the image of a project-making author, the subject of choices, who selects the expressive means most appropriate to reach a certain artistic effect. Shklovsky goes on to write:

> In our phonetic and lexical investigations into poetic speech, involving both the arrangement of words and the semantic structures based on them, we discover everywhere the very hallmark of the artistic: that is, an artifact that has been intentionally removed from the domain of automatized perception. It is "artificially" created by an artist in such a way that the perceiver, pausing in his reading, dwells on the text.[28]

For Shklovsky, art's purposefulness does not mean, however, a purposefulness that the artist is conscious of. The purpose of the technique may not be fully evident to the author in the moment in which he or she puts it to work. What counts is that such purposefulness is inherent in our manner of conceiving and enjoying art, the fact that the sign of artistry resides precisely in an artistic intentionality presumed to be behind every technique, and evaluable on the basis of the difference that we perceive between this artistic operation and those that have preceded it.

In the past, a similar (and paradoxical) copresence of the artist's purposefulness and unconsciousness was the very definition of genius. But something unprecedented occurs in modern art; the lack of awareness is destined not to last long. Temporality is not extraneous to the processes of modern enjoyment, which, even from this point of view, tend to incorporate the history of the forms and of the manner in which they are perceived. As Calvino's "authorial experience" *once again* paradigmatically reveals, over time the late-modern writer cannot help but become aware both of what he does, and of how it is perceived, enjoyed, and defined. The eye of the critics and readers, who eventually learn how to recognize the specific formula of a writer, to define and to evaluate it, is introjected into the author himself. From whichever side one considers it, that of creation or that of the act of enjoyment, the self-observation of the literary system is a single circuit that absorbs into itself the entire process of artistic communication; creation reflects the processes of enjoyment and vice versa.

In the preface to his *Theory of Prose*, Shklovsky relates a conversation that he had with Aleksandr Blok. Shklovsky had just finished giving his lecture when the poet said to him, "It's the first time that I've heard the

---

28. Shklovsky 1929b, p. 12.

truth spoken about poetry, but it seems to me that what you're saying is dangerous for the poet, once he knows it."[29] Shklovsky replied that one can't say that the poet really works unconsciously. He may work with less awareness than a scientist because he is unable to repeat the experiment, but the best way to put it is that in the poet's work there are some elements that are incomprehensible *at first*. But sooner or later the poet is destined "to know" what he has done. Even the scientist, moreover, as Einstein writes in his autobiography, sometimes finds himself amazed by what he is discovering. The reason is that the discovery runs up against a world of concepts that have stabilized in us. But before long that conceptual world is modified so as to be able to receive and integrate the new element. This, Shklovsky concludes, is the spiral of consciousness. Something of the kind happens also in artistic creation. The poetic construction has at first some incomprehensible elements, which astonish the artist himself because they are in conflict with his (and our) usual coordinates. But here, too, what at first astonishes ultimately goes through a process of integration, which brings an end to the astonishment. In short, the mode in which the new emerges is indeed, as the romantics held, unconscious; nevertheless, it does not stay that way long. Similar to science, "poetry, too, knows itself within a certain lapse of time." Once again, here we have no trouble recognizing the typical dialectic of defamiliarization that we have already described, though put into focus this time from the artist's perspective and his or her processes of self-consciousness. After a certain lapse of time, the new no longer astonishes; that which was estranging is no longer so. In this way, even the artist is destined to become aware of the new that he or she has unconsciously discovered. But the most interesting thing is that this inevitable process of self-consciousness coincides, for Shklovsky, with the elaboration of the poetics that underlies an artistic operation, and with the definition that critics or those who enjoy art might give it: "Poetics is beyond consciousness, poetics rounds out the poetic construction. I think that the work of the literary scholar accelerates the progressive motion of poetic consciousness." This is how things stand for Shklovsky, which is to say for his particular theory of literature, one which is not universal but rather altogether modeled on modern artistic logic (and ultimately too simple to falsify by bringing forth examples of art from the past that, through time, have preserved their opacity almost intact). Nevertheless,

29. Shklovsky 1929, Preface to *Theory of Prose* (not included in English translation). See Shklovsky 1976, pp. xix–xxi, from which come the following citations as well.

it is just because of this consonance with the spirit of the times that Shklovsky's idea of literature can help us grasp the uneasiness of the late-modern moment.

Calvino, too, was notably affected by the way Pavese defined him based on *The Path to the Nest of Spiders*. But it does not always take a critic's definition to awaken the writer's self-consciousness. The late-modern author has internalized the defining eye of the critic, or the shrewd reader, or worse, the eyes of all possible critics and readers. With or without the intervention of the critic to explain his techniques (and so encourage the process of self-observation), this type of writer can't help but become aware of that which initially he discovered in an unconscious manner since the entropic process is nevertheless inherent to the dynamics of modern art. So if every innovation is destined to become, sooner or later, convention, it also needs to be said that it does so exactly at the moment when it is recognized as formula, as an explicit, and by now defined, poetics. The elaboration of a poetics on the part of the author (i.e., the awareness of what he has done), or its comprehension on the part of the critic, nullifies the estranging value of the technique. That which is known and defined loses its capacity to astonish. Note the short circuit that is thus established between the framing of an artistic operation in a poetics and its decline into convention. Not only because through the definition of poetics the new is explained and thereby integrated, but also because in this way it is fixed into a formula that will be recognizable in the future and thus felt as a style, or worse, imitated, parodied. Which also means that every poetics is there to be surpassed. The self-consciousness of poetics ends up having a circular effect on the processes of creation; it causes art to pass into another phase of the spiral, propelling it in its progressive motion. It is an entropic process that the original avant-garde movement made visible and problematic by inverting its stages, provocatively putting the poetics before the work. The avant-gardes thus made perceptible this virtual object (poetics), on which the self-observation of modern art is concentrated, and which unifies in a single gaze the eye of the author and that of the enjoyer. Not only is this object virtual, but it is also situated on a level of logic superior to that on which the texts exist in their sensible concreteness. Just the same, through its virtuality and from its location on that secondary level of literary communication, poetics exerts all its powers of mediation, like a new currency that measures the artistic value of works.

CHAPTER 6

"This Is Literature!"

If someone calls it art, it's art.
DONALD JUDD

What makes a verbal message a work of art? Now there's a question that has driven generations of theoreticians crazy. It is often traced back to Jakobson, who formulated it in 1919, promoting it to the rank of a fundamental issue of literary theory. A century earlier, however, Hegel had already posed an analogous question in his *Aesthetics:* "We must take on the task of separating *poetic* representation from *prose.*"[1]

Whether it was philosophical aesthetics or literary theory that posed the question for the first time, the sure thing is that it is not one that has always been posed. Only modern literary communication has made this issue crucial. It's not that earlier poetry had no need to mark out its own identity and boundaries in some way: the system of genres already implicitly guaranteed such demarcations, and did so without much trouble. However, when the metacommunicative function of genres began to fade away in the modern epoch, or indeed, was turned into its opposite, the identity of literature became an open problem. That does not mean it became a difficult problem, but just a problem that keeps getting posed *over and over,* for each individual work. "What is it about *this* text that

---

1. Jakobson 1958, pp. 85–86. Hegel 1836 (Italian translation, p. 1084).

makes it a work of literature?" is the question that modernity has inscribed in artistic practice itself. Every modern work must furnish reasons why it should be granted the right to be considered art. And that is a right that is never won once and for all, but is forever open to dispute.[2] The set of all such reasons claimed by the work, or that the act of enjoyment supposes to be claimed by the work, is poetics. And it is by way of poetics that the dispute over the artistic value of a text develops. As a result, in the modern period the constitutive problem is not merely theoretical (i.e., one that theory may or may not pose). It is instead the fulcrum of artistic communication, the inherent stake at risk in every act of enjoyment, the very motor for the adventure of art.

What Makes Literature Literature?

Twentieth-century literary theory instead posed the problem of literature in a general way, to be resolved once and for all on the ground of theory, by means of describing "the literary," in other words, that which constitutes the specificity of literature. Such theoretical elaborations are sterile, and it would not be worth the trouble to examine them except that the question itself, and the fact that it has been posed, is for us already a significant phenomenon. What distinguishes literature from nonartistic practices is no longer, in the modern epoch, something obvious or to be taken for granted; on the contrary, it explicitly emerges as problematic, requiring those who think about art to come to terms with it directly.

Jakobson wrote that the fundamental task of "poetics" (understood here as the theory of what makes literature literature) is to define the specific difference that sets apart the artistic use of words from other verbal practices. It is, of course, completely legitimate for literary theory to pose as fundamental the definition of its own object. However, there are

2. I borrow the term *dispute* from Rino Genovese, who understands it as "the proliferation of arguments around works according to conflicting criteria about which it is impossible to reach universal consensus." Dispute, then, would appear to be the specific trait of art since the beginning of the romantic movement, which is to say, of art that has abandoned the "generically aesthetic code" (based on the opposition beautiful/ugly) in favor of a plurality of codes (for example, ancient/modern, innocent/sentimental, famous/unknown, etc.) which are left to collide in dispute. "Unlike what happens in the simple quarrel over aesthetic judgments (already accepted by Kant), dispute derives from the conflict between different codes in which each code is endowed with its own particular power of generalization" (Genovese 1989, p. 154).

various ways of doing so, and searching out a property supposedly common to all literary works is neither the sole nor the most obvious among them. Why should we search for the "literariness" of a work rather than consider "literature as a set of concrete exemplars"? And why not view literature as a system of genres, as had always been done from Aristotle to Romanticism?

Genette explains it this way: in order for me to know that an animal is a dog, I do not have to be familiar with its breed, which moreover may be unaccertainable; similarly, I may not know exactly whether some text is a novel, but I will have no doubt about whether it is literature or not. This is also the basis on which Genette justifies his own choice of dealing with art and the artistic in general: "Paradoxically or not, it seems to me that the *artistic*, as to its general action, is definable with greater certainty than any one of the 'arts.' "[3] Consequently, there would seem to be a *logical* necessity to justify such an inquiry, not a *historical* one. I, on the contrary, would say that the only necessity for such an inquiry is historical. If theory in the twentieth century started to inquire into what makes literature literature, it is because it can no longer consult the genres for an answer.

That this is the way things stand for us is by now obvious, given the phenomena discussed in the preceding chapters. But literary theory of a formalist-structuralist stamp ignores the transformation of the genres and so refuses to recognize the historicity of the phenomena into which it inquires; it reflects on notions that originated in modern art, while passing them off as ahistorical and universally valid. The concept of "dog" is as old as the hills; the concept of "literature" as an abstract class is altogether modern. How then would the ancients have been able to recognize a text as belonging to a class for which they did not possess the notion? The idea of literariness is not innate to our experience of literature, in the same way the concept of dog is to our experience of the animal world. The ancients certainly knew how to recognize dogs without specifying their breed, but as for literary texts the same cannot be said. If they did know how to recognize literary texts, it was, on the contrary, because they knew how to recognize their genres: tragedy, epic, comedy, and the rest. Not only is literature as a general class of all possible forms of verbal art a modern notion, but above all (and I am compelled to emphasize this point), the need to define literature *independently of genres* is a typically modern preoccupation. It could only have been born at the

---

3. Genette 1994, p. 3 from which comes the following citation also.

moment in which literature becomes an open class, no longer delimited by the system of genres. Only by taking account of this new condition of literature, stripped of its formerly distinctive marks, can one understand why modern literary theory, born at the dawn of the twentieth century with the Russian formalists, was confronted with the necessity of defining a general criterion for what makes literature literature.

The Aesthetics Solution

Even before literary theory, however, eighteenth-century aesthetics had defined a criterion for the delimitation of artistic phenomena equally universal and metahistorical. It resolved the constitutive problem for all the arts by anchoring them to the concept of the beautiful (understood by Kant as "purposiveness without purpose") and so gave rise to the definition of a specific sphere of human experience, that in which aesthetic judgments are formed, whether they concern objects of art or objects of nature. The specificity of the aesthetic sphere is therefore based on its distinction from other spheres of human experience or activity, and knowledge. A similar approach, which we might call functional or even anthropological (and which responds to the question "what does man do, or which of his faculties are involved whenever he judges an object beautiful or sublime, whenever he beholds something endowed with, or to which is attributed, an aesthetic value?") survived in much twentieth-century thought,[4] and at times reemerged even in modern literary theory in the "structuralist tradition," which is now stuck at the impasse to which Jakobson led it, as Genette's recent thought demonstrates.

Defining the artistic in a general way might also seem reasonable considering that today many works (performance pieces and video installations among them) are considered art despite the fact (and without anyone being terribly concerned about it) that no one has succeeded in determining which art they belong to. In such a context, Genette writes, to insist on the plurality of arts could cause a taxonomic blockage and a conceptual impediment, so that, in his opinion, even the Crocean theme of the unity of art might prove liberating, "because it leaves to a relational criterion . . . (and not necessarily Croce's), the task of defining not the arts but the artistic character of a certain practice or object." But if

4. Cf. for example, Mukařovský 1966.

Genette takes it for granted that the artistic is more easily definable than are the arts, it is because he believes that it can be given a definition "of a typically functional order": that is, a definition of the same order as that which Kantian-inspired aesthetics has always furnished it, by anchoring art to a particular sphere of activity, endowed with its own functional characteristics, peacefully defined within its own boundaries, and institutionalized. Literary theory, when it poses the constitutive problem, tends to presume it already resolved on the basis of notions "imported" from aesthetics, elaborated for an art that may no longer even exist.

As Hamburger notes, Hegel was probably the first to insist on the need to differentiate poetry from everyday discourse.[5] But it must also be mentioned that for Hegel the problem was posed not in a general sense, in relation to every form of poetry, but specifically for that of his epoch. Unlike "primal poetry," modern poetry lives and develops in competition with "prose" (in whose sphere Hegel also included philosophy), that is, in competition with a sphere of consciousness and knowing capable of expressing the true and the absolute even in nonpoetic form, by means of "intellectually ordered representations and cognitions."[6] And in such a context, which is completely "prosaic" both in its conception of the world and its mode of expression, poetic discourse not only must "detach itself from everyday discourse," but also know that it is doing so, developing itself therefore "as consciously different from the prosaic." Thus Hegel was well aware of the historicity of the problem, of its specifically modern dimension, which is something that instead gets obfuscated by both eighteenth-century aesthetics and modern literary theory in the search for universal criteria with which to lay down boundary lines.

However, the solution of eighteenth-century aesthetics was not destined to reign for long.[7] One reason was that "the beautiful" actually did put art on the same plane as other beautiful, though not artistic, objects (such as sea shells, mountain views, or sunsets).[8] There was also another reason. The sphere of art is defined here on the basis of aesthetic experi-

---

5. Hamburger 1957, p. 18.

6. Hegel 1836 (Italian translation, p. 1089).

7. With romanticism the beautiful/ugly code was already vanishing in favor of a plurality of concurrent codes, as mentioned above. See Genovese 1989. However, see also Carchia 1983.

8. For Hegel, in contrast, the naturally beautiful (which the ancients were, moreover, uninterested in) was deficient in comparison to that beauty realized in a work of art (Hegel 1836, Italian translation, pp. 171 ff.); and, in fact, aesthetics here is a theory of art, not a science of perception or the senses.

ence understood as *aisthesis* (sense perception), but from romanticism on, *aisthesis* was no longer able to describe how modern art nails down its own constitutive specificity. "Beautiful art" is dead, Hegel said. In the epoch of the reflectiveness of art it would be impossible to anchor artistic value either to the beautiful, or to a particular sensible value, since other processes had arisen, other mediations of a conceptual type which surpassed *aisthesis* (to which, nevertheless, not only eighteenth-century aesthetics but also its modern revival remain attached). So that the aesthetic experience which is spoken of today often has the redolence of a nostalgic reevocation, of a celebration of the "aesthetic virtues" of the past, which at most can be cited by artistic practice. Just as in the "return to painting" trend of much contemporary art, what gets restored is not so much the painting as references to it, a visual citation of it.[9] It must be added that the beautiful form, the "aesthetic relation," where it does survive, has now acquired the after-taste of aestheticization, which renders grotesque Genette's pretense of considering the artistic as a particular case of the aesthetic. In the category of nonartistic beauty he would also have to include all kinds of merchandise, shows, spectacles, and gadgets, and perhaps find himself illustrating his notions ("aspectual attention," for example) by pointing to a designer watch, the packaging of expensive chocolates, or the sand dunes of a vacation resort. In Genette's theory, however, there is no trace of the aestheticization of the living world.[10]

Breaking Away from Aesthetics

Twentieth-century literary theory, born with the formalists, gathered under the flag of the rejection of aesthetics and its claim to unite all the arts around the value of the beautiful. However, its "breaking away" from aesthetics does not go in the direction of an integration of all the conceptual aspects of art; instead, it immerses itself in the materiality of linguistic signs, in the forms and morphological aspects of verbal art in general, hoping to find there the markings of what makes literature literature. It thus does not abandon the terrain of *aisthesis*, but rather seeks,

9. On the "rebirth" of painting, cf. Kosuth, "Necrophilia mon amour" (1982), now in Kosuth 1966–1990, pp. 204–205. For a different opinion, cf. Clair 1983.

10. In compensation, his neo-Kantianism leads him to define the aesthetic as a branch of general anthropology. Genette 1997, p. 11.

and with greater perseverance than did aesthetics, the sensible aspects of verbal art, from within their linguistic specificity.

Jakobson talked about the fundamental task of *poetics*, not the theory of literature. The theory of literature born out of formalism and nourished by structuralism has often defined itself as "poetics" in the ancient sense of the term,[11] in direct opposition to an aesthetics which by then was justly considered incapable of taking account of many things. Let us try then, to take the bearings of these notions: (1) poetics in the classical sense, (2) the theory of literature, (3) aesthetics. Their differences and oppositions conceal much more than a simple question of terminology.

The distinction between poetics and aesthetics is obviously modern since aesthetics did not exist before the eighteenth century. That is not because before then people did not discuss subjects like the beautiful, the sublime, grace, the judgment of taste, or the nature and function of art; it is simply that such topics were not the object of a specific discipline, but were discussed either in the realm of metaphysics (for example, the beautiful) or, in the case of art, in the realm of poetics. By "poetics" what was meant then was any discourse about poetry (not *literature*, which is a later concept), the concrete modes of artistic production, the rules, as well as the nature of art, and the criteria for its evaluation. If we read the first paragraph of Aristotle's *Poetics*, all these things will be found listed together among the topics to be treated:

> Our subject being Poetry, I propose to speak not only of the art in general but also of its *species* and their respective *capacities; of the structure of plot required* for a good poem; of the number and nature of the constituent parts of a poem; and likewise of any other matters in the same line of inquiry. Let us follow the natural order and begin with the primary facts.
>
> *Epic poetry* and *Tragedy*, as also *Comedy, Dithyrambic poetry,* and most *flute-playing* and *lyre-playing,* are all viewed as a whole, *modes of imitation.* But at the same time they differ from one another in three ways, either by a *difference of kind in their means,* or by differences in the objects, or in the manner of their imitations.[12]

11. The appellation was most widely used in France: *Poétique* is the name of a journal and a collection of literary theory directed by Todorov and Genette. Even Valéry, moreover, judged the term *poetics* appropriate for indicating the study of "artistic practice" in general, as long as it was understood "according to its etymology," that is, as "the name of everything that has to do with the creation or composition of works," and not in the restricted sense of a collection of rules or precepts that concern poetry (see chapter 2, n. 25, of this book).

12. Aristotle 1947, p. 623 (italics added).

Poetics therefore describes above all else the forms of poetic activity, its genres (tragedy, epic, comedy, dithyrambs, etc.) distinguished on the basis of their objects or themes (characters "superior" to us, or inferior to us), their specific styles (high, low), and their specific methods (imitation by means of words, rhythm, music, or dance, variously combined or separate). And the discourse is not limited to describing what has already been done, but also treats the capacities inherent in each of the forms (thus, for example, as regards the *mythos,* or story, Aristotle distinguishes between the main plot and accessory motives, and develops too a theory of the *fabula,* from which the modern analysis of fiction draws many of its concepts). In addition, Aristotle's poetics treats the manner in which story lines should be composed so that the poem is well-made: how to compose a tragedy, how the plot should be constructed, and other themes, and in this we find its preceptive aspect. But there is more: in saying that all these forms are imitations, Aristotle also formulates his own idea of poetry, which is also a defense of poetic art against Plato's condemnation of it. By way of the theory of mimesis, Aristotle demonstrates the cognitive value of poetry and its superiority to history (which is always an account of the particular, whereas poetry is "vision of the general"), culminating in the theory of catharsis (passing beyond the passions by means of knowledge), which in its turn is also a demonstration of the superiority of tragedy over the other genres.

This technical treatment of verbal art is then also the first treatise on aesthetics and poetic theory; its individuation of methods goes hand in hand with a general theory of dramatic poetry (particularly of tragedy); its detailed precepts aimed at providing practical instructions to writers go hand in hand with a meditation on the nature of art (imitation) and on its function (vision of the general, catharsis). In Aristotle's poetics, in short, reflection on method is united to matters more properly called aesthetic, and these two inspirations remain together within poetics until the eighteenth century, that is, until the time when the judgment of taste with regard to artistic production and the beautiful in general become the object of a specific discipline. From that time on, every "aesthetic" question (anything that goes beyond method and precepts) was kept outside the field of poetics.

The modern literary theory born out of formalism intends to be a poetics in the ancient sense insofar as it rejects that separation of tasks, and in confronting the formal and technical aspects of literature, it also wants to include those aspects that are more properly aesthetic. It does not limit itself to indicating how literary texts are made, to describing their forms and techniques, but through linguistic inquiries also tries to define the aesthetic use of language.[13] As a result, not only is poetics unleashed from that purely preceptive-normative ambit within which philosophical aesthetics had confined it, but at the same time, aesthetics completely dissolves in poetics. Against the ambitions of aesthetics to found art on something anterior (or ulterior) to artistic practice, poetics claims the immanence of the aesthetic to artistic practice itself, to that *poiein* which, as Valéry used to say, is realized in some works. Thus Jakobson could say that the fundamental task of poetics is to answer a question that once had been the prerogative of aesthetics. Aesthetic qualities are presumed to be immanent to the concrete artistic product, and are investigated on the basis of the linguistic qualities of the texts, their formal and structural aspects. That, however, can only destine the inquiry to failure.

The Impossible Return to Aristotle

Modern poetics, in its claim to reconnect with ancient poetics, is actually faced with a problem that Aristotle never had, and that no ancient poetics would ever have posed for itself: what is the criterion that in general permits the inclusion of a text within literature, in other words, within the class of all possible literary facts, independent of the genres? This problem is typically modern. Aristotle never speaks of verbal art as an abstract category; he speaks only of tragedy, comedy, epic, and the other genres, which is to say, of the particular poetic genres, lined up in a tradition. He speaks, in short, of the concrete members of a class that had not even been imagined yet (it would be some time before the modern concept of literature, which now seems so natural to us, was formed). And those "members" were distinguished by clear markings, generic markings (theme, style, means of imitation), besides the marking that has always served to neatly differentiate the artistic use of language from its practical use: verse.

As Hegel noted, "poetry is older than artistically elaborated discourse in prose."[14] Initially, the sole possible language for verbal art was that of verse, exactly because it was the furthest removed from everyday language. In the realm of the verbal arts, which was not by mere coincidence referred to as "poetry" for centuries, prose (i.e., an artistic lan-

---

13. As Jakobson writes, modern poetics not only studies the technique of artistic creation, but also "artistic creation in its originality and aesthetic significance."

14. Hegel 1836 (Italian translation, pp. 1087–1088).

guage not in verse) arrived on the scene late. That habit of calling verbal art poetry has been carried on mechanically until our own time. Thus Jakobson speaks of the "poetic function" of language and not of its "literary function," and the science that studies literature goes on improperly being called "poetics," without acknowledging the gap that separates the verbal art of the past from that of today. The first stage of verbal art, then, passes necessarily through its dissimilarity to nonartistic discourse. And perhaps, even before verse, what served to distinguish the singer's words from the sphere of the quotidian was musical accompaniment. Music (with which Aristotle is still concerned in his *Poetics*, where it is included among the means of imitation, alongside of words and rhythm) provided a frame for the words so that they were perceived as belonging to a sphere unto themselves, the sphere that today we would call the "aesthetic" or "artistic." Then came verses, rhythm, rhyme, that is, the clearly perceptible formal signs of dissimilarity.[15] Even in Aristotle's time, however, things were not so simple since there were also treatises written in verse. But here I have mentioned verse only as a supplementary mark to artistry. The fundamental mark remained, in a more developed literary system like the one described by Aristotle, that entrusted to the genres.

The ancient theoreticians, therefore, did not find themselves confronting the supreme problem of modern literary theory simply because they were dealing with poetic genres, whose artistic mark was intrinsic and self-evident, and not with an abstract class encompassing all possible literary creations. This "minor" difference, overlooked by the majority of theoreticians who today have gone back to inquire into Aristotle, has, nonetheless, major consequences. The problems that modern poetics is called on to solve are not the same as those that Aristotle was concerned with. Verbal art today is a much more complex phenomenon, one which can contain not only things that are not versified but also things that are not codified; it is concerned with a literature centered on the values of "making it new" and leaving the canons behind. It is, moreover, a phenomenon in motion, which over time can include and then exclude the same object, or vice-versa, first exclude it and then reclaim it, as has happened, for example, with certain texts of pulp fiction, which have been reinvested with value by postmodern taste. To stick to the modern period, however, there is the case mentioned by Jakobson of the Czech writer Mácha (1810–1836), whose diary, left unpublished by the author

15. Cf. Lotman 1970.

(his contemporaries would not have considered it literature), ended up nonetheless being published and appreciated as a literary work in the twentieth century.

Thus, for modern literary theory, defining the criterion of what makes literature literature becomes an extremely thorny, yet unavoidable, issue. Unavoidable because, for the new discipline that calls itself "poetics," the problem coincides with its very foundation. Thorny because this specificity, given the features of modern literature, can no longer be sought for in the characteristics of genre. It will be necessary to define instead a criterion that allows us to join together disparate artistic practices, deprived of codified marks. It will be necessary, in short, to define the membership criterion of any individual creation (independent of generic characteristics) to the "open" class of all possible literary creations. That is just what modern theory fails to do. By addressing its question to the language and formal structures of texts in search of an artistic mark that is immanent to them, literary theory has merely succeeded in providing comically tautological answers, thus making it an easy target for the darts of skeptical pragmatism.

Dissecting the Body in Search of the Soul

The twentieth century, it is said, was not an epoch of universal aesthetics but one of contending theories based on the various arts (theories of painting, music, literature, and cinema), each of which draws its own legitimation from the specific medium that distinguishes the art in question, that is, form and color for painting, sound for music, verbal language for literature. One no longer speaks of the arts as joined together through reference to the aesthetic value of the beautiful, or through that which characterizes the sphere of the aesthetic in the unity of culture; instead, each individual art is differentiated on the basis of its expressive medium. Thus Jakobson wrote: "Poetics deals with problems of verbal structure, just as the analysis of painting is concerned with pictorial structure; since linguistics is the global science of verbal structure, poetics may be regarded as an integral part of linguistics."[16] The discipline that defines itself as "poetics" is therefore fundamentally a theory of lit-

16. Jakobson 1958, p. 86.

erature, insofar as it is the theory of a particular art, a theory born in opposition to the generalizing claim of aesthetics.

This breaking away from aesthetics is not of equal intensity in every theory of art; it is perhaps less severe with regard to the figurative arts, but there is certainly a clean break when it comes to literature. The modern theory of literature constitutes itself radically as an autonomous discipline, professing to reformulate on its own, on the basis of its "specificity," questions of aesthetics in the strictest sense. Therefore even the ancient question of what art is, and of how to distinguish it from nonart, which philosophical aesthetics posed for all arts, is now approached from within the "material" that distinguishes this specific art, which is to say, language. The constitutive problem is thus reduced to the search for what characterizes the aesthetic use of language. For that reason, however, defining what makes literature literature becomes an impossible mission, in which theory appears valiantly committed to lifting itself up by its own bootstraps. An unrealistic task, it carries within itself the germs of its own inevitable frustration: like looking through the viscera of a dissected body in search of its soul.

I do not mean by that, as Bakhtin may have believed, that philosophical aesthetics succeeds in explaining the phenomena of modern art better than does formalist theory.[17] What I do mean is that aesthetics in its own fashion solved the problem of the delimitation of art in a clear-cut way, even if it is inadmissable for us today. The modern theory of art is incapable of solving it. Having at its disposal neither the "classical solution" (the system of genres, which rather than a solution was more a way of not posing the problem) nor the solution of aesthetics (the beautiful), it reformulates the problem from within the linguistic specificity of literature, in other words, in a manner that is in and of itself destined to failure.

Jakobson attempted a functional definition of poetic language that attracted a great deal of attention. As his theory is widely known, there is no need to rehearse it here. What may be useful to look at, though, is the oppositional scheme that underlies and defines it. Just as philosophical aesthetics sought the specificity of the aesthetic in a sphere of human activity, defined in opposition to other spheres (the sphere of morals or

17. Bakhtin polemically called formalist theory "material aesthetics" because, in rejecting aesthetics as a guiding discipline, it grabbed onto linguistics, and overvalued the "material" moment of art (cf. "The Problem of Content, Material and Form in Verbal Aesthetic Creation" in Medvedev 1978).

practice, the sphere of knowledge or science), structuralist poetics seeks the specificity of the aesthetic use of language in opposition to its practical or communicative uses: "Language," writes Jakobson, "must be investigated in all the variety of its functions. Before discussing the poetic function, we must define its place among the other functions of language." If in its practical use, language is a medium (for the transmission of information, for the communication of thought), in its aesthetic use it is an end unto itself, characterized therefore by a kind of "autotelism," as Todorov calls it, rightly connecting this idea of poetic language back to its romantic roots.[18] The practico-communicative end obviously does not altogether disappear in poetry, but passes onto a secondary plane. Thus, if in the communicative use of language our attention glides over the sounds of words and their letters, or over how the sentences are constructed, in the poetic use the materiality of sound and construction demands notice. Instead of being a transparent medium aimed at its referents, poetic language attracts attention to itself, becoming a physical object. "Poetic language tends at its limit towards the phonetic word," writes Jakobson. However, since similar phenomena can, after all, also take place in nonpoetic uses (consider advertising and all the "aestheticized" languages of the mass media), Jakobson finds himself forced to insert the concept of "dominant." By so doing, the poetic function can certainly be detected even in an electoral slogan (as in the famous "I like Ike," with its repetition of the same diphthong, its rhyme, paronomasia, and alliteration), but as Jakobson reassures us, in such cases it remains only a secondary function, which reinforces the instrumental effectiveness of the message. In poetry the aesthetic (or "autotelic") becomes the dominant function.

This functional characterization of poetic language enjoyed great success in meditations on literature, and not only in the structuralist camp, but also in some theories of a psychoanalytical bent that flourished in the 1960s.[19] Its fortune may have hung on the fact that it "rationalized" in

18. Todorov 1984.

19. The theories of Francesco Orlando (cf. Orlando 1973 and 1982) and of Julia Kristeva (cf. Kristeva 1975), though having notable differences from which one can abstract only in the most general way, both presuppose a vision of poetic language borrowed from the formalists and Jakobson (high rate of figures of speech, emphasis on the sonorous shape of the words, message oriented not to the referent, but intransitively to itself). It is thanks to these traits that literature can become, for Orlando, the formal basis for a return of the repressed (or of the "aberrant" logic of the unconscious, which he calls, along with Matte Blanco, "symmetrics"); for Kristeva, it is the location in which another type of articulation of discourse is insinuated (the "semiotic"), which brings back into the

pseudoscientific terms (in the shadow, one might say, of the laws of linguistics) an idea of poetic language that was essentially romantic, and that the late-nineteenth century and early-twentieth century poetics, from Mallarmé to the avant-gardes, had updated. The theory of the poetic function of language is moreover in line with that idea of "prolonged hesitation between sound and sense" of which Valéry spoke: the poetic use of language would emphasize the sonorous shape of the words at the cost of their signification, deepening the dichotomy between signs and their objects. But all this really tells us is that the functional definition of poetic language is not so much a theory but an idea of literature, thus a poetics in disguise (since not in all forms of verbal art does language actually acquire this "autotelic" density). Today it has been abandoned by most, criticized above all for its claim to bear on its shoulders the solution of the constitutive problem.[20]

There was a subsequent, more sophisticated version of autotelism elaborated by theories of a semiotic bent. In this version, autotelism no longer characterizes poetic language but the literary text as a whole, which is supposed to be, unlike the nonartistic text, more highly "structured," richer in internal connections, in elements that refer to each other. This "superstructuration" is supposed to be realized at diverse levels or "rungs" (thematic, symbolic, ideological, stylistic, syntactic, lexical, phono-timbric, rhythmic, metric), each of which supposedly contributes to producing that "hypersemanticity" typical of literary communication. In a literary text, in short, everything is pertinent, "everything signifies," from the level of its sounds to that of its meanings. This is tantamount to saying that a literary text is above all perceived in itself, autotelically, in the cohesion and connectivity of its internal references.[21] But this semiological and textual version of the specificity of literature is surely no more satisfying than the other if employed as the criterion for determining what makes literature literature. One can always raise the objection that the "superstructuration" does not belong to the literary text as its objective quality, but rather as the product of an attribution. In short, it is the attitude the appreciator takes in the face of a text that has already been attributed with an aesthetic

---

limelight the pleasure principle and the unconscious processes of immediate gratification.

20. Besides Fish 1980, about whom we shall speak shortly, see also Di Girolamo 1978 and Brioschi 1983.

21. All these notions, including that of "semantics at many rungs," are found in Lotman 1970. However, see too the reformulation of it made by Corti 1976.

value that induces him or her to notice, and so construct, such connections in the text, as Stanley Fish has provocatively "proven."

Fish's Experiment

Stanley Fish was teaching two courses, one following right after the
other in the same classroom; the first was on the relationship between literary criticism and linguistics, the second on English religious poetry of
the seventeenth century. He was teaching the second group of students
how to identify Christian symbols, and to recognize the poetic intention
(mostly didactic) hidden within them. On the blackboard during the earlier class, Fish had written a list of the names of linguists organized ver-
tically, in a column: Jakobs-Rosenbaum/Levin/Thorne/Hayes/Ohman
(the last followed by a question mark since he could not recall if it was
spelled with one or two *n*'s). When the second class arrived, he told the
students that what they saw on the blackboard was a religious poem of
the kind they had been studying, and asked them to interpret it. One stu-
dent began by saying the poem was probably a hieroglyphic in the form
of a cross. Shortly thereafter, "Jakobs" was interpreted as a reference to
Jacob's ladder, an allegory for the ascent to heaven. However, in this
case, the instrument of ascent was not a ladder, but a rosebush (Rosen-
baum), probably an allusion to the Virgin, among other possibilities. I
will go no further into the stages of the interpretation, which as one can
imagine, ended up being anything but banal; it actually turned out being
highly complex and based on multiple levels of the "text."[22] From this in-
cident, Fish concluded that every communication takes place within a
situation, or context, and that finding oneself in a given situation means
being already in possession of a structure of presuppositions, of practices which are considered to be pertinent to the goals and objectives of
that context. Thus it is not so much the literary text that imposes the
manner in which it must be perceived, but a particular mode of perceiving that determines the emergence of the literary text. There is enough
here to put any definition of "literariness" founded on the objective
(functional or structural) characteristics of the poetic text into fatal crisis.

Of course, Fish's "experiment" proves nothing. In no way does it
prove the thesis that he would like to assert, that literature is a conventional category. The *pars construens* of his reasoning is no more satisfying

---

22. Fish 1980, pp. 322–325.

than that which it criticizes. In order to explain how, "in the absence of formal criteria," literary texts can be identified, he takes the easy road of conventionalism, unburdening himself of all his skeptical habits as he sets off down it. In short he resolves the constitutive problem by tying the recognition of the literary to "decisions" of the community of readers, to their tacit consensus on what is to be taken as literature.[23] However, if what discriminates between art and nonart is indeed entrusted to the criteria on which the community of appreciators *agrees*, no work that glaringly deviates from the canons could ever aspire to be considered as art; neither the bottle rack that Duchamp exhibited in 1914 (which certainly had to be disconcerting to much of the public), nor the list of linguists that Fish "exhibited" on his blackboard proclaiming it to be a poem, which visibly departed from the parameters shared by the community of interpreters. Even for Duchamp's bottle rack, the community of critics, not unlike the students of Fish, set themselves to searching for hidden and obvious meanings, dragging in the symbolism of alchemy and whatnot.[24] As a result, far from the conclusions that Fish draws from his "experiment," I like to interpret it as a kind of skeptic's performance piece aimed at unmasking "idols," in this case, including those to whom Fish remains devoted.

Profiting from a Tautology

Thus interpretation, evaluation, and all the other moments of modern artistic communication exist only if put into motion by a metacommunication of the type "this is art" since everything can be art, and "if someone calls it art, it's art." The problem then is to figure out how such a metacommunication comes about. In premodern literature it was the genre that implicitly spread the message: "This is literature." But when literature became an "open" class, it necessarily triggered off new processes for identifying literature considerably more complex than had been the generic identification of the past. The genre is constituted by the

23. Ibid., pp. 11–17. The criterion that I am proposing is not based on convention but on a linkage: the attribution of an artistic intention. That means that the attribution of literary value does not depend on an agreement upon what literature is, and in fact can very well be produced (as often happens in contemporary literature) even in cases under dispute (see. also, p. 160). For a more exact critique of conventionalist solutions in the field of communication theory, see Benedetti 1989.

24. Cf., for example, Paz 1985.

series of formal and thematic continuities that can be found in a corpus of similar works. Its characteristics are therefore more general with respect to the singularity of each work, but at the same time it does possess precise distinctive markings of a formal and thematic type, which is something that literature as a class obviously cannot possess. In addition, while the genre signals that a text is literature, implicitly it also communicates the "reasons" why it is such. Every single tragedy, every single chivalric epic has, insofar as it belongs to a genre, its own reasons for being inside of literature. Reasons which we need not inquire into again each time we find ourselves faced with the singularity of a work. Modern literature continually finds itself confronted by this problem of legitimation. Each single text over which the dispute is reopened must resolve it anew, resolve it on its own account, itself furnishing the reasons why it aspires to be considered a work of art. These reasons are concretized precisely in poetics, in the idea of literature that one supposes has guided the artist. The phenomenon that I have described as the mediation of poetics finds here, in this unavoidable process, its raison d'être.

Any object (beautiful or ugly, harmonious or dissonant, unusual or repetitive, deviant or conforming to one's expectations) can aspire to being valorized as art as long as there is an idea of literature capable of giving it an artistic meaning, like a certain idea of realism, or expressionism, or estrangement, or experimentation. Even that which is so "old" that it is by now experienced as cliché, even that which has already been devalued insofar as it is "generic," can aspire to artistic value as long as it is refurbished with an idea of literature that justifies it, that is, through a poetics that renders it necessary once more (for example, an ironic revalorization of pulp fiction). Which also means, however, that everything, even the "bygone" sonnet, which once enjoyed immediate acceptance as poetry, if reused by a poet today, can only be appreciated *reflectively*, which is to say, mediated by the reasons for which it aspires "again" to an artistic value. Thus each modern work not only ceaselessly reproposes the question, "What is it that makes *this* text a work of art?" but also asks to be approached in a reflective manner, so that its "concept of itself," which justifies it and makes it enjoyable as literature, can be abstracted from it. Poetics is thus not simply a reflection on art that orients our judgment, but also a reflection of art on itself, required of each work in order for its own artistic claim to be justified. But since poetics can only be attributed to a subject, the investment in the author-function finds again in these processes of identifying literature its strongest raison d'être.

Things are so similar in the other arts that one might say that the distinction between art and nonart in almost all of its fields today turns on the same hinge. Not only cinema, "the young art," has had to resort to the authored/genre designations in order to distinguish between a commercial production and one that instead aspires to an artistic value. Even more striking examples are found in what used to be called the figurative arts. In our epoch, painting and sculpture have attained such a high degree of complexity that the metacommunication, "this is art" can no longer be entrusted to the intrinsic artistry of their products. In these fields, too, establishing lines of demarcation is a major problem. Above all, it was the development of the art industry that made new processes for identifying art, no longer based on intrinsic criteria, necessary.[25] Spreading colors on a piece of canvass or sculpting stone, wood, or metal are no longer intrinsically artistic activities. Thus other (extrinsic) factors of discrimination have necessarily intervened, among which are the museum and the gallery. The exhibition of an object in a place designated for art is equivalent to attributing an artistic value to it. And that is something that can also be exploited, as we shall see shortly, for the purposes of paradoxical operations that oblige us to reflect on the mechanisms of art themselves. With dadaism and the birth of conceptual art, the problem of distinguishing art from nonart emerges in a glaring way. Standing in front of a "readymade" (an ordinary object exhibited as a piece of art), one can no longer appeal to the intrinsically artistic practices of painting or sculpture because here the artist has neither sculpted nor painted anything. Even so, the object, not in itself artistic, provocatively asks to be accepted as a work of art, with which it shares two fundamental traits: (1) it is "authored"; (2) it is exhibited in a context that testifies to its artistic nature (gallery or museum). These two modalities for conferring artistic value are so powerful that they can grant the status of art to a blatantly nonartistic work, a urinal, for example. Both the exhibition of the work and its being "authored" here play the role of a metacommunication of the type "this is art."

As Kosuth writes, in commenting on the statement by Judd featured as the epigraph to this chapter: "A work of art is a tautology in that it is a presentation of the artist's intention, that is, he is saying that a particular work of art *is* art, which means, is a *definition* of art. Thus, that it is art is true *a priori*."[26]

25. Such phenomena are described by Simmel, in addition to what Benjamin (1936) says about them. But according to Riegl, as Benjamin himself recalls, the problem had already been posed for the art of the late Roman Empire (Cf. Riegl 1901).
26. Kosuth 1966–1990, p. 20.

All this brings us back once again to the intentionality (whether true or presumed) of the artist, which one supposes to be at the origin of the work; it brings us back, in short, to the author as subject of meaningful choices. But what must be added to Kosuth's observation is that the tautology is there in order to be detautologized. Even if art is always true, the reasons why "x is a work of art" can be infinite, differing from work to work. The artist's intention that we suppose to be at the work's origin carries with it a reflection on art and on its history: it carries with it the attribution (and so the construction) of a poetics capable of conferring an artistic meaning and value to that which the artist has created, or at least of reaffirming it within the dispute. No matter how aberrant it may appear to us, modern artistic logic arrives at this extreme situation: that of deriving aesthetic enjoyment from the possibility of arguing, evaluating, but also of imagining and constructing the infinite possible reasons, differing from one work to another, which make it so that "x is a work of art." And modern artistic communication is centered on this profiting from a tautology. So this supposition of the artist's intentionality is not merely what makes us understand and appreciate the work, but is also the motor of a complex construction, of that "secondary labor" described by Borges, on which largely depends the pleasure that late-modern appreciation derives from art.

Dispute

The work of modern art thus implicitly communicates the premises that legitimate it as art: what its motivations are, why a certain form of expression is chosen in preference to another, what place that operation will occupy within the history of forms and of poetics (for example, whether it is a work of tradition or transgression, neorealist, neo-avant-garde, or postmodernist). In short, modern art justifies itself by means of the implicit theorization of its own poetics, which thus becomes the premise on the basis of which the work asks to be evaluated and accepted in the artistic system. That is why I have used the term *metacommunication*. Despite the prefix, which could call to mind a communication that has itself for its explicit object (just as metalanguage is a language that has language for its object), metacommunication is instead something that develops "normally" in an implicit way. When someone is telling a joke it is obvious that a metacommunicative message of the type "this is a joke" is sent out in some way by the speaker, and yet it is not necessary for the person to stop the conversation and say, "From this point on I am telling a joke." How then is one to understand it? Here is a vexing muddle both for philosophers of language and for ethologists who study communication among mammals. It is controversial, for example, whether or not animals possess special signals for indicating that a bite is aggressive or playful. There are those who say that they do, and then the problem is resolved; there are also those who maintain that animals only bite in one way, which can be playful or aggressive, and that the game therefore implies a form of implicit metacommunication of the type "this bite is not a bite." From which results the paradoxical nature of the game, on which we will not dwell:[27] what is important to underline is only the fact that the possibility of an implicit metacommunication is recognized. Implicit metacommunication gives "instructions" on how the communication should be understood, for example, seriously or as a joke; or on the respective roles of the speakers, but in every case without interrupting the communication that is underway.

In art, too, metacommunication can be implicitly contained in the artistic communication itself. The artist makes a move, and by so doing also communicates (i.e., metacommunicates) his position within the artistic system (the manner in which he confronts the existing tradition and codes). The selections that he has made within the artistically possible and the history of forms (stylistic, formal, thematic; even choice of "genre," as in the case of the recycled genres) function for the appreciator as premises for the evaluation of the work. Starting from such selections, which are considered as meaningful choices, the reader attributes intentions to the author, programmatic aims, even if the latter has never explicitly expressed them. In his turn, the author (as occurs in many late-modern writers, and once again I invoke the emblematic case of Calvino) may perceive himself, sometimes in a paralyzing manner, through the reader's attributions; he knows that every element of the work, from its theme to its style, will be considered as an indication of his poetics. A whole, closely woven metacommunication then develops between the author and the reader by means of the works, a metacommunication concerning what position the work should take in the artistic universe, with respect to other works, and to the possible ones it has ruled out. When a work posits itself as a work of art, it not only communicates about something, but also metacommunicates the premises on the basis of which it wants to be accepted and evaluated.

27. On this subject, besides Bateson 1972, see Benedetti 1992.

Obviously, in certain cases such metacommunication may be declared openly. In the art of the twentieth century it was almost the rule that that is what happens. What were the avant-garde manifestoes and programmatic declarations if not messages of the type "this is art" thrust explicitly at the act of enjoyment? But for this very reason, explicit poetics are to be considered as a secondary phenomenon, if not really a critical awareness, at least a reflected use of the modern mechanisms of the attribution of artistic value. At this level, as we have already explained, poetics no longer concludes but rather precedes the poetic construction in the form of a manifesto. Does modern enjoyment need to extract from the text the idea of literature that legitimates it in its artistic claim? Does it need to attribute a supposed project-making nature to the author? Well then, all this is done in a single gesture by the author herself, who now becomes openly project-making and shamelessly strategic. The "noise" of the avant-garde manifestoes and the programmatic declarations could thus be considered as a paradoxical denunciation of the role of poetics in the processes of identifying literature. In more recent times this reflected use of the mechanisms of valorization is also adopted by the culture industry: the display of poetics is exploited as a means of commercial promotion.

Before leaving the avant-gardes, however, it needs to be pointed out how in some cases the metacommunication "this is art," in becoming explicit, can also explode in paradox. Readymades, for example, not only oblige us to become aware of the mechanisms with which modernity confers artistic value to works, but also lock those mechanisms into a conflict from which there is apparently no exit. If indeed all art objects, by definition, distinguish themselves from objects of practical use, then Duchamp's *Fountain* (which, being a urinal in reality, is not only an object of practical use, but of a rather base use to boot) is not a work of art. Yet if we refuse to consider it art, despite its having been displayed in a context that attests to its artistic value, we would be forced to question the artistic value of everything inserted into analogous contexts. Even the status of a painting by Leonardo, which, like most great works, is exhibited in a museum, would become subject to doubt. In other words, if the urinal is art, then everything can be art; but if it is not art, nothing is. We find ourselves, in short, in that condition of blockage typical of every paradox: the distinction between art and nonart cannot be determined with impunity because no matter what we do, we fall into contradiction. Thus, pushing the metacommunication "this is art" onto the primary level in some cases seems to go hand in hand with a critique of the institution of art, or with an inquiry into the foundations of art,[28] but its effect is ambiguous, as it also seems to go hand in hand with the banalization of art.[29]

In the twentieth century the constitutive problem tended to come out into the open in both the theory and the practice of art. Separating art from nonart no longer works implicitly, not even in painting and sculpture. It is ever more relegated to the *decision* of the artist, the museum curators, or to the dispute of the critics, the cultural journalists, the strategies of promotion. And if the dadaists and conceptualists have set the dispute in motion problematically and paradoxically, the culture industry today turns it into a profitable means of promotion. What stands inside and what stands outside of art, the very criteria for determining inclusion or exclusion, are therefore the object of a continuous dispute. Even so, one thing remains clear: the dispute in no way causes the attribution of artistic value to break down. The nonartistic nature of the readymade does not prevent its being granted artistic investiture. The blockage only exists for theory when it obstinately goes on searching for objective markings of artistic (or literary) quality inside the works. In contrast, artistic communication always "knows" how to determine the distinction between what is and what is not art, today as in the past, without ever falling into the impasse of indeterminacy. In modernity, the concrete artistic processes adjust themselves to the change in conditions, delegating to the mediation of poetics what the genre system can no longer do. Artistic practice, nevertheless, goes on playing with the constitutive problem, opening itself up to a continuous dispute over what is outside and what is inside art, and at times purposely provoking a paradoxical indeterminacy, yet always making it profitable for its own operations.

28. According to Kosuth (1966–1990, p. 25), the "purest" definition that can be given to conceptual art is: "inquiry into the foundations of the concept 'art.' "

29. The critique of the institution of art itself is ambivalent. Duchamp's operation, for example, could have no effect outside the framework of the museum or gallery, in other words, without the contextualization that its exhibition as a work of art grants.

CHAPTER 7

Malaise and Its Remedies

I'd like to be a machine.
Andy Warhol

The Eye inside the Author

Unlike theory, contemporary artistic practice does not seem to have ever misunderstood the imposing role of the author, which it has often experienced in all its crushing weight, and sometimes targeted as an enemy to be defeated. In late-modernity, the author's position becomes problematic for art itself; like the diseased limb or organ in which the symptoms of a systemic disease converge, the author becomes the agonized site of art, wherein lies the malaise of modernity.

I think it is worth mentioning that the initial impulse for this meditation on the author, which is aimed at questioning the dogma of the author's irrelevance, came to me as the result of reading several contemporary writers. Time and again I found myself faced with literary texts that more or less directly alluded to the phenomena that I have described under the name of authorialism, yet I was unequipped with a conceptual grid capable of putting it all into focus. It was only when I came across Calvino's story "A Sign in Space," that all the tesserae suddenly arranged themselves into a comprehensible shape. What is described in that story is not so much the "signs in space" as the one who traces them there, the one who leaves signs of himself in the space of literature, in short, the author as the subject of choices within the realm of the artistically possible.[1]

And that description is from the author's own point of view. I found before my eyes the record of a "lived authorial experience," an experience painful in its own way, even if set down with Calvino's usual ironic detachment. What can be read between the lines of that story is the anxiety of a writer who is gradually being closed into an identity constructed by his readers, an identity that comes back to him with almost paralyzing effect. Moreover, that anxiety is one of Calvino's recurrent themes, perhaps the most authentic of his entire opus.

So, is there a "malaise of the author"? And what might its causes be? In order to explain Calvino's uneasiness, his fear of being "petrified" in an image, his obsessive need to control that image, to be continually adding new touches to it, it was first necessary to take another look at the myth of the author's death, to demystify the idea of the dispersion of authorial identity in literary writing. It was necessary to redefine the type of author-function implied in the processes of today's artistic communication, the value accorded to the supposed choices of the artist, and the role of poetics. Later I encountered further indications in the work of Gianni Celati, following his arguments on the art of fiction and the excess of strategy that falsifies the position of the modern author. As it turned out, it was not true that the writer, when writing, enters into her own death, nor does she go through the *desoeuvrement* of which Blanchot speaks. Once the problem was put into focus, I found that many other aspects of contemporary literature began to look clearer, suggesting the outline of a phenomenology much wider than that accessible through the work of Calvino or Celati. I began to realize that nearly everywhere artistic practice in some degree registers the hypertrophy of the author-function, and always as something from which it must defend itself; at times the artist exhibits this looming threat ironically in order to explode it in its contradictions, at other times he or she attempts to negate it with special deauthorializing techniques.

Obviously Calvino sees the phenomenon from a perspective "internal" to the processes of art. But it would be mistaken to think that such a perspective is irrelevant for a theory of the author. Observation internal

1. "A Sign in Space" is one of the stories in *Cosmicomics*. Its protagonist, Qfwfq, travels through intergalactic space leaving signs, which are then erased by Kgwgk. For an analysis of that story, see Benedetti 1998, pp. 63–88.

to the artistic system not only discloses the point of view of the artists, but also that of those who enjoy their works, which is reflected in the artists' point of view. It is as if the author were seeing himself through the eye of the reader who is pointing his spyglass at him: that eye intent on reading every peculiarity of the work as authorial choice, each choice revealing an artistic intention, the same situation that is so irksome to another of Calvino's characters, Silas Flannery, in *If on a winter's night a traveler*. As a fundamental characteristic of modern literary communication, the writer introjects the eye of the reader in the same way that Qfwfq introjects that of Kgwgk, the mysterious inhabitant of another galaxy who enjoys imitating and laughing at the signs left in space by Qfwfq. But it is the writer himself that judges his own signs and his own image as author, sometimes finding that image to be ridiculous. It is he who is observing himself through the eye of the reader. Nor is such self-observation an epiphenomenon, since it is through this exchange of gazes that the attribution of intentionality necessary to modern artistic valorization is fulfilled. The reader (or viewer) needs to suppose an artistic intentionality at the origin of the work in order to be able to approach it as a work of art. Thus the selections of the artist, which on their own may even be random or barely relevant, become for the person who enjoys the work, and consequently for the artist watching himself through the eye of that person, meaningful choices, which express an author's purpose, poetics, and style. And these characteristics help shape the author's identity, to which, in turn, the author reacts. It is precisely with such reactions that we are now concerned.

In this chapter, then, we are viewing those same processes from an "internal" perspective, taking account of the manner in which they are observed and "elaborated" by artists. Once again we will be talking about authorialism and the hypertrophy of the author-function, but approaching them from the side of creation, a point of view not frequented by modern literary theory, which is accustomed to studying the text as a semiotic device capable of interacting "on its own" with the reader, or as a machine for provoking interpretations. The removal of the author to the advantage of the text or reader is also the removal of the problematics of creation to the advantage of an aesthetics of reception. Reception provides for only two elements to be at play: the text and the reader. From my perspective, however, which is based not on reception but rather on *attribution,* there are three elements at play: the text, the reader, and the author. And the author enters into play not only as an instance to which are ascribed attributions, but also as an eye in which the eye of the reader is reflected. The author's perspective, therefore, can not be over-looked in the complex dynamics of modern artistic communication. Late-modern literature observes itself through the eye of the author and incorporates this gaze into itself. And insofar as it is reflective and self-critical, late-modern literature mostly talks to us about creation and its impasses.

Bound Writings

An aspiring author is engaged by a literary agency to write stories. The contract provides that she rigorously stick to one of thirty-nine composi-tional methods prescribed by the agency. Here's the one chosen by our character:[2] go out walking on the outskirts of the city between nine in the morning and three in the afternoon with your eyes glued to the ground; pick up all the objects you find on the sidewalk, excluding cigarette butts and paper litter; go back to the office and write a story that contains all those objects in the exact order in which you pull them out of your bag! Of course, no one has ever adopted such a "method" of writing. Nonetheless (and this is what makes it a nice bit of metaliterary humor), it is very similar to, in its total arbitrariness, the actual methods em-ployed by numerous artists, from the dadaist (and later surrealist) tech-nique of the *found object* to the abstruse rules of OuLiPo.[3] No matter how fictitious, this situation serves to introduce us to the deauthorializing practice to which this chapter is mainly devoted: the practice of bound writing.

Bound writing is produced when the artist programmatically im-poses on himself a constraint that limits the range of choice. Bound by the chance "finds" and by the altogether aleatory order in which they are pulled out of his bag, the writer will not be completely free in choosing either the story's characters or its plot since the found objects will in large part impose these on him if they are to be plausibly woven to-gether. If then with a bit of luck he has picked up "easy" objects, he will be able to get a true-to-life or realistic story out of it, but they might turn out to be such disparate items as to be linkable only by means of an ab-

---

2. The episode is from a novel; see Salabelle 1992.

3. Ouvroir de Littérature Potentielle, or "Workshop for Potential Literature," is the name of a French avant-garde literary group active in the 1970s. Writers associated with it, such as Raymond Queneau, François Le Lionnais, George Perec, and Italo Calvino, are noted for their experimentation with various kinds of literary constraints. [trans.]

surd or fantastic tale. As a result, not even the genre is left completely to the writer's discretion. Chance, therefore, which in and of itself is wide open, when it is taken up as a method of composition limits the artist's range of choice. But we would have the same limiting effect, too, if in lieu of chance, we set an arbitrary rule having no intrinsic artistic aim, such as, for example, writing a story in which a specific letter or group of letters of the alphabet never appears. Unlike the one described above, this second method of writing has been tried out: called a lipogram, it was elevated to a literary technique by the OuLiPo writers and made famous by Perec's novel *La Disparition*.[4] What characterizes bound writing is therefore not simply the reliance on chance but the assumption of a constraint, whatever kind of constraint it may be, as long as it succeeds in withdrawing a good portion of the task of thinking up or composing the text from the author's discretion. That made it one of the most commonly used tactics of deauthorialization in the twentieth century, and not only in literature. Since modern artistic communication heavily emphasizes authorial choices, transforming the artist's selections (which may, in themselves, be merely random) into meaningful choices (i.e., whatever the choices, they are assumed to be indications of an artistic intention), deauthorializing practices go to work exactly on that site.

From the matches soaked in varnish that Duchamp, using toy cannons, fired against *The Bride Stripped Bare by Her Bachelors, Even (Large Glass)* in order to determine the points at which to put the nine holes, to the notes that John Cage wrote out on the pentagram corresponding to the points in which the paper showed some imperfections, artistic practice has come up with various methods in order to "abolish" the author's intentionality by means of the randomness of chance. Cage's work offers an impressive repertory of such methods: from the specially prepared piano, whose wires have been modified with foreign objects (nails, erasers), making it impossible to know in advance the sounds of his music and thereby reducing the composer's control over the work; to the score for twelve turned-on radios, where all that is indicated is the choice of frequencies to tune in, the duration and level of the volume, but obviously not the sounds which will be heard. One last "method" worth mentioning: in composing the scores of *Music of Changes* and *Imaginary Landscape no. 4*, Cage left each choice (such as materials and length) to

4. Perec 1969. As is almost the rule among those who have tried their hand at bound writings, Perec, too, has published several essays describing his choice of constraint: cf. *Histoire du lipogramme* and *Un roman lipogrammatique*, in OuLiPo 1973, pp. 73–89 and 90–92.

the *I Ching* (first published in English in 1950).[5] The debt to dadaism is evident here, and Cage himself recognizes Marcel Duchamp, whom he had met in New York in the 1940s, as the precursor to the aleatory method for eliminating the author's choice in artistic operations.

Chance, however, as is clear in this brief survey, requires a method in order to be produced. Randomness is not so easily found in the universe of human subjectivity, and thus neither in artistic practice; the most difficult thing that can be asked of a subject is to carry out operations that are totally random, whereas for a properly programmed machine, it is quite simple. At best, a person might be able to do operations that are not consciously controlled, but that opens the doors to the unconscious, which, as is well-known, does not work by chance, or to the free unfolding of spontaneity, which is always susceptible to being interpreted as individual expression. The only way for really getting around the choices of the author, including those which are unconscious, is the adoption of an arbitrary constraint: putting newspaper clippings into a bag which are later pulled out blind and stuck together in that order; allowing oneself to be guided by the faint spots resulting from the manufacture of a piece of paper, by the responses of the *I Ching,* or by whatever other rule. Such methods can at times get very complicated and writers such as Queneau, Perec, and others from OuLiPo offer us myriad examples of them.

This is the reason why, strictly speaking, the automatic writing of the surrealists, despite its clear descent from dadaism, cannot be considered as "bound." Instead, this method appears to be aimed more at opening the way to the writer's "unconscious choices" (and consequently is a "serious," not an ironic technique) than at excluding them.[6] The same is true for those artistic practices like *action painting,* where the color is dripped or spattered onto the canvass, leaving ample space to chance and gestural automatism. Here too, the absence of an arbitrary constraint makes

5. Philip K. Dick, too, made use of the *I Ching* to compose the plot of his novel *The Man in the High Castle* (1962). Philippe Sollers, on the other hand, constructed his *Drame* not so much on the book's responses as "on the structural matrix of the *I Ching:* sixty-four sequences alternately equal and unequal, divided between *he* and *I*" (See *Tel Quel,* 1974, p. 46).

6. In opposition to the automatic writing of the surrealists, Raymond Queneau wrote: "Another very wrong idea that is also going the rounds at the moment is the equivalence established between inspiration, exploration of the subconscious and liberation; between chance, automatism and freedom. Now *this* sort of inspiration, which consists in blindly obeying every impulse is in fact a form of slavery. The classical author who wrote his tragedy observing a certain number of known rules is freer than the poet who writes down whatever comes into his head and is slave to other rules of which he knows nothing" (cited by Calvino 1988, p. 123).

such practices more favorable to the reclamation of the individual's creative freedom than to its restriction.[7] Only by *having himself constrained* by something that imposes gestures that are obligatory yet independent of his intention can the artist truly be said to be guided by chance. There is a tendency then for aleatory techniques to turn themselves into true and proper rules, provided they are clearly arbitrary, that is, deprived of any artistic strategy save that of excluding every artistic strategy. As a result, the aleatory spirit that supports bound writings lends itself "naturally" to the use of rules, even rigorous mathematical rules that nonetheless remain arbitrary in relation to the ends of art. A good example of the "mathematization of chance" is Sergio Lombardo's *Quadri stocastici*, painted in the early 1980s, in which both the composition and distribution of colors follow mathematical functions applied to sequences of random numbers. In literature too, over the decades that now separate us from the first dadaist contrivances, bound writing has seen a large number of variants and of improvements in that direction: the technique of the *cut-up* used by Burroughs presents itself as a simple random technique, but in Balestrini the method of "cutting and combining," used by him in almost all of his production, adds more complicated rules toward randomizing the composition and assemblage of texts.[8] Often the arbitrary constraint makes for a "bizarre" rule, sometimes expressible in a pseudomathematical formula, as in the technique known as "S+7," adopted by several members of OuLiPo, which consists in constructing a new text by starting from an already existing one (literary or not), and substituting every noun (S) with the seventh noun that follows it in the dictionary;[9] or it slides towards "puzzle-making," as in the case of the li-

7. On this last type of artistic practice, Bürger speaks of the "immediate production" of chance, distinguishing it from the "mediated production" that passes instead for an exact calculation (1984, p. 77). I believe, however, that the distinction between the two is more precisely the presence or absence of a constraint, which is what sharply differentiates their spirit as well.

8. The technique of the cut-up used by William Burroughs in the novels *Naked Lunch* and *The Soft Machine*, consists in cutting up pieces of a text (conversations, newspapers, his own and others' writings) in order to then insert them, without any system and at times with hallucinogenic and chaotic effects of association, into the novel he is writing. Nanni Balestrini, on the other hand, cuts and assembles the pieces following precise rules: for example, in *Funerali di Togliatti* (*Togliati's Funeral*), he cuts sentences of a length predetermined by a gardening manual in order to then combine them in a systematic manner according to rules defined by himself; or in *Tape Mark I*, according to mathematical parameters inserted into a computer.

9. Cf. J. Lescure, "La Méthode S+7," in OuLiPo 1973, pp. 139–144; and R. Queneau, *Contributions à la pratique de la méthode lescurienne S+7* (Contributions to the Practise of Lescure's S+7 Method), ibid., pp. 145–147.

pogram. Or again it becomes a true and proper mathematical structure, like the "orthogonal Latin biquadratic of the order of 10," which Perec used in combination with other rules of composition to write the novel *La Vie, mode d'emploi* (*Life, a User's Manual*).[10]

However the "rules" of the OuLiPo writers are only one case of bound writing among many. Going back in time, we should mention Raymond Roussel, and in particular his famous text, even though it is a self-commentary, *Comment j'ai écrit certains de mes livres* (How I Wrote Some of My Books). In this book, published posthumously in 1935, Roussel reveals the "manufacturing secret" for several of his texts, setting down the famous *procédé* that consists in taking two homophonic sentences and then devising a story that begins with the first and concludes with the second; or by letting himself be guided towards "unforeseen creation" by homophony and phonic combinations.[11] These arbitrary rules are supposed to have "ordered" the writing of many of his works, from his earliest childhood stories to *Impressions d'Afrique*. The resonance of this constraint-bound technique, and above all of its delayed revelation, can be easily measured by the quantity of "self-commentaries" that subsequent authors, playing on Roussel's title, have published: from Butor (*Comment se sont écrits certains de mes livres* [How Some of My Books Wrote Themselves]) to Renaud Camus, who in 1978 put out a *Comment m'ont écrit certains de mes livres* (How Some of My Books Wrote Me);[12] from Calvino (*Comment j'ai écrit un de mes livres* [How I Wrote One of My Books])[13] to Bénabou, *Pourquoi je n'ai écrit aucun de mes livres* (Why I Have Not Written Any of My Books).[14] Notice how those that came after Roussel turned the expression around: how "[the books] wrote themselves," how "they wrote me," why "I didn't write [them]" in order to ironically stress the author's "vacation." Calvino alone returns to the active form, which might merit some comment if it did not run the risk of overinterpreting a title. There is one question, however, that we can pose: is it possible that Calvino, who, while still in

10. Perec 1978. For English translation, see Perec 1987. Perec himself describes his compositional rules in *Quatre figures pour "La Vie, mode d'emploi"* (Four Figures for "Life, a User's Manual"), in OuLiPo 1981, pp. 387–392.

11. Cf. Roussel 1935. There have been differing readings on the importance of the *procédé* within Roussel's work: cf. Foucault 1963 and Roscioni 1985.

12. These two items come from Genette 1987.

13. Calvino's article (Calvino 1984), published in French, explains the compositional scheme of *If on a winter's night a traveler* with the aid of diagrams (and in a kind of "OuLiPo-Greimassienne" writing, as Greimas describes it in his introduction).

14. Benabou 1986.

his "combinatory" phase (coinciding more or less with the writing of *The Castle of Crossed Destinies*), had been inclined to experiments of this type, no longer believed that a simple arbitrary constraint could really extract the author from the game? Moreover, it is not so much by adopting bound writing as by embracing the effect of the apocryphal that he plays his most important match against authorialism.

The more recent use of bound writing based on precise and arbitrary rules is less flashy. One example that depends less on "puzzle-working" than those of OuLiPo, yet whose origin in the latter is still recognizable, is the rewriting of De Amicis's *Sangue romagnolo* (Romagnole Blood) in seven different versions entitled *Sette cuori* (Seven Hearts).[15] Finally, we could also mention Manganelli's *Centuria* (Century) (1979), a book that contains one hundred one-page novels, which, besides the constraint of its fixed length (which Calvino compared to the rule for sonnets), also imposes on itself the prohibition against presenting any of its characters in more than one "novel."

Artificial Genres

Some varieties of bound writing might also appear as surrogates for the traditional genres to such an extent that they deserve to be defined as *artificial genres*. Through the self-imposition of a rule, constraints are constructed to which the writer must submit, just as formerly one had to submit to the metric, thematic, and verse-making rules of the sonnet, or to the drama-constructing rules of tragedy. The only difference between these schemes is that unlike the latter, which are embedded in tradition, the former are artificial constructs, cooked up at their desks by the artists themselves, and consequently altogether arbitrary. As Le Lionnais wrote in OuLiPo's first manifesto:

> Every literary work is constructed starting from an inspiration (or so at least the author would have us believe) that is thought to fit for better or worse within a series of constraints and techniques. . . . The constraints of vocabulary and grammar, the rules for writing novels (chapter divisions, etc.) or classical tragedy (the three unities), the general constraints for writing poetry, those of the fixed forms (as in the case of the *rondeau*

15. *Sangue romagnolo* is a story that appeared in the 1886 collection *Cuore* [Heart], a widely read book in the period following Italy's reunification. [trans.]

or of the sonnet), etc. Must we limit ourselves to the well-known recipes and obstinately refuse to imagine new formulas?[16]

Inventing new constraints to substitute for the old ones is exactly what OuLiPo's "creative effort" strives toward under the banner of the idea that "constraints are good."[17] OuLiPo is no more than the most striking example of a general *craving for constraints* provoked by the collapse of the genres, as well as the empty freedom of the modern artist, about which Hegel said: "The artist is the I which on its own poses and dissolves everything."[18] The need to channel their own freedom of choice has also brought some contemporary writers to constructing rules, less flashy yet equally rigid, to govern the writing or simply the arrangement of the writings (for instance, collections of stories). Think of the almost maniacal attention that Calvino paid to ordering the "pieces" internal to texts such as *Marcovaldo, Invisible Cities,* and *If on a winter's night a traveler,* as he himself declared in many self-commentaries.

In this type of bound production, we see how the genre (or rather, what pretends to be so since what we are dealing with are artificial constraints) returns to having a brutally normative function. The need to be bound reveals a desire to go back in time to when the genres really functioned as programs for the construction of texts, retreating down the road that in modernity led to the exaltation of the author's "freedom of choice." The freedom from the canons of genre (since the possible form a text might take is no longer guided by tradition) places on the author, and his or her poetics, the responsibility for almost every selection to be made. To adopt an arbitrary rule represents for the modern writer, then, a return to the "prerogative" that genre literature used to have before its modern devaluation dragged it down. And that is diametrically opposed to the spirit of modernity. Indeed, these arbitrary genres are the sign of a refusal of modernity, and the "odious" freedom it has conceded to artists. Often, it is also accompanied by an ironic awareness of the paradoxical nature of the matter: the rule of the lipogram certainly constrains the artist, but it is a rather silly rule, almost a game of puzzle-

16. OuLiPo 1973, French version, p. 16.
17. J. Lescure, *Petite histoire de l'OuLiPo,* ibid., p. 27.
18. The genial irony of the romantics, according to Hegel, is the expression of an I for which "all constraints have been broken" and which looks on "the vanity of everything concrete, every ethicality, everything having a content in itself" (Hegel 1836, pp. 99–100).

making, a grotesque parody of those metric and compositional rules that used to guide the writing of a sonnet or the other true and proper genres.

Genius Returns as Game

If there is a value attributed to such "methods," it is usually that of a stimulus to creativity. Douglas Hofstaedter, for example, in an interview in which he talked about the themes of one of his books, asserts that creativity always takes place "within certain constraints that condition it, and by which it is at the same time stimulated."[19] The interviewer wanted to know what he meant by constraints. Hofstaedter then mentioned a book of poetry by Giuseppe Varaldo, *All'alba Sharazad andrà ammazzata* (At Dawn a Man Shall Ax Shaharazad), which, similar to its title, is made up of verse composed with words that contain only the vowel "a," or only some other vowel. In short, it is a latter-day version of OuLiPo's lipogram, something many others have already experimented with.[20] That bonds stimulate creativity is an idea that is as true as it is vague, one that can be invoked for all kinds of things, from the conventions of genres to those of metric schemes, or to cite more recent forms, from the requirements of expressive power to the programmatic aims of any particular "movement." But compared to the latter, there is something very peculiar about OuLiPo's "rules" or the techniques based on randomness, which cannot be ignored. There remains something infantile about them; they are unnecessarily complicated or they veer toward puzzle-making; and these are qualities that clash with a particular idea of creation. If we do not account for this peculiarity of theirs, which is intrinsically paradoxical or ironic, we will totally fail to grasp their "raison d'être."

Canons, thematic regulations, expressive requirements, and programs all have their intrinsic raison d'être in either tradition or the poetics of the writer. In contrast, what characterizes bound writing, above and beyond all its variants, is its gratuitousness, its lack of any artistic purpose except that of excluding every possible artistic purpose. Sometimes such arbitrariness makes bound writing seem absurd. However, it is by virtue of their gratuitousness that those constraints fulfill their purpose, by

19. The book in question is *Fluid Concepts and Vague Analogies* (Basic Books, 1995). The interview appeared in "la Repubblica" on June 29, 1995.

20. That includes Umberto Eco, who also wrote the preface to Varaldo's book, which was published by Vallardi.

blocking the author's "control" over his or her own techniques. They serve not to stimulate creativity, but to make the strategic author disappear, and if they do serve creativity in any way, it is only for this reason. What is essential in these practices is that the author relinquishes responsibility for the principal poetic operations, which can no longer be considered the product of his or her choices, whether conscious or unconscious. In short, bound writing reveals its own true nature only if one considers it as a deauthorializing practice, and only if one takes account also of its intrinsic paradoxical nature, which especially inclines it to the ironic display of the destruction of genius at the hand of the mechanisms of modern enjoyment. Its aim therefore is much more ambiguous than how it is sometimes described: the "serious" attempt to expel the author's intentionality from the processes of creation goes hand in hand with scorning the idea of creation as we have inherited it from the romantics.

As is seen in many of the cases mentioned, the "method of fabrication" is usually exhibited as an integral part of the work. Bound writing tends to emphasize, and with an almost didactic zeal, the constraint out of which it is generated. From Duchamp to Cage, from Roussel to the members of OuLiPo, from Calvino to Balestrini, this artistic practice goes together with and draws value from revealing the particular method that has been followed, providing its detailed description, and in some cases, even prescribing it as a recipe for future artistic productions. But since the bond is almost always banal and "insipid," its revelation, as Foucault observed apropos Roussel, serves to deepen the mystery rather than diminish it.[21] Its apparent ingenuity takes on the tone of a grotesque, or at least ironic, mordent, which allows us to infer an acute diagnosis of the characteristics of modern enjoyment. The very fact of its acting on that site where the author's choices take shape presupposes, moreover, that the mechanisms of modern artistic communication are by now reflected.

Recipe for a Work of Art

We find a rather clear illustration of such contradictory instances in the practice of the dadaists. Despite the strong presence of a project-making subject, the author of manifestoes and proclamations, it was precisely

21. Foucault 1963.

the artists who identified with dada who initiated the attack on the author: the insertion of chance into their processes of creation, the "invention" of the collage, the readymade, automatic writing, and multiauthored writing began of a series of practices aimed at standing in the way of the project-making nature of the "creator subject." As can easily be seen, however, what we have here is a paradoxical attack. This is not only because the dadaists, with their proclamations, were at the same time making a strong investment in project-making, and thus too in the author-function, but above all because those same practices that were presented as the means to negate authorial strategies, exhibited ironically the "poverty" of their method as well. Openly declared and flaunted as "recipes for art," the aleatory methods and arbitrary rules immediately take on a desecrating tone toward the act of creation, which, seemingly, they should have defended from the excess of modern art's strategy. Take the famous dadaist recipe for creating a poem:

> Take a newspaper.
> Take some scissors.
> Choose from this paper an article the length you
> want to make your poem.
> Cut out the article.
> Next carefully cut out each of the words that make up
> this article and
> put them all in a bag.
> Shake gently.
> Next take out each cutting one after the other.
> Copy conscientiously in the order in which they left
> the bag.
> The poem will resemble you.
> And there you are—an infinitely original author of
> charming sensibility
> even though unappreciated by the vulgar herd.[22]

In Tzara's text two almost opposite things are easily discerned. The first is that poetry is an activity for which one can provide the recipe. Ostensibly, then, it reproposes exactly what genius was against: a rule for art, a "precept" to be followed. On the other side, however, the recipe contem-

22. Tzara 1920.

plates among its techniques the recourse to something that stands, even if now only ironically, on the side of genius: chance, insofar as it is external to the intentionality of the artist. Chance gives back to art that rule which, as Kant said, art cannot find on its own. Words cut out of the newspaper were to be ordered on the page unforeseeably, without the author's aim, artistic strategy, or even technical ability playing any kind of role. Like nature, chance gives art a rule that has no underlying concept as to how the work should be, or how it should be achieved.

But unlike the nature that is expressed in genius, chance, in order to be put into action, has need of a strategy: it needs to be maneuvered like an artistic technique aimed at attaining a certain effect. Naturally, for genius, too, a technique was necessary (mastery of the rhetorical devices and of all the instruments of art), without which the artist would not succeed at being guided by the nature that *dictates* within him. Furthermore, the arts have always known and tranquilly practiced this paradox, representing it, and by so doing holding it at bay, first through the notion of the sublime,[23] then through that of the genius. However, mastering a method in order to favor spontaneous creation is a paradox different from the one we are describing here. A method, although learned through practice, is in itself blind, and has no particular aim. With Tzara, it is a question of adopting a strategy that has an aim, which is precisely that of realizing a nonstrategized artistic practice. Thus the vicious circle of dadaist practice. Art, by now aware of the mechanisms that valorize artistic works, and thus of the importance accorded to the author's intentionality, intentionally tries (through a programmatically adopted constraint) to expel that intentionality.

Dadaism was an avant-garde movement unlike any other. It was already penetrated by the signs of that self-reflection that characterizes late-modern art. Dada, moreover, was born after all the other movements, after cubism, expressionism, futurism, abstraction, and with an openly polemical relation to each of them. This time, however, it was not the "usual" critique that every avant-garde group had, until then, aimed at the art of the past (or at art contemporary to it, but already felt as past), a critique which, as Shklovsky said, gave each new poetic school the character of a revolution. For the first time, the dadaists seemed to want to break out of this logic. Each avant-garde group, like a new social class (to stick to Shklovsky's metaphor), announces the revolution that

23. On that subject, see Benedetti 1990.

will be carried out in the art of the future, a future it already claims to represent. Thus, the futurists proclaimed themselves the standard-bearers of the art of the future. For the dadaists, however, there is no future; indeed, their motto is "abolition of the future," as Tzara's *Manifesto* of 1920 states: "Dada is the chameleon of rapid and opportunistic change. Dada is against the future. Dada is dead."

The logic of modernity is driven by the search for differential value, and so by the principle of change, which the avant-gardes greatly accelerated. But each avant-garde group contributed to that change from within the movement of art, without observing its mechanisms from the outside. The dadaists seem to have gained this external view. In a kind of deutero-learning, artistic practice no longer limits itself to resolving this or that problem of art (which form to adopt in order to produce a shock or other result) but considers the entire class of such problems according to its constant "laws." Thus the necessity for change, which supports modern art in the succession of its poetics, is now observed from an external vantage, reflected on and thematized ironically in dadaist "poetics." This process was reflected on to such a degree that dada, in its poetics, even contemplates its own end.

Years after the movement fell apart, Tzara spoke of its "voluntary end." An end, as it is often said, that was desired the moment dadaism began to become institutionalized. But in contemplating its own death, dada not only had faith in its fundamentally skeptical and antidogmatic spirit; much more, it was expressing too a polemical reaction to the logic of modernity. By presenting itself from the moment of its birth as a movement already dead, dada assumes in itself and in a reflective manner, that which "naturally" happens to all modernist movements, destined *without knowing it* to be "surpassed" by other "new" trends, which in their turn will assert themselves in the name of art's future. It brings to mind the already-cited point made by Mukařovský: "The present is perceived as a tension between the past norm and its future violation destined to become part of the future norm." But dada will not wait to become part of the future norm in order to die a natural "modernist death." Dada declares itself already dead at the very moment of its birth.

Beyond the compulsion to change, the other load-bearing elements of the logic of modernity were also criticized and rejected in the usual paradoxical manner: the role accorded to poetics and its consequent authorialism. The attack on the author, moreover, can only go hand in hand with an awareness of the mechanisms of artistic valorization typical of modernity. And these are exactly the mechanisms that now come to be reflected on and made to "explode" in artistic practice itself. In his 1922 "Conference on dada," Tzara said, "You are mistaken if you take dada for a modern school, or for a reaction against the current schools." In effect, the dadaist manifestoes never propose a poetics in the true sense of the term, that is, in the same way as one can speak of an expressionist, cubist, or futurist poetics. Dada had no precise artistic physiognomy, but finds its common denominator in an attitude or, as Breton said, in a state of mind.[24] And as critics have furthermore recognized, what is called dadaist art is not something that is defined or clearly stated, but a mixture of ingredients that could already be found in other movements.[25] That fact, however, is not the weak point of dadaism, but rather what makes it profoundly different from all the other avant-garde movements. Dada rejects the search for a stylistic coherence, or for a formal model that would provide the movement its "differential position" and raison d'être within the history of artistic forms, because it is exactly out of these *formal* reasons, one following the other in the *querelle* of poetics, that the logic of modernity is engendered. "I write a manifesto and I want nothing," Tzara wrote in the 1918 *dada manifesto.* "Those who are with us preserve their freedom. We recognize no theory. We have enough of cubist and futurist academies: *laboratories of formal ideas.*"[26] The themes of plasticity that were of interest to other artists were really of no interest to the dadaists, who thus seem to reject the imperative of modernity to construct a differential *aesthetic* standard, an imperative to which cubist, expressionist, futurist, or abstractionist poetics fully responded. The conceptual art of the 1960s would get its start from the same kind of refusal to consider formal reasons as the essence of art. In perfect harmony with the dada spirit, conceptual art would end up by questioning the identity of artistic value and aesthetic value (based on the formal, morphological aspects and the sensible appearance of art). As Kosuth would

24. "Cubism was a school of painting, futurism a political movement: DADA is a state of mind" (A. Breton, in "Littérature," May 1920, p. 17). And Theo Van Doesburg said that it was impossible to answer the question "What is dada?" because dadaism doesn't belong to the category of *new forms* of art like impressionism, futurism, cubism, expressionism; dada is not an artistic movement (cf. Doesburg 1923).

25. Even in its name (a meaningless neologism with strong infantile connotations), dada underlines the absence of a poetics, distinguishing itself from, and at the same time criticizing the seriousness of, the names assumed by the other avant-garde movements. On the name "dada," see Magrelli 1990.

26. Tzara 1918; the italics have been added.

claim, "It is necessary to separate esthetics from art," since the function of an artistic object in the context of art can include things that have nothing to do with their morphological or "physical attributes."

> "Modern" art and the work before seemed connected by virtue of their morphology. Another way of putting it would be that art's "language" remained the same, but it was saying new things. The event that made conceivable the realization that it was possible to "speak another language" and still make sense in art was Marcel Duchamp's first unassisted readymade. With the unassisted readymade, art changed its focus from the form of the language to what was being said. Which means that it changed the nature of art from a question of morphology to a question of function. This change—one from "appearance" to "conception"—was the beginning of "modern" art and the beginning of "conceptual" art.[27]

The dadaists, then, were not interested in elaborating any "differential markings" assigned to formal aspects of artistic practice, which is the first example of the rejection of poetics, understood as the valorization of the differential reasons that motivate the artist to choose one particular form of expression over another. And only an artistic subject that had deeply reflected on the dialectic of modernity and the role it grants to poetics could have expressed such a rejection.

Return to Meter

The "weapons of dada," as Arturo Schwarz defines them, are irony and paradox. However, that does not mean that all bound productions take on the same kind of polemical attitude toward the institution of art. If Duchamp uses random techniques as a means to display the arbitrariness of the very concept of art, Arp instead seems to exploit their "artistic moment" in his consideration of a creation spontaneously generated: after having torn up a drawing he had been working on, Arp was attracted to the "beauty" of the chance composition produced by the fallen pieces. Both in his poetic texts and in his collages made by using aleatory arrangements, Arp pursued an "immediately" creative goal and an intrinsically artistic object. Stripped of its ambivalent guise, chance seems to have been used here "seriously" to assist genius, or to furnish a surro-

27. Kosuth 1966–1990, p. 18.

gate for it. The same can be said for surrealist automatic writing, where chance is interpreted as a way of favoring unconscious creative energy, or for the techniques of *action painting* (abstract expressionism), where the reduction of the conscious creative act is aimed at favoring the irrational, unconscious or "primitive" dimension of the artist, which amounts to a new, and undisguised, exaltation of genius. As I have already said, however, these artistic practices are not to be considered as located entirely under the heading of bound productions.

Even in the bound writings found in more recent literature, one observes a greater element of seriousness, or perhaps a "return of innocence." The arbitrary constraint ceases to be theatrical and overtly displayed, and the war on the author for the most part sets aside ostentation and desecration in order to become a true and proper desubjectivization tactic.

Parise's *Sillabari* (Primers), which is a collection of stories ordered alphabetically on the basis of the first letters of their titles (for example, *Altri* [Others], *Amicizia* [Friendship], *Amore* [Love], *Anima* [Soul], etc.), is an example of such a tactic. This ordering of the collection makes it a simple and exemplary case of outflanking the author's power to make choices by recourse to an arbitrary constraint (which here does not extend to the process of thinking up or writing down the individual "pieces," but is solely limited to their organization and presentation).[28] Certainly the idea of the "syllabary"[29] refers above all to those elementary lessons about life to which the stories, as little samples, are humbly meant to draw us. But just as important is the alphabetical order that goes along with the "syllabary" form: this is definitely *chosen* by the author (Parise could as easily have let the stories follow each other in an undetermined order, as happens in most collections), yet it is also, among all possible orders, the most arbitrary there is. It depends neither on a meaningful intention of the writer (as would, for example, an organization by theme or conceptual development), nor on some charac-

28. The idea of alphabetically arranging the contents of a book can also be found in *Dictionary of Accepted Ideas*, which is composed of citations from other authors, though it is used with intentions that are much less "peaceful" than those of Parise (see chapter 8, n. 14, of this book). Commenting on Flaubert's "choice," Sartre said that "the alphabetical order is a confession of impotence" (Sartre 1971, vol. 1, French text, pp. 633 ff.). Flaubert, however, adopted the alphabetical ordering consciously, as the sole truly meaningless system that marginalizes the author since neither the book's content (which comes from other books) nor its organization was actually his own.

29. A primer organized according to letters and syllables that is used to teach students in the first years of elementary school to read and write. [trans.]

teristic of the subjects that are treated (obviously neither life, nor learning about life, follow an alphabetical order). In short, it is at the same
time both arbitrary and binding, and for that very reason it attains the
desired effect, which is an exposition not totally guided by the author's
strategy. It should be pointed out that not even a genuinely random
order would have attained the same result since that would nonetheless
have left the reader the possibility of supposing an implicit authorial organization, one not immediately visible, or perhaps purposely concealed. Instead, the alphabetical order hinders this attribution also; it
confers on each of the stories the sign of an arbitrary approach to the elementary experiences of life, underlining the humble position of the
writer faced by the complexity of what he is observing. Due to this "serious" deployment of the constraint, used discretely and without showy
display, and due to other aspects of his writing that we will not go into
here,[30] Parise in the *Sillabari* draws much closer to the poetics of grace
than to the "tradition" of bound writings that flows from Roussel and
dadaism down to the participants of OuLiPo.

Of greater interest for the purposes of our argument, however, is the
recourse to regular metric schemes (sonnets, sestinas, and other forms)
found in some poets of the 1980s. For the poet, obviously, metric
schemes have always represented an objective constraint, one endowed
with its own artistic purpose, and therefore something quite different
from the bonds that we have up to now been dealing with (which by definition must meet the requirement to be arbitrary). Whereas that was
true for earlier epochs, when metric schemes were perceived as inherent
to poetry, it surely does not hold in the modern "tradition," which is by
now accustomed to perceiving metric schemes as obsolete, and sometimes even in conflict with the artistic value of a poem. So when we encounter them, we regard them not only as unusual but also as arbitrary.
Certainly, they are not arbitrary in the same manner that lipograms or
certain random practices are; nevertheless, metric schemes are arbitrarily
adopted by the writer, who picks them out once again from the trick bag
of the artistically possible, thus deviating from the modern literary system. Here, too, as we shall see more closely in the case of Gabriele Frasca,
to whom the following section is dedicated, the reason for such a
"choice" consists in the attempt to exclude the artist's choices. Closed
metric forms and highly constrictive poetic genres adopted in an artistic
system that instead concedes to the poet the maximum freedom of form

---

30. For more on Parise, see Benedetti 1994.

answer to a need for bonds, a need which is at times even dressed in an ethical value, under the name of the "need for discipline."

"Long Live the Chain!"

If there is a return to meter in Frasca's poetry, it is as rigorous as it can possibly be: strict rules that rein in poetic expression are imposed without any deviation or license. The cage is built not only out of metric schemes but also out of rhyme schemes and rhythmic patterns. At times there are rhymed hendecasyllables according to the scheme AB BA AB BA, as in the poem *giunto al frigo, l'aprí, non c'era molto* (reaching the fridge, I peeked in, there wasn't much there). At other times we find the most musical meter of the Italian tradition, that is, *ottonari* (octosyllabic lines): "si nascose in un androne / per sfuggire quel concerto / basta solo avere un tetto / ad un morto senza nome" (he hid inside a passageway / to get away from that concert / a roof is all you really need / for a dead man with no name).[31] Elsewhere there are more sophisticated regularities that depart from true and proper meter; they are based more on accentuated rhythm and pauses, but that does not take away from the fact that the rhythmic scheme is just as recognizable and rigorous, or better, hearable: "queste ansie già secche nel presto / risucchio del giorno se prime / a dirsi rifarsi nel gesto" (anxieties already withered at dawn / suck the day right down the drain when pressed / to say make yourself over again).[32] They appear to be *novenari* (lines of nine syllables), but in reality the line of verse is structured into three feet, each with an identical rhythmic pattern, almost hypnotic, which forces us to make long pauses inside each line at the end of each foot. Then there are the rhymes, these too not left to chance but made obligatory by regular schemes, which are immediately recognizable even in their variations. In the *Rimasti* (as a verb, the title means "you rhymed"; as a noun, it means "remainders" or "leftovers") section, the rhyme scheme is that of the Italian sonnet; in 3 and *Trismi*, Dante's terza rima (hendecasyllables whose rhyme scheme is aba bcb cdc, etc.) is used. At other times the scheme is

---

31. Frasca 1995, section entitled *Quarti* (Quarters), p. 66.

32. Ibid., *Trismi* (this title not only refers to the Latin root "tri-" meaning "three" but also plays on the Italian word *trismo* meaning trismus or lockjaw), p. 128, where the word *lime* (the noun *lima* means "file," as in the steel tool used for cutting bars or smoothing surfaces, but the verb *limare* can also mean "polish" or "give the final touches to") appears: "furia del *labor limae* [Latin for "the act of polishing"] del gesto che incide una materia indurita."

that of the sestina, in which the final words of each line of the preceding stanza appear in variously reversed orders in the following stanzas, so that in going forward, the rhyme is also looking back and criss-crossing. There are no true and proper sestinas in *Lime*, but there are numerous references to the sestina, or variations on it. The poems of *Rimastichi* (the verb *rimasticare* may mean chew over, brood over, or rehash), for example, make use of the sestina system, though with stanzas that are based on four verses, the fourth stanza of which (i.e., the last four verses of the poem) faithfully reproduces the scheme of the first.

All these schemes and regularities, beyond being obvious to eye and ear, are often signaled by the titles of the collections, at times somewhat cryptically. Thus, *Trismi* refers to its triadic structure. *3* may get its name not only because it comes third in the book, but also because it is composed of three stanzas, each of three lines, hinged on three rhymes. And something similar occurs in *Quarti* (Quarters), *Quartetti* (Quartets), *Facili rime* (Easy Rhymes), and others. All of which goes to show how much value is placed on the cage of rhyme and rhythm, which, it must be said, entraps poetic expression. In regard to *3*, however, there is something else that needs to be pointed out. Here the terza rima scheme is combined with the *retrogradatio cruciata* (backward-looking reversals) of the sestina form, in such a way as to present us with a sort of closed terza rima that cannot be taken beyond the ninth verse (abc cab bca), making it quite different from Dante's scheme (aba bcb cdc ded . . . etc), which can be carried on virtually without end.

Frasca's choices thus consist not only of unbreakable regularities, but, what's more, of closed regularities, as is shown by his predilection for the sestina, which not only appears in his poetry[33] but also in his prose, as the subject of a book-length scholarly study.[34] The sestina is the closed genre par excellence; it constitutes a microcosm penetrated by a constant tortion toward closure, where rhyming words keep recurring, ineluctably, like idées fixes; it is a closed microcosm, with rules, constraints, and variables, from which there is no exit, criss-crossed by reiteration, strapped down by the obligation to repeat. That might also serve as a description of Dante's circles in Hell, or the closed microcosms that stud the work of Beckett, equally infernal in their being governed by unbreakable and arbitrary rules, imposed by no one knows who.[35] An anal-

33. Cf. Frasca 1984, which includes a "sestina sextuplet."
34. Cf. Frasca 1992.
35. For a perfect example, see *Le Dépeupleur* (Beckett 1970). Both Dante and Beckett, moreover, serve as constant references in Frasca's poetry. Cf. Frasca 1988.

ogous closed situation, for example, is this one, described in a poem from *Senza meno* (Absolutely):

> pietraia. sia in un rombo. mura ai lati.
> piccoli corpi adesi. alle pareti.
> nel centro musica. ottoni. orchestrati
> malaccio. una dozzina. urla. divieti.
> minacce. a tempo alfine. non per molto.
> stesse urla. a tempo. stasi. stesso volto[36]
> [a pile of rocks. make it a rhombus. rock walls on the sides.
> little bodies stuck together. against the walls.
> in the center there's music. brass winds. symphonized
> a dreadful mess. maybe a dozen. shouts. calls
> to stop. threats. finally all in time. but not for long.
> the same shouting. all in time. stasis. the same face][37]

Here, as in a mathematical problem, the coordinates are given along with boundaries, variables, and parameters; or, as in a circle of the damned, you find the repetition of the punishment: to keep in time, as the brass dictate, in the rhomboid roar surrounded by walls. What comes through here is the evident triumph of structure, the regularity of a closed form, which even has a thematic correlate. The rigid structure also stands for the infernal aspect of our quotidian existence.

The return to metric forms is certainly not a phenomenon limited to this poet, nor is it even something very recent. One need only think of Zanzotto and his *Supersonetto* (Supersonnet), or in more recent years, of Giovanni Raboni, Patrizia Valduga, or Gianni D'Elia.[38] The reappearance of sonnets, octaves, rhymed hendecasyllables, even "hexameters,"[39] seems to be part of a kind of inversion of the trends typical of the "modern tradition"; contemporary poets seem to be going back to metric schemes and more or less regular rhythms. How is one to evaluate this throwback to the good (or bad) old rules that formerly guided the art of writing poetry? And I say "throwback" because it is well understood that modernity has gone in an altogether different direction, violating the institutionalized forms, and doing away with virtually all rhyme and metric schemes.

36. *Lime*, op. cit., p. 34.
37. Translation of these and previous lines of Frasca's verse by wjh.
38. Cf., for example, Raboni 1986 (in which one finds a version of Arnaut Daniel's sestina, *Lo ferm voler qu'el cor m'intra*) and 1993, Valduga 1989, D'Elia 1993.
39. Cf. for example Toti Scialoja 1994, and Cudini 1999, pp. 253–254.

An initial answer to the foregoing question can be found in a more general phenomenon, one that goes well beyond the sphere of poetry. Over the last several decades, with the change of aesthetic values brought on by the postmodern, the tendency to reclaim the more or less codified traditional literary genres, or even the degraded ones of pulp fiction, has cropped up everywhere. Thus we have the recycling of the sixteenth-century mannerist treatise,[40] the love story, the detective thriller, the novel in its most conventional aspect. It is a conspicuous tendency which, as has been seen, in a certain sense overturns the modern axiology. Modernity, centered on the differential value and the struggle against convention, always looked on the genres with an evil eye to the point of stripping them of any artistic function. The regular metric forms met with the same fate insofar as they were traditional norms that spawned generic conventions. As a result, even the "return to meter" in poetry can in part be included, and so understood, within the more general recycling of genres that characterizes postmodern taste. I say "in part" because, if this is surely the case for some of the above-named poets, it is, nevertheless, not true in the case of Frasca, nor for any of the other poets who have shared his experience since the early 1980s, such as Tommaso Ottonieri, Lorenzo Durante, and Marcello Frixione.[41]

The first difference that leaps to the eye is the separation between the "serious" use of meter and its ironic or "citational" use. The latter is in a certain sense less disconcerting to the late-modern reader. If modern sensibility has taught us to experience regular meters as conventional and artificial, their use for the purposes of citation does not at all force us to change that way of perceiving them. It merely makes us ironically reaccept the artificial. Thus the modern aversion to regular metric forms is not nullified, but only exploited for a particular artistic operation. The "serious" use of meter (or at least one that is not ironic) presents itself as

40. See, for example, Manganelli's *Hilarotragoedia* (Tragicomedy) and *Nuovo commento* (New Comment) in which the author incorporates the stylistic methods of writers such as Torquato Accetto, characterized by peculiar syntax, nonlinear argument, and a passion for digressions.

41. In 1984 these four published a small volume entitled *Beat: Riscritture da King Crimson* (Beat: Rewritings from King Crimson) (Editoriale Aura) in which rock lyrics were recast in the meters, sonority, and lexicon of ancient poetic traditions. In the work of Ottonieri, the metric regulation is less open even if equally unbreakable: the traditional meters are combined with "internal" rules, almost instinctive, in a kind of "physical metricism" (cf. Ottonieri 1985 and 1998). In his "materic" prose there is also a constraint: the solely physical use of heterogeneous linguistic material, aiming at a kind of pantheistic writing, without person and "without author" (cf. Ottonieri 1994). Cf. also Frixione 1992.

a more mysterious artistic fact, and one loaded with "constructive" motives, which would seem to require from the reader a different approach to enjoyment. Frasca's poems are a perfect example of this latter phenomenon.

Frasca's use of meter is not merely the ironic, or "necrophilic," use of something the modern tradition had devalued. First of all, the metric constraints that we have described do not all belong to tradition. As we have seen, we also find among them noteworthy innovations in rhythm and rhyme. However, what is more important is that these metric constraints are rigid, and furthermore, closed. Each composition has a regular scheme of rhyme and rhythm imposed on it, which is maintained from beginning to end, without deviation. In conclusion, what results is not so much the *manipulation* of traditional forms as the *inexorable action of the bond*, and a poetic expression that chooses to have itself bound.

Is freedom, then, not always a good thing? The opening scene of Buñuel's *The Phantom of Liberty* comes to mind. It is set in Spain in 1808, the year of Napoleon's invasion. Some captured Spanish guerrilla fighters are about to be shot. In the face of the firing squad, a few seconds before dying, a cry issues from their lips, "Long live the chain!" (in the Italian version it is translated as "Down with liberty!"). It is a paradoxical cry, yet not without some historical veracity: as is well known, Napoleon invaded Europe in the name of liberty and the other values of the French Revolution. In every field, modernity has always moved to the cry of "Long live freedom!" The peoples of the world claim their independence in the name of liberty, individuals in the name of the freedom of conscience or feeling. The artist has always taken increasing liberties with respect to the norms of literary tradition, in the name of who knows what, but it is certainly something personal, unrepeatable, internal to oneself or one's feelings, something that can be expressed only by breaking open the coercive forces imposed by the institution of poetry. Wherever there are constraints, there is a tendency to force them and break out of them. The same is true for the rules of meter.

The modern tradition has never abandoned meter, though it has assigned it a particular role to play in poetic writing: that of a chain that is there to be broken. The cage of stressed meter is sometimes respected and sometimes transgressed. There are rhymes and no rhymes (imperfect, hidden, or missing rhymes); the rhythmic scheme is there, and the next thing you know, it's being broken by a dissonant rhythm, or by the rhythm of prose. Rhythmic expectation is continually being created so that it may then be frustrated. All in order to stage the spectacle of the poetic self that breaks the chains, the expression that breaks the form, as Adorno put it.

In the poems of Frasca, there is instead a form that forces the expression. After so many romantic, neoromantic, expressionist, and neoexpressionist claims to freedom, here is a poet who seems to do everything possible in order to limit his own expressive discretion, freely choosing to imprison himself in rigid and unbreakable bonds. So here too we hear a hymn to the chain, represented in this case by the strict, closed metric scheme. And that, it must not be forgotten, besides limiting the freedom of the poet, is also a flare launched in the direction of the act of enjoyment. A signal that says: if "this is poetry," it is only because there are metered verses and rhymes. And so we go back to the opposition authored/generic. There is no escape from that opposition. If poetry is not "generic," it means that it must be "authored," or better, "poeted." This poetry, which at all costs wants to submit to a generic discipline, reveals itself to be an attempt to expel the strategic author, whose artistic intentionality supposedly attests to the artistry of the product.

If we search for the "meaning" of the particular late-modern use of meter that we have traced in the poems of Frasca, what we find, I believe, is this: the attempt to restore the rules of genre that bind poetic expression. It is no longer aimed at the artistic institution in a desecrating key; on the contrary, it resonates with the longing to relegitimize a poetic practice, to reenchant it. From this point of view, Frasca's operation has something spiritually in common with the practices of writing to which I have given the name the "search for grace."

Grace and the Apocryphal

The problematization of the author that characterizes late-modernity is, as can be intuited from this survey of bound writings, a complex event, so much so that in going over it we encounter the fundamental articulations of twentieth-century art and its toughest theoretical and aesthetic issues. The kernel of the problem is precisely the excessive valorization of authorial choices, perceived by artists as destructive for art (the strategic author that consumes every bit of unreflected space in artistic practice). But it is not only in bound writing that artists have sought relief from authorialism. Late-modern artistic production invents quite a rich array of "stratagems" aimed at avoiding or retarding the introduction of the author-function, whether on the side of creation (in order to reclaim even just a tiny zone of nonreflection) or on that of enjoyment (in order to block the author from being frozen into an image). In more recent years, following the collapse of poetics, as I have already mentioned, at least two other types of remedy can be identified: the search for grace and the apocryphal effect.[42]

By the *search for grace*, I mean all those literary practices aimed at reclaiming a slice of what is not willed, or better, what is not strategized, though without the adoption of arbitrary rules (which are still based on decision-making). The road taken by the artist in this case is that of narration without destination (in Walser's sense), or the narration of "reserve" (in Celati's sense), but also that of the discipline of meter (in Frasca's sense); in each case it is a matter of desubjectivization. A perfect example is the late narrative work of Celati, starting from *Narratori delle pianure* (Storytellers of the Plains). In a less pure form, we can also trace it in Parise's *Sillabari*, or in Calvino's *Palomar*, with its idea of giving voice to the "unwritten world." The form of short short stories, a certain minimalism in regard to style, or the revaluation of the craftsmanship of writing, are common to the narrative result of this second group of "remedies."

Of the three fundamental aesthetic concepts—beauty, the sublime, and grace—the last, understood by Schiller as immediacy constructed without effort, as a union of the voluntary and the involuntary,[43] seemed to have completely disappeared from modern theories of art. In modern poetics one could resort to either beauty or the sublime, which oriented in various ways the opposition between avant-garde and tradition. In late-modernity, however, grace seems to have made a comeback, having been called on by many writers with the aim of realizing, as Benjamin wrote in regard to Walser, the perfect fusion of will-lessness and intention.[44] Of course, in addition to Walser, the other inevitable point of reference for this utopia of writing outside of a project, outside of a duty to write, is Proust and his idea of "nonsearch."[45] The purpose is without doubt similar: to give voice to an experience that is almost structured "on its own" in the work, beyond the strategic domain of the writing subject. However, the "expedients" used are quite different: the impor-

42. Having already treated the apocryphal effect elsewhere (cf. Benedetti 1998, pp. 89–114) as well as the poetics of grace (cf. Benedetti 1993, pp. 7–33), I will limit myself here to summarizing their characteristics in order to draw some general conclusions.
43. Cf. Schiller 1793.
44. "Robert Walser" (1929) in Benjamin 1996, vol. 2.
45. On which, see the chapter "Proust e la '*noluntas narrandi*,' " in Benedetti 1984.

tance of hearing the language, its oral quality, the craftsmanship of the writing, and the discipline of meter indicated by the more recent writers as a means for producing the writer's "obliviousness of self" have little to do with the complex "strategy of no strategy" set up by Proust. Whereas in the work of the great French novelist, the nonsearch was realized by means of the laborious construction of a cathedral, today a sort of "return of simplicity," resolved entirely on the plane of style, seems to smooth the way for such operations.

Besides, what was already extinct for Benjamin (an experience that is precipitated outside the domain of the subject, and that Proust tried to salvage through a nearly impossible "striving for the miraculous"), in the later writers becomes a condition to be "restored" with stylistic artifices and shortcuts. The expression "search for grace," slightly paradoxical in itself, well reflects the contradictoriness into which fall these late-modern attempts to desubjectivize the creative act, that is, to revive artificially a nonreflectivity that modern artistic logic has already destroyed.

Finally, under the name of the *apocryphal effect* we place all those writing practices characterized by the ironic detachment of the writer from his or her own voice, in other words, by the display of an inauthentic style. Various expedients are used to produce this: from the caricature of a style to the adoption of a noncontemporary form of writing (one clearly belonging to another epoch, as for example, in the work of Manganelli), to the co-presence of diverse forms of writing within a single work, so as to exclude the possibility that any one of them might be "authentic," that is, the author's own. The apocryphal effect makes the very concept of authenticity problematic, almost frustrating it from within. Such an effect is produced when the author, as Calvino puts it, invents a fictitious author in order to make him or her responsible for the author's own work. For its ironic use of forms, for that tendency to take advantage, at its limit, of all possible styles, without distinguishing between different epochs and different personal inclinations (which is another way of frustrating authorial choice), this group of practices covers, in part, what is usually called postmodernism.

All three deauthorializing tactics are aimed at taking effect on that problematic site where the supposed choices of the author take shape. This is obviously because modern literary communication stresses such choices in its processes of artistic valorization. Nevertheless, in each of the three cases the common target is attacked with a different weapon. While the apocryphal effect multiplies the author's choices to the point of falsifying them, rendering them transparently inauthentic, bound writing aims instead at expelling them from the creative act. That brings bound writing closer to the search for grace, though there is an important difference: the search for grace does aim to reclaim a slice of the unwilled for writing, but without adopting arbitrary rules invented at the worktable. The poetics of grace at times also imposes some constraints (e.g., brevity and meter), but it does so by drawing them from a distant tradition (the oral tradition, the poetic tradition of the past, etc.), and so dressing them up with a pseudonatural guise, the absence of which, to the contrary, bound writings flaunt. With respect to the apocryphal effect, both bound writing and the search for grace might in addition appear as more "archaic" practices, which attempt to right the evils of modernity by acting directly on the processes of creation, when instead authorialism lurks also, and even more insidiously, in the processes of attribution. In reality, this may be true of the search for grace, which is plainly distinguished by its greater seriousness, its attempt to pursue the unreflectedness of creation after it has already been destroyed. Also, in certain cases (for example, Celati), the search for grace is strengthened by a sort of "return of innocence," in its effort to revitalize narrative art by unexpectedly carrying it back, in the age of mass media, to its sources in the oral and epic traditions. Bound writing, however, is also flawed, as it often lends itself to a paradoxical and mocking game aimed at the mechanisms of modern enjoyment.

Finally, it can be said that bound writing and the search for grace are based on the principle of "it's not me who *chooses*," whereas in the case of the apocryphal effect, the principle is instead "it's not me who *speaks*." In all three cases, nevertheless, it is "it's not me" that comes first: it's not me, but rather a constraint external to me (bound writing); it's not me, but rather a reservoir of experience from which I draw (grace); it's not me but rather someone else, a fictitious self constructed as a character (the apocryphal effect).

Desecration and Reenchantment

In the war on the author, therefore, two attitudes can be isolated: one serious, one paradoxical and ironic. In both cases the strong role of the author as subject of the choice of poetics is targeted. But whereas the latter denounces that role by flaunting it, and so at the same time pointing to the death of art founded on genius, the former seriously tries to revive an art "without strategy," impeding in various ways the intervention of the author's intentionality in the act of creation. An example of the first attitude in its pure state can be found in certain readymades by Piero Manzoni, like that entitled *Uovo con impronta* (Egg with Imprint) (which is a hard-boiled egg that bears the impression of the author's thumbprint),[46] where it is precisely the "power" which modern artistic logic confers on the author that is displayed and targeted: the ability to transform into art whatever it touches, whatever is exhibited by him as a work of art, whatever bears the impression of his artistic intentionality. Or, in another work by the same artist: *Base magica* (Magic Base),[47] a pedestal capable of transforming into art everything that is placed on it, including the author Piero Manzoni, who turns himself, through a paradoxical short-circuit, into his own work. In contrast, the abstract expressionist technique of drip or action painting, which takes away from the painter intentionality and the possibility of control over the painting, is a good illustration of the second type of attitude.

Still, it often proves difficult to isolate these two moments in concrete artistic practice since most of the time they are found mixed together. Are the random techniques of dadaist desubjectivizing practices aimed at reclaiming an art without strategy, or are they just a "little game for boys," simple and ridiculous, aimed at debunking the idea of the subject as creator? This ambivalent mixture, in which the attempt to substitute genius is mixed with the display of its disappearance, is a characteristic perhaps unique to late-modern art.

It would seem, however, that over the last two decades the ambivalence has been increasingly resolving itself toward the serious attitude (and once again, a good example is the later work of Calvino, where he has set aside both the combinatory game and the apocryphal effect in favor of an "unwritten world," the inexhaustible object of description). Whereas the aleatory practices inaugurated by the dadaists tended to exhibit the author's role in a desecrating tone in order to explode it in its contradictions, more recently artistic production has for the most part set aside the exhibitionism and the desecration. In certain cases, even bound writings end up enveloped in a new seriousness, reducing to a minimum their inherent dose of irony. The war against the author has ceased to be theatrical and exhibitionist to the point of sometimes coinciding with a true and proper "reenchantment" of literature and art, harmonizing

46. See photograph section of this book.
47. See photograph section of this book.

with the aestheticization of the everyday world of life, merchandise, and consumption, and most of all with the culture industry's demand for aesthetically enjoyable objects, endowed with the quality of "aura."[48]

The risk of an artificial reenchantment of literature is most visible, however, in the search for grace, which sometimes (as in the late Calvino) is nothing more than an attempt to reimbue a lifeless literature with a fake aura. Moreover, it should not be forgotten that these results of the search for grace follow on, or coincide with, the display of inauthenticity brought on by the postmodern and by the practices of the apocryphal effect, which in a certain sense they complement. Here, creation is given up for being irretrievably lost, in unison with that kind of mournful elaboration pervading the late-modern, which is nicely summed up in the formula: the "impossibility of the new." This mourning is over what is now deemed impossible: tilling virgin lands cleared of history, thinking what has never been thought before.

48. Thus César's cast polyurethane droplets, the "residue" of performances, survive the "author's gesture," in order to remain as "works," which can be enjoyed and sold, or exhibited in museums.

CHAPTER 8

Endless Mourning

We live in an epoch without future.
The expectation of what is to come is no longer hope, but anguish.
Simone Weil

The Two Deaths

The modern epoch has produced two great terminal myths: the death of art and the death of the author. Even though they arose nearly two centuries apart from each other and are different in content, there is an intimate linkage, so much so that the second death appears to us as a continuation of the first, almost as its "perfection," at least in the sense that paranoia or phobia might be viewed as the perfection of an anxiety.

The death-of-art theme is consubstantial with modernity, the fruit of the reflection which inaugurates it, part of which is the "historicization" of artistic processes. Hegel was the first to make it explicit, but it was already stirring in the thought of the late eighteenth century. As soon as one starts talking about "epochs of literature,"[1] it follows that there will

---

1. Such is the title of one of the four short treatises inserted into Friederich Schlegel's *Dialogue on Poetry* (1800), from which comes also the following: "Art is based on knowledge, and the discipline of art is its history. It is an essential quality of all art to follow closely what has already been formed. Therefore, history goes back from generation to

not only be a history, a continuity, a development, but also an origin and . . . an end. Modernity is unable to conceive art except through its history. But it is precisely the insertion of artistic phenomena into a temporal continuity, in which there is evolution, accumulation, and difference, that makes it possible to conceive the end of art. The modern epoch is self-described by its historical condition; it incorporates history in its very manner of perceiving itself, fixing its own identity in relation to the epochs that have preceded it. Based on the comparison between ancients and moderns developed by classicism, there arose an idea of history as decadence, as the loss of ancient perfection, from which originated some of the fundamental concepts of preromantic aesthetics. For Schiller, ancient art was "naïve," whereas modern art was "sentimental," marked by its reflectiveness. This way of looking back also contains within it a certain nostalgia, to the degree that we are made aware of the superiority of ancient to modern literature, so that the entire romantic effort consisted in trying to bring the "most remote antiquity" back to life.[2] That august past was supposed to be reborn, palingenetically, through its miraculous regeneration in the new condition of the moderns. Thus late-eighteenth-century thought on art often reveals an implicit sense of epigononism, which from then on would remain inherent to modern sensibility. Sometimes openly declared, sometimes feared though not overtly mentioned, the idea of an end of art is the result.

Since then, the negative myth has never ceased to resurface in diverse forms; it accompanies the triumphal march of the modern, with its hymns to evolution, progress, technical and artistic innovation like a subdued countermelody. In the twentieth century, it reemerged in almost regular cadences with the avant-gardes and the postmodern. With each successive reprise, it takes on different aspects and connotations, but it still has the effect of breathing life back into a certain form of art, each time relegitimating a brief reprieve, a short extension of its life, despite its declared terminal agony. At the beginning of the century, the death of art at first had a utopian face; for the avant-gardes, art was supposed to extinguish itself, but only as a separate sphere (as museum or

---

generation, from phase to phase, always farther back into antiquity, to its original source." English translation in Wilson 1982, p. 84.

2. "One could summarize all the essentials in which modern poetry is inferior to the ancient in these words: We have no mythology. But, I add, we are close to obtaining one or, rather, it is time that we earnestly work together to create one. . . . Why should what has once been not come alive again? In a different way, to be sure. And why not in a more beautiful, a greater way?" (ibid., p. 96).

institution, as the deputized site of aesthetic experience), in order then to "dissolve itself" into life and spread its own alternative potential there. In the early sixties, the neo-avant-garde overthrew that utopia using sarcasm to show how art had already been degraded into commercial merchandise while at the same time taking on the task of accelerating the end of art in a kind of paradoxical suicide. Finally, the postmodern has deployed the death of art at the very core of an ironically necrophilic artistic practice. This third stage was in many ways crucial. For the first time, the end of art is neither feared, nor predicted, nor viewed as imminent: it *has already happened,* and without any tragedy. All art is felt as posthumous; its current products are nothing but relics.

As with each previous return of the death of art myth, even this latest has had its productive effects. It has made possible the relaunching of artistic activity on a vast scale, reopening many of the roads that modernity had truncated. Painting returns to the figurative; literature reclaims the narrative genres or poetic traditions that modern sensibility had previously devalued as conventional or declared off-limits. Turning its back on the death of art is just what worked the "miracle." If all is dead, everything is possible again. Since art has exhausted every possibility of innovation and is by now incapable of producing the new, writing can "liberate itself" in an ironic traffic with the old forms. The detachment from a strong idea of art has thus been able to free artistic activity from all kinds of scruples and taboos: not only may we again feel free to tell stories and write novels, but even lyric poetry comes back, despite Adorno's sentiment that Auschwitz had rendered it inconceivable.

Such liberalization has, however, not only come at a price, but at a price so high as to be simultaneously a condemnation. There is no longer anything that is truly created; every form is an imitation, a citation of someone else's work. As John Barth says, one can only write "novels that imitate the form of the Novel of an author who imitates the role of the Author."[3] But even where the postmodern self-description of art does not reach such extreme formulations, its motto is always on the point of turning into its opposite: "If everything is possible again, it is because everything is dead." With that, art condemns itself to necrophilia. The medicine turns out to be a poison. Sure, it allows one to elude the modern artistic logic centered on the value of the new and to get around its paralysis, but only on condition that creation no longer exists.

3. Barth 1967.

It is right here, at the climax of this third passage, this third and ulti-
mate rewrite of the death-of-art motif, that the myth of the author's
death steps onto the stage with an important role to play.

A Medicine against Genius?

What stakes were in play on the arrival of this second death myth, born
at mid-century, when the signs of a self-critical and (I would say) self-
paralyzing vision of the modern had already been circulating for some
time? To all appearances, the war on the author unleashed in the 1960s
was a battle against the grand unity of "man-and-work," and its psy-
chologistic degenerations; it was a definitive and liquidating gesture
made by literary theory in opposition to the framing notions of
nineteenth-century criticism and hermeneutics. These at least were the
declared motives, ones still accepted today as key to understanding the
phenomenon, even by those literary thinkers who have recently begun
to distance themselves from them. There are theoreticians who now criticize the excesses, and who may even attempt to reintroduce the figure of
the author in a moderate way, yet in retrospect they still tend to justify
the earlier excesses as having been necessary given the advantages that
art theory and literary criticism supposedly thereby derived. Against the
"deconstructionist aberrations," which conceive literature as "the appropriation of the text on the part of the reader," Maurice Couturier, for example, reassigns the author an important role as a necessary partner in
the exchange between two subjectivities that is literature. He maintains
that the antiauthor militancy, no longer current, was nevertheless necessary in Barthes's time in order to make the "Copernican revolution" that
supposedly freed literary criticism from the idea of the author as guarantor of meaning.[4] I, on the contrary, believe that the outbreak of that
theoretical agitation was less "innocent" than Couturier depicts it. It was
not merely an attack on the old, but also, and more than anything else,
an elaboration of something new. The death-of-the-author myth contributed to the generation and spread of an absolutely unprecedented
idea of literature, one which still dominates the Western literary scene to
this day.

4. Couturier 1995, pp. 12–13 passim.

But let's take a closer look at the presumed target of that ambiguous "war of liberation." Was there really any need, in the middle of the twentieth century, to refute once again the notorious form of "criticism" based on biographical data against which Proust had already launched a radical attack in his *Contre Sainte-Beuve*? It is true that Sartre's existentialism had forcefully returned the intentionality of consciousness and its "freedom" of expression to center stage. Furthermore, psychoanalysis as applied to literature, or rather to the author, had ended up by reaccrediting the worst forms of psychological and biographical interpretation, prone to completely skipping over every artistic specificity of the works, which tended to be reduced to the same level as psychoanalytical symptoms.[5] Assuming however that there was a need to clinch Proust's refutation with new arguments, how to explain the fact that this new battle cry often assumed quasi-epic tones? They are revealed, for example, in this passage by Barthes:

> the modern *scriptor*, having buried the Author, can therefore no longer believe, according to the pathos of his predecessors, that his hand is slower than his passion . . . ; for him, on the contrary, his hand, detached from any voice, borne by a pure gesture of inscription (and not of expression), traces a field without origin—or at least with no origin but language itself, i.e., the very thing which ceaselessly calls any origins into question.[6]

The war on the author also had another target, one repeatedly invoked by all the "combatants," artists and theoreticians alike: the romantic creator-genius. "Una medicina contro il genio" (A Medicine against Genius) is the title of an article by Giorgio Manganelli (dated 1969), in which, taking as his point of departure the publication in Italian of *Handbook of Literary Rhetoric*, he attacks the romantic idea of the "divine creator," in the name of a literature without author, redefined as a "rhetorical warehouse."[7] But what need could there have been, in the second half of the twentieth century, to cast oneself so vehemently against that romantic hypostasis of the author as genius? Why rail against a target al-

---

5. It was precisely to oppose the reduction of literary texts in those years to a symptom of the author's unconsciousness that brought Francesco Orlando to write the most convincing paragraphs of his "Freudian theory," basing himself on Freud's *Wit and its Relation to the Unconscious* rather than on *Writings on Art and Literature* (cf. Orlando 1971 and 1973).

6. Barthes 1968, p. 52.

7. Now in Manganelli 1994, pp. 67–71.

ready hit so many times before, first of all by Hegel? Hegel had shown the ambiguous and contradictory relation of genius to irony, and even arrived at comparing genius to the effects produced by a bottle of champagne. Though apparently dominated by enthusiasm (by the poetic frenzy of the ancients), the romantic genius is in reality, according to Hegel, an exasperated subjectivity, which sets itself up as something "supreme." This hypertrophic ego, placed above all that would limit it, not only dominates nature, but negates it, as it implies the relativity of all things by comparison to the artist's "divine geniality."[8] Genius was subsequently ridiculed through its own prosaic and unintentionally parodic substitutes; if not exactly champagne, drugs have certainly substituted for genius over various generations of artists, from De Quincey to Burroughs.[9] What was ultimately to hit the bull's eye, and this time with intentional desecration, was twentieth-century artistic practice itself, which focused on other mocking surrogates of genius: chance and arbitrary constraints, both used (like drugs) in the very act of creation, in order to mitigate subjective control over the work.

By the 1960s, then, the romantic idea of unconscious creation was already a notion too weak to require serious refutation. One can therefore reasonably suspect that the medicine against genius which late-modernity strove so hard to find with its "reduction of the ego" epic in reality served as a cure for an altogether different malady. Moreover, the romantic genius itself had been a response to, or, if you like, a remedy for, a modern queasiness that the late-modern is far from being cured of.[10] Late-modernity did not seek remedies *against* genius, but rather a remedy to substitute for it, since it was no longer available, or had simply been revealed as ineffective.[11] It is in this key that the myth of the au-

8. Hegel 1836 (Italian translation, pp. 75 ff). English translation in Hegel 1970, pp. 96ff.

9. For Baudelaire, De Quincey's opium could already be read as an attempt to regain geniality artificially: "The Gambler who has found a sure means of winning is called a swindler; what then should we call the man who wishes to purchase happiness and genius for the price of a few coins?" (Baudelaire 1860, p. 73).

10. A. Vaillant, too (*Entre personne et personnage. Le dilemme de l'auteur modern*, in Chamarat and Goulet 1966, pp. 37 ff.), maintains that the genius of the romantics was a reactive formation to an uneasiness, which he describes, however, in sociological terms, as a "crisis of legitimacy." It struck writers immediately following the French Revolution, with the advent of the culture industry, on which their survival now depended. The romantic poet supposedly reacted to that "with the pathetic assertion of his own moral or spiritual superiority and the privileges due to the author of genius."

11. It should be recalled that even Gadamer's hermeneutics is explicitly posited as capable of substituting for the romantic aesthetics of unconscious creation (cf. chapter 1, and n. 20 of this chapter).

thor's death must be interpreted: as a last resort, a last spasmodic reaction to the death of art; last not only chronologically, but also for its pretense to undo the knot of epigonism *definitively* by once and for all giving up for lost everything that was feared to have been lost: art, creation, the new. The myth, in short, cuts the knot of epigonism by recourse to a reassuring catastrophe.

Internalized Epigonism

The Latin word *auctor* comes from *augeo,* which means "increase," but also "generate," that is, to give birth to something that was not there before.[12] An author is anyone who produces a work that contributes to the increase of intellect, art, or knowledge. Where there is a work, there is an author. Where there is no author, there can only be absence of work. This then is what the expression "death of the author" literally says once free of the veil of euphoria in which it is wrapped: it says creation no longer exists. If artistic activity is authorless, it is because the possibility of giving birth to the new has vanished; in other words, it means that our condition as epigones is considered to be confirmed once and for all.

And one need not search for such a "truth" in the very deep or hidden layers of the myth. It is there, in clear view, in its most familiar statements. Barthes writes:

> Similar to Bouvard and Pécuchet, those eternal copyists, at once sublime and comic, and whose profound ridiculousness indicates precisely the truth of writing, the writer can only imitate a gesture that is always anterior, never original. His only power is to mix writings, to counter the ones with the others, in such a way as never to rest on any one of them. Did he wish to *express himself,* he ought at least to know that the inner "thing" he thinks to "translate" is itself only a ready-formed dictionary, its words explainable only through other words, and so on indefinitely.[13]

The writer-no-longer-author is then not only, as is said, someone who has thrown aside, almost as if it were an out-of-style suit, the "genial divine irony" of the romantics, or the exaggerated expressive freedom of Sartre; above all, she is also someone who has internalized her own condition of epigone to the point of adhering to the role of a *bricoleur* who

12. Cf. Benveniste 1973. On the Latin usages of the term, cf. Agamben 1998.
13. Barthes 1968, p 53. [See Cindy Sherman images in photo insert.]

mixes preexisting writings, or that of an "eternal copyist" of the already written. And if Barthes's explicit reference to the impossibility of an original gesture were still not sufficient to prove it, the fact alone that he entrusts the task of designating the "truth of writing" to Bouvard and Pécuchet would allow us to intuit how the myth develops in the sign of an epigonism no longer opposed but openly embraced. In those two characters, incapable of doing anything other than ingesting and regurgitating, copying and recopying commonplaces (or better, "received ideas," as the French expression more explicitly puts it),[14] Flaubert has staged the progressive paralysis of modern culture, its sense of being condemned to cite what has already been written while it picks and chooses with no sense of hierarchy in the immense warehouse of literature and renounces any new organization of ideas. In welcoming that image as emblem of the writer's condition, Barthes ironically transforms its tonality but not its content: what Flaubert despises is exactly what Barthes adheres to; it is accepted as a destiny. The myth of the author's death seems, in effect, to do just this: it converts the anguish of the epigone into euphoria, even while it transforms his or her condition from contingent to inevitable.

The myth of the author's death certainly lacks the power to make the strategic author or author-image (which, as has been seen, artistic communication and the culture industry need more than ever) disappear; however, it has the effect of profoundly modifying the status of the artist in the collective imagination. The writer is no longer someone who generates or increases, but merely a *scriptor:* a scribe, a scrivener, a copyist, a craftsman, a collector of preexisting writings, a librarian, a *bricoleur,* a prop-man for the literary bazaar. The list of expressions coined to define his or her new condition is richly varied, but at the same time stunningly homogeneous, because it all goes under the banner of a single verdict: no one will ever be able to add anything to that "museum of images" over two thousand years old, which constitutes the history of art for us moderns.[15] Late-modern culture experiences itself as the extreme appendix of

14. Flaubert's unrealized intention was to make the *Dictionnaire des idées réçues* part of a second volume of *Bouvard et Pécuchet* containing citations from the books read by the two characters, placed in alphabetical order and juxtaposed in their contradictory assertions. One can thus trace back to this project many of the guiding images of late-modernity: not only the use of other authors' writings, the idea of the "book of books" (cf. Foucault, "Fantasia of the library" in Foucault 1966, p. 88), but also that of the dictionary or encyclopedia as the oppressive condensation of a history without progress.

15. The expression belongs to Malraux 1951, but the concept was innate to the historicization of art made by eighteenth-century aesthetics. Winckelmann, for example, writes:

a past greatness to which nothing can be added except comments, blas-
phemous appendices, ironic embroideries, false movements. The idea of
the author's death definitively sanctions such a condition precisely in the
metamorphosis it imposes on the notion of the writer.

This second myth reveals itself to be even more funereal than the one
which has accompanied modernity since its birth. The "death of art"
may also mean that one form of art dies in favor of another; or that it is
indeed art as a whole that dies, but so as to favor philosophy, as Hegel
wanted, or some other form of expression or knowledge. "Death of the
author," on the other hand, is like a nuclear explosion that creates a des-
olation around it and leaves the earth sterile for who knows how long. It
means that in no form of expression or knowledge will there be any increase, any new birth. One then arrives at an understanding of the role
played by the myth of the author's death at the moment of that last transition, when the demise of art is deemed an event of the past, and it is
taken for granted that all is over and done with. Thus, late modernity
was able to celebrate a definitive liquidation of art by removing its most
vital organ: the very idea of creation.

The Absent Work and the Already Inscribed Word

To those who are familiar with the theme of *désoeuvrement*, or absence of
work, it may seem strange that I use the expression here in a negative
sense, as an equivalent to the impossibility of creating. Indeed, in the
work of Bataille and Blanchot, the expression appears with altogether
different connotations. Whether it has to do with revolutionary action
(theorized by Bataille as "acephalous")[16] or literary writing (theorized
by Blanchot as "impersonal"), *désoeuvrement* always has the value of a
desubjectivizing catharsis realized by means of a sacrifice of the self. It is

---

"The artist needs a work drawn from all mythology, from ancient and modern writers,
from the mysterious wisdom of many nations, from the monuments of antiquity preserved on gems, coins and utensils, by means of which poetic form has been given to general concepts. This wealth of material should be conveniently classified and, with proper
application to particular cases, be adapted to the instruction." (Winckelmann 1755, p. 65).

16. Bataille does not use the term *désoeuvrement* but others close to it like *inachèvement*
(incompleteness) or *acéphale* (acephalous), tied to the theme of sacrifice, self-castration,
the refusal to rival the father, as well as to themes of political struggle (cf. Bataille
1936/1939). And it is probably from Bataille that Foucault picks up the concept, asserting
in the appendix to *Histoire de la folie* (*Madness and Civilization*) (Foucault 1961), that the absence of the work, understood as a "reserve of meaning" (like a word that is self-implied
and signifies no more than language itself), is what, after Mallarmé, relates madness to
literature.

supposed to be this sacrifice that, in a culture dominated by the values of individualism and strategic behavior, repotentiates the experience of the sacred or the work of art. For Blanchot, the work's absence is that impersonal space in which the writer places herself, which allows writing to connect with a truth "that is beyond the person."[17] So it is not depicted as an impossibility to create, but on the contrary, as the necessary condition for there to be once again something resembling the creation of the classical writer (who, as Blanchot says, sacrifices his or her own voice in order to give voice to the universal), despite an artistic logic that instead values everything that is individual and oriented to the "search for difference." Whereas the logic of modern art induces us to suppose that the subject makes use of writing as its own instrument for attaining certain results, which are dominated by subjectivity, Blanchot speaks in a utopian manner of a writing that instead eliminates the arbitrary and the artist's choices, obligating him to submerge himself on behalf of a neutrality having neither form nor destiny, "that lies behind everything written." Thus, *désoeuvrement* can be considered as a reaction to the excess of modern art's reflectedness, and the auspice of its desubjectivizing catharsis, a cure capable of weakening subjective, strategic control over the work. It is the utopia of "what matter who's speaking!" which, starting from Proust, runs parallel to the "noisier" poetics of the avant-garde. Not far different from that "striving for the impossible" to which Proust consecrated himself according to Benjamin, what Blanchot pursues is the possibility of a writing undertaken outside the current strategies of the subject who writes. In this sense, he is able to say that "the writer is dead from the moment that the work exists": a death wished for as a way of restoring the conditions of partial unreflectedness, which is the only situation in which creation can take place.

But it is not of this death and this absence of the work that the death-of-the-author myth, as subsequently developed in the sphere of poststructuralism from Roland Barthes on, speaks. What is portrayed to us instead is a death by strangulation on the part of a culture overstuffed with history. Yes, impersonality does get realized, but only parodically, in the form of being condemned to drawing on or being spoken by (as Pierre Menard is spoken by Cervantes's *Don Quixote*) those works that have already been written. The writer-no-longer-author is really not he who submerges his own ego in favor of the "anonymous, impersonal affirmation" that is the work; he is rather the writer-librarian who rewrites and mixes together preexisting writings, someone incapable of

17. Blanchot 1955.

producing the new. Certainly the myth continues, in all of its multifarious formulations, to stress all that which can be supra-individual in the act of writing: sometimes it is the language, understood as the site on which the subject "never ceases to vanish"; sometimes it is the writing itself, depersonalized, as the site on which the traces of a mute difference are voicelessly inscribed. Yet, looking a little closer it is easy to see how the theme of the work's absence begins to undergo a curious twisting into epigonism. The supra-individual entity that is supposed to sweep away the strategic subjectivity of the artist, strangely, or better, surreptitiously, comes to coincide with the already written word. One reads in one of the many apologetic writings on the subject: "Drowning the author in the textual ocean, god is chased out of his own creation and reduced to the level of scribe of a Word already written and catalogued in the Borgesian library."[18]

And if the god of creation now appears in the lower case, the already-written Word gains, in contrast, a capital letter. The already-written Word, in its turn, is refigured as an infinite *library*, an *encyclopedia*, a "ready-formed dictionary," a closed totality, already complete, already elaborated, to which it is impossible to add anything.

The "medicine against genius," described by Manganelli, also openly heads in this direction: the "rhetorical trove" is actually conceived by him as a *warehouse* capable of holding "literature as a whole, divided and ordered in modes and forms, subdivided in examples, placed on infinite mental shelves." In this way literature becomes "a *deposit* of possible literary situations," which one can endlessly go through on an "uneven and *labyrinthine* route."[19] And so the exalted desubjectivization, instead of opening up writing to the unpredictable realm of the possible, locks it into a "ritual," an infinite play of refrains and citations.

The utopia of a desubjectivized writing, which, from Proust on, has never ceased to reappear, even if in the most diverse forms, certainly has no easy realization (as Proust himself, moreover, shows us). But here it is not so much a matter of the impossible actuation of a utopian principle as of its mocking realization in the form of being phagocytized by the already given, by what has already been written or already thought. Instead of its being freed from the narrow constraints of individualism and

---

18. From the introductory note of R. Silva in *Tel Quel* 1974, pp. iv-v.

19. Manganelli 1994, p. 71, italics added. The idea of literature that inspires Manganelli's argument is explicitly epigonal: a literature conceived "as the articulation of a rhetorical figure, the tenth trope: irony. To make the eternal demon of literature into a game, a ceremony, a coat of arms, only with this exorcism can we face up to literature!" An art of the word, therefore, exorcised by irony, practiced only insofar as it is dead.

of strategic subjectivity, what we get is the impossibility of original writing. The myth then preserves, superficially, all the utopian valences of the absence-of-the-work concept, but only as the euphoric mask of an epigonal sensibility.

It must be pointed out, though, that even Blanchot's work contains the epigonal version of the work's absence, if not yet actively, at least, potentially, on account of its being oriented toward language. From the moment in which the supra-individual entity that is supposed to wipe away subjective control over the work is identified with something finite, the paths of the labyrinth are opened, or rather, closed up. Language is, through antonomasia, the closed system that contains in itself all things expressible, even if not controllable, by the subject. Furthermore, Proust's attempt to preserve in writing a nonsubjectively dominated experience operated through altogether different channels from that of "being spoken" by language. After Proust, however, that utopia mostly takes, and not solely in the work of Blanchot, or in the domain of French, the route of language. Even hermeneutics starts, with Gadamer, to think desubjectivization as a *being played by language* (which is exactly what Gadamer substitutes for genius). That already prefigures the epigonal turn, since the supra-individual (or, to use Gadamer's terms, the Hegelian objective spirit) is transferred into the finite entity of language,[20] which has the characteristics of a closed system and locks the possible into a paradigm. From the very idea that literature is nothing other than the infinite texts that language can generate, widespread among theoreticians and writers in those years, comes, like a corollary, the paradoxical image of a monkey that, over an infinite period of time, through hitting the keys of a typewriter by chance, would be able to "create" the masterpieces of world literature. Such inventions comically reveal the closure of possibilities hidden behind the apparent images of infinity as suggested by the analogic model of language when this model is used to explain the processes of creation.

Claustrophilia

The idea of the author's death is born as a euphoric myth, one which hails the phenomenon it describes as a liberation: the liberation of writing from the tasks of expression, representation, and from categories such as sense, subject, and truth; the liberation of literary criticism from

20. Gadamer 1960, pp. 10 passim.

the fetters of the author's psychology; the liberation of reading from the "principle of authority," or from the need to decode the work in search of the meaning intended by its author. Freedom even from the chronology of history, from that "progressive" history that animated the modern vision of culture and art. Again, Barthes:

> I savor the sway of formulas, the reversal of origins, the ease which brings the anterior text out of the subsequent one. . . . Proust is what comes to me, not what I summon up; not an "authority," simply a *circular memory*. Which is what the inter-text is: the impossibility of living outside the infinite text—whether this text be Proust or the daily newspaper or the television screen: the book creates the meaning, the meaning creates life.[21]

But as soon as one scratches the surface exaltation, and this is even true in Barthes's own work, a subterranean sense of oppression becomes evident. There is something claustrophobic about the impossibility of living outside of the infinite, yet closed, text by which we shall all be woven together. It is a nightmare, a sorcerer's spell. Everything is text; everything is circular memory. As Derrida writes: "Wherever it is found, if it is found, it is text." A text that has no beginning, and which, according to Barthes's image, is accessed by several entrances, none of which is more important than the others. Everything is inside, "textualized," like a labyrinth outside of which there is nothing. There is no other space in which the work can take place. Nor is forgetfulness possible. But as Nietzsche would say, he who does not forget, can neither act nor think.[22] Like Funes, the Borgesian character with prodigious memory, so the late-modern writer: paralyzed by the inability to forget anything. History, no longer progressive, piles up around one in an unwieldy heap: and the writer, no longer author, is asked to assume the role of an ironic (or melancholic) librarian of that immense accumulation.

Wherever it takes form, the myth of the author's death sports a euphoric look. Sometimes, it even surrounds itself with a subversive glow,

---

21. Barthes 1973, p. 36. Manganelli, too, presented his "rhetorical warehouse" as "an anti-historical vision of literature" (1994, p. 70).

22. For Nietzsche the hypertrophy of memory paralyzes rather than favors the life of the spirit, producing among other things, "the belief in being late fruit and epigones" (Nietzsche 1874, pp. 16 passim). A concise and convincing critique of the concept of the end of history, treated as a memory disorder, can be found in Virno 1999, in the chapter, "Il fenomeno del *déjà vu* e la fine della Storia" ("The Phenomenon of Déjà Vu and the End of History").

as happened in the late sixties, in the *Tel Quel* group. Here Barthes's semiology, reelaborated by Julia Kristeva, intersects with Jacques Derrida's "new theory of writing," hailed by Philippe Sollers as a "revolutionary work" that overthrows every tradition of metaphysical thought: a writing "without subject," "that denotes an operation that is not an operation," and from which the presuppositions for an act of generalized subversion can supposedly be drawn:

> By stressing the text, denouncing the metaphysical valorization of the concepts of "work" and "author" . . . we have touched the central nerves of the social unconscious in which we live and, in short, the distribution of symbolic property. What we are proposing intends to be as subversive towards "literature" as was Marx's critique towards classical political economy.[23]

And yet, even the emphasis on the subversive leads to the same approach: a definitive presumption of the end of literature,[24] and above all the end of creation, which is liquidated by Sollers with no beating about the bush as "a myth of bourgeois ideology." Nor is it difficult to trace the same sad verdict in the work of Derrida: that continuous deconstruction, and dislocation of concepts and their reinscription in other chains much resembles an endless wandering through the paths of a labyrinth with no escape. And the labyrinth, once again, is nothing but our oppressive sense of history, the "woven tissue" or interminable text constituted by everything that has already been said and thought before us: "I do not believe in decisive ruptures, in an unequivocal 'epistemological break,' as it is called today. Breaks are always, and fatally, reinscribed in old cloth that must continually, interminably be undone."[25]

Thus, neither in literature, nor in philosophical thought and epistemology, will anything ever be added to that "ancient fabric" that one can only keep trying to undo. All that remains is to pass over ground that has already been trod, like Borges's Pierre Menard (who, while not copying, rewrites *Don Quixote* in exactly the same words as Cervantes), contenting oneself with the infinite "mute differences" produced through such

23. Sollers, in *Tel Quel* 1968, p. 40.

24. "That which until now was called 'literature' belongs to a closed epoch that is giving way to a nascent science, that of writing" (ibid., p. 42; from which comes the following citation also).

25. Derrida 1972, p. 24. The concept of "epistemological break" which Derrida is arguing against is probably that of Bachelard, later taken up by Thomas S. Kuhn.

repetition. Here the infinite is provided not by an unlimited opening of the space of the possible, but by the reiteration of journeys through an enclosed space, an interminable losing of oneself and repeating of oneself, an eternal retracing of one's own footsteps. In poststructuralist philosophy, one reads the same verdict as that in poststructuralist thought on literature; in no form of expression or knowledge is there to be any further generation.

This is what the myth of the author's death drags along with it unawares, or better, half-aware, since the absence of the work in its unhappy and nonutopian formulation is not actually removed from consciousness. All that poststructuralist thought speaks of, in its multifarious elaborations, is merely our supposed irreversible impossibility to create. But what gets left out is its affective valence: the anguish that it generates. What gets repressed is not the lost object, but the fact that it constitutes a loss. Therein lies the reason for the fundamental ambivalence that accompanies the myth of the author's death in almost all its formulations: whatever else it might express, it expresses our supposed condition of epigones, but reelaborated in a euphoric tone. Bouvard and Pécuchet, the Borgesian library, the labyrinth, Pierre Menard: images and symbols that in their original formulation allude tragically to an impossibility to create, are now taken up ironically, and transformed into exultant banners.

We should not be astonished by the contrast between what the myth says literally and the gay tones with which it is usually formulated since its "work" consists precisely in its euphoric elaboration of a loss. Late-modernity's bereavement is over the impossibility to create; it perceives itself as a terminal culture. The myth of the author's death, which poststructuralism has disseminated across much of contemporary culture, is its elaboration: an interminable labor of mourning. Its "usefulness" consists precisely in transforming the tragedy into irony. Just as the death of art is transformed into a euphoric event, an event that has already taken place, so, too, epigonism. No ruptures, no tears, only dislocations. Dislocation substitutes for creation, but at the same time, it animates the immobility of the epigone; it closes the realm of the possible inside the already given, but simultaneously transforms into claustrophilia the claustrophobia which results from that enclosure.

Thus, if it is true that the myth of the author's death is an attempt to definitively whisk away the paralyzing sense of epigonism, it must also be said that it is a curious way of freeing itself, given that it ends up by confirming that condition as an irreversible fate. If we wanted to continue with the Freudian metaphor of the work of mourning, it would then be necessary to specify that here we are confronted by a peculiar type, a process that is not reconstructive but pathological, like the one Freud noticed in manic-depressive syndromes. The lost object (the possibility to create) does not get reconstructed under another form, but attacked, vilified, ridiculed. That can already be seen in many writing practices of a dadaist stamp which "abase" the creative act to the point of making it into a game of chance, governed by randomness or arbitrary rules, perfectly derisive substitutes for genius. It is seen again in the 1960s, in the emphasis with which the condition of copyist (i.e., the opposite of creation) is celebrated. Finally it is seen, in more recent years, in the "escape routes" tried by other late-modern writers: the road of ironic citation, the road of the hybridization of preexisting writings, the road of the apocryphal effect (another way of attacking the idea of creation: the Proustian "deep self" is frustrated by means of the ironic principle, "it's not me who is talking"). In all these cases the loss is healed through detachment from that which is considered to have been lost, through an ironic detachment from the very idea of art, and from all the correlates that lay embedded in its notion: creation, greatness, authenticity, the absolute. As a result, the appeasement that it brings is, in its turn, traumatic. The remedy consists, then, in adjusting a weakened idea of literature: a literature without author, without creation and declaredly epigonal.

Literature "Reconfigured"

The myth of the author's death did not remain restricted to the formulations of a small number of philosophers or theoreticians of art. It branched out into critical methodologies and has produced a homogeneous set of notions, all related to each other, which penetrate diverse theories and diverse fields of knowledge, from deconstructionism to hermeneutics, from literary theory to new information technologies. The network of its concepts is so homogeneous as to render it easily identifiable as a single corpus. And each of those concepts contributes in its own way, through capillary and decentralized action, to the normalization of the impasse, to the mournful inversion of the realm of the possible.

At the top of the list of those related concepts is the triumphant notion of the text, with its myriad derivatives: intertext, hypertext, metatext, architext, hypotext, among others, plus the related abstract nouns (intertextuality, etc.). But even before the proliferation of its nomenclature, what is most significant is the substitution that it brings about. The notion of text has actually reached the point of replacing that of work. In that substitution, which moreover is overtly theorized,[26] one can read the loss that afflicts late-modern thought. The text, as is so often heard, is supposed to be the theater of a meaningful practice without subject, or a production whose subject is plural and in which the person who writes is displaced and lost at the very moment he or she utters something. But as has been seen, it amounts to a rather peculiar depersonalization, one which consists in being spoken by the already-written. Resorting once again to the fictional world of Borges (whose capacity to describe the magic tricks of late-modernity, and to incarnate them in memorable characters and situations surpasses almost all others), the *Don Quixote* of Cervantes is a *work*, that of Pierre Menard is a *text*. However, what Borges constructs as a paradox (oozing with the anxiety of the epigone) has now been flattened out, transformed into a positive and regulative notion by various theories of the text.

The text without author is in effect a "normalized," frozen paradox. In it there converge two things that normally should be distinguished as belonging to different levels of logic. On one side, there is the product of the act of writing (that perceptible object, which we read, and which formerly would have been called a "work"); on the other, the act of writing itself, immersed in the same woven tissue of citations from which every text comes. Indeed, not only is the succession of sentences to which we attribute a certain internal coherence called "text," so is its source, the subject who approaches it, whether as author or interpreter,[27] which is another distinction that tends to be annihilated by the textuality in which everything is systematically immersed. But it is exactly in such a collapse of logical hierarchies that the impossibility of creation and the paralysis of late-modernity take hold.

In the cancellation of the difference between an activity and its product many other cancellations can be read. The text is a connective tissue in which the confines of the work disappear, and where the difference between original elaboration and citation, between creation and repetition of the already-written, is annulled. Claustrophilic epistemology conceives no other reality outside of the great signifying process that is

26. Cf. Barthes 1971.

27. "This 'I' which approaches the text is already itself a plurality of other texts, of course, of codes which are infinite" (Barthes 1970, p. 10).

the text, understood as social space for production of meaning in light of the already-written. That erasure is usually valorized as the suppression of every metaphysics based on concepts such as meaning, subject, and truth. Above all else, poststructuralist notions of text and intertextuality suppress the gaps between discourses,[28] which are exactly what the notions of author and work serve to produce through the processes of attribution that we have described. Intertextuality thus comes to be the amniotic fluid in which the differences between work and comment, between author and critic, between author and reader, between creation and the act of enjoyment, even that between greatness and mediocrity, get thinned out and watered down. But a horizontality of such magnitude does not easily conceal the condition that it sets up. If there is no longer a difference between text and comment, it is because everything is always and irremediably comment on the already-written.

Late-Modern Learning

Far superior to pathological mourning, which in our discourse is little more than a metaphor, is the concept of deutero-learning, which can help us understand the paralyses of late modernity. Beyond providing a graphic image of its obstructive results, it also gives us the possibility of understanding the "logic" that underlies it, or better the fallacy on which it is based.

Let's go back to Derrida's statement: no ruptures or tears, only dislocations. What comes through here is not only the melancholy of the epigone, but also his anamnesis. Rupture is nothing other than the process of thought as conceived by the differential logic of the modern; which is to say, modernity conceives thought as a continual supersession of itself (Shklovsky's continual "revolutions," or Bachelard's epistemological breaks). And if such ruptures are now held to be useless, it is because it has been learned that each one gets fatally reinscribed in the same "woven fabric" that it was supposed to tear apart. In short, there is an eye that has learned to recognize the class of *ruptures and tears* and that is now able to discern the "law" that causes them to repeat. But it is exactly the fact of perceiving rupture as an event that repeats itself, in an interminable series of analogous events, that empties such events of their meaning: it demonstrates the futility of continuing the series ad infini-

28. Cf. Foucault 1971.

tum. In other words, what is at work here is that paralyzing deutero-learning, which according to my hypothesis, represents the emblem of late-modernity. It consists in gaining self-critical consciousness of what have been the propulsive mechanisms of the modern, that is, the new as a surpassing of the old, as a transgression of the norm, as estrangement. These mechanisms, which, operating implicitly (and thus silently, semi-visibly) since romanticism, had made the life of art possible in the form of continual innovation, are now stripped bare and perceived as worn out.

Although the debate over the postmodern stressed the exhaustion of the differential logic of the modern, it was only the latest theorization of a process initiated long before. The conviction, or at least the suspicion, that the law of innovation and shock was destined through entropy to use up all its resources made its appearance early on. Traces of this way of perceiving the affairs of art are already apparent in the work of the futurists, to the extent that they began to see how the mechanism of perpetually "killing the fathers" drove modernist evolution. And they saw it not in its productive aspect, as described by Shklovsky, but in its sinister and repetitive aspect, as is clear in these lines by Marinetti:

> Our successors will gather against us; they will come from far off, from everywhere, dancing to the regular cadences of their first songs . . . they will hurl themselves upon us murderously, driven by a hatred that will be the more implacable, the more inebriated their hearts are with love and admiration for us.[29]

The dadaists' awareness of this fate was even stronger. In addition to incorporating the "death of dada" in their slogans, they did not wait for their "natural" modernist death at the hands of their eventual successors, but voluntarily broke up, decreeing the end of the movement themselves. However, it is later on, in the post-avant-gardist reflections on literature and art, that such learning flares up in the sharp and virulent manner attained by the postmoderns: "It's sad, *mon cher* Luís, but it's no longer possible to scandalize anybody."

Thus Breton to Buñuel in 1954 after Max Ernst had won the Grand Prize of the Biennale in Venice.[30] A few years later, Barthes would write:

29. *Manifesto del Futurismo,* 1909, in Marinetti 1976, p. 8.
30. Buñuel 1983, p. 114.

"A 'provocative' *language* is readily accommodated by literary institutions: the scandals of language, from Rimbaud to Ionesco, are rapidly and perfectly integrated."[31]

As with the awareness of the self-referential aspect of literature, so too the idea that there is no longer any norm to combat, that instead transgression itself has been transformed into a kind of new convention, or a new academy, becomes part of the standard equipment of late modernity: it is its baggage, or if you prefer, its burden. It is a kind of second-level learning that brings into the visual field of thought what had once been the implicit law of the modern, now perceived on all sides as destined to a blind alley. It records the impossibility of being original, not merely in the form of a historical contingency, but rather in that of a collapse, an implosion of that very logic on which modern art stands.

History Reconfigured as Labyrinth

The paralysis of late-modernity starts here, in this deutero-learning that changes history into labyrinth. Modern artistic logic has as its guiding idea the supersession of what came before, thus a progress, even if through discontinuities, jumps, continual revolutions. That permitted it to include history within the very process of artistic valorization without being crushed by it. By celebrating the new as differential value with respect to the already-written, history was turned, so to say, into an interest-bearing account for the benefit of art. Late-modernity, however, no longer has such means at its disposal; for it, the historical process has gotten jammed, along with the possibility of producing further "difference." If for the romantics, the history of poetry was a tradition, which means an accumulated body of knowledge, a technical patrimony that leaves behind sedimentary layers (including even the literary genres)[32] and so poses no obstacle to renaissances, for late-modern culture history is instead an immense, overstuffed library, to which nothing can now be added. What comes down from the past now takes on the oppressive

31. Barthes 1960, p. 149.

32. "A school of poetry will be discovered . . . in its own history. The teachers of all times and of all nations have opened the road for us; they have left us an immense capital," wrote Schlegel in the same pages in which he foresaw the birth of a theory of genres and of poetic schools (Schlegel 1800, p. 32).

guise of an encyclopedia, of a "ready-formed dictionary," of a labyrinth coextensive to the world, which one can only go through over and over again, and which, through another euphoric shift in metaphor, is simply called "intertext."

It has often been said that such a description is the fruit of a "posthistoric" vision of the facts of art.[33] Whether the image is that of library, dictionary, or rhetorical warehouse, the intention is supposedly to put "a deposit of possible literary situations, in some ways historically neutral" at the writer's disposal, all equally available, independent of their position in history.[34] But in no way can it be said that such a perspective will really free us from history. The only thing that it "liberates" us from is the idea of a consecutive line of works, one after another, according to an evolutionistic model. History, in and of itself, however, is in no way dissolved; on the contrary, for this very reason it begins to make its oppressive weight felt, like a pyramid that looms at our back. Having taken away the idea of progress, history becomes simultaneous, it curves around the subject, it turns into a labyrinth.

Many speak of postmodernity as a new era that has supposedly left the modern behind. And yet the description of art elaborated by it fails to escape the range of action of that crushing sense of history that runs through all modern art. The only thing that changes is that in place of the "salutary" (as long as it was functioning) *surpassing* of the old, now what we perceive is the *accumulation* of the old. Taking the death of art for granted, as I have already said, is a decisive passage. From a certain point of view, this might even appear to us as the first major turning point that there has been in reflection on art since romanticism. And yet that change is insufficient to bring about a true leap beyond the modern conception. Despite a reshuffling of the pawns, the board and the game itself remain the same as when modernity first opened. The museum of twenty centuries never disappeared from the background; it is still there, and by now it is totally copresent, all stacked up as if in a warehouse, or a library of Babel, but for this very reason more oppressive than ever. Thus late-modernity ends up in a dead end, which might also be described as a double bind with regard to history: whatever we do, we remain prisoners to the already-written or the already-thought.

33. Cf., for example, Danto 1992.
34. Manganelli 1994, p. 70. See also the passage from Barthes cited earlier in this chapter.

Double Bind

In taking up, and in a sense liquidating, the menacing problem limned by Marinetti, Calvino wrote that "a *precursor* is . . . one who does before others what the others will later do better than he."[35]

In this extract from a letter of 1960, the dead end we have been discussing comes through clearly. This way of viewing things obviously presupposes late-modern deutero-learning: the "old" propulsive mechanism of art, its proceeding through continuous "killings of the fathers," is now visible and thereby emptied of meaning. It is useless to continue the series of innovations now that the "law" of innovation is already familiar, now that it is known that sooner or later we will all be surpassed and kicked out in our turn. (Nor is anyone ready to reassume the role of "martyrs of the new," those who sacrifice themselves to the now dubious law of supersession, as futurist rhetoric called for.) But at the same time, in that slightly cynical, and surely partial, mode of defining innovation, we can also read the double bind that I have been talking about. If one cannot innovate, what way is there open for literature? It is obvious that once posed in these terms, the problem has no visible solution. Because if you can't innovate, you still can't not innovate without by so doing resigning yourself to epigonism. If you innovate, you will soon be made part of the future norm, but if you don't innovate, you are already part of the norm of the past. In short, every possible route seems to be blocked off in this jam.

Late-modernity is littered with double binds of this kind. Even revolutionary action seems to get caught up in it. Buñuel recalls that in 1968, in the streets of Paris, one would find slogans lifted from the surrealist armory written on the walls: "power to the imagination," "to prohibit is prohibited." He adds, however, that even the students of 1968 were unable to put them into practice, transform them into actions, except by choosing terrorism, which is another dead end. Action, in short, had become impossible, just like scandal.

In addition to slogans, May 1968 had other things in common with the surrealist movement—the same ideological themes, the same verve, the

35. Calvino 1991, p. 334; a response to Calvino's remark is found in Moresco 1997, p. 274.

same schisms and romance with illusions, and the same difficult choice
between words and actions. Like us, the students of '68 talked a lot and
did little. But I don't blame them at all. As Breton might have said, action
has become impossible, just like scandal. Except by choosing terrorism, a
choice some made. But here, too, there is no escape from the phrases of
our youth. . . . I do not forget having once written that *Un Chien Andalou*
was nothing other than an open call for assassination.[36]

The double binds that ensnare late-modern culture are paradoxical com-
mands of the type "I order you to disobey," made by those in power or
by the institution of art. Revolutionary action, like the transgressive logic
of modern art, ends up in a dolorous paradox: if you disobey, you are
obeying; if you innovate, you are an epigone; if you scandalize, you remain inside the norm; no matter what you do, you are prisoner to the
already-given. This is the way late-modern learning is: modernity sees
itself in the mirror and is paralyzed by its own gaze. But one doesn't end
up in such a condition spontaneously. On their own, thought and behavior tend to find ways out of double binds. If need be, they invent escape
routes where they don't already exist, without falling into the trap. In
order to get trapped by a paradoxical order, in an eternal oscillation between two opposite poles (like Bateson's image of the hammer of an elec-
tric bell vibrating between one electrode and the other), in order to get
stuck in such a highly improbable condition, there must be special circumstances interfering with all the possible ways out. In reality there is
no irreversible fate that weighs on late-modernity so as to lock it into this
dead end. If it is trapped, it is only because it itself has barred every possible exit.

What brings on paralysis is precisely admitting the impossibility of
the new. Here we get a measure of how ambiguous and deficient this
kind of self-criticism of modernity can be. It is obvious, actually, that
starting from such an admission, the roads that could open up to literature and art are infinite. If one can no longer proceed in the search for
further difference, it means that the time has come to free oneself of that
"task," and to invent a new direction for literature and art. Yet this is precisely what late-modern learning fails to come up with. Instead of totally
abandoning the differential logic of the modern, it remains prisoner to it,
even while declaring its impasse. Like an orphan that won't stop crying

36. Buñuel 1983, p. 125. The English translation by Stephen Heath has been slightly
modified.

for its dead parents, it is incapable of conceiving the new in a manner completely different from the way the romantics had conceived it (and after them, the avant-gardes), to the point of deducing from the impossibility of this particular new, the impossibility of the new in general. The impossibility of producing further difference is wrongly generalized as an impossibility of exploring virgin lands, of thinking the unthought, of creating a work. The vicious circle of late-modernity derives from such a fallacy. And it is a circle of its own construction. The myth of the author's death tells us that nothing fresh can ever be thought, and it says it with a sinister circularity, both as diagnosis and as therapy. The impossibility of the new is both the loss to be worked out and the means to work it out; both the ailment to be cured and the medicine with which to cure it. In effect, the sole way "open" to this kind of modern criticism that fails to overturn its own premises is to take the end of art for granted, accepting the condition of epigones without reservation, transforming art and literature into a funeral service with the corpse on display.

Not one of the solutions that late-modernity has elaborated (the myth of the author's death, the postmodern description of art that assumes the end as having already arrived, the poststructuralist theories of the text) offers an escape from the impasse of modernity. They are only adaptations to a double bind, in other words, to an impossible condition. But the adaptation to a double bind is pathological: as Bateson would say, it leads to schizophrenia. The myth of the author's death (and the depotentiated idea of art born from it) transforms art, as it transforms the world that art allows us to see through it, into the *idios kosmos* of a schizophrenic (like those worlds into which many of Philip K. Dick's fictional characters find themselves thrown). In this parallel universe, neither originality nor repetition exist since every word is citation; neither work nor comment exist since everything is comment on the already-written; neither authenticity nor inauthenticity exist for every voice is apocryphal; neither greatness nor mediocrity exist for everything is epigonal. It is a tomb-world, where everything that happens has already happened, and where nothing can happen ever again.

But all this is no more than an evil spell cast by a fallacious description, the product of a self-critical gaze that is at the same time self-paralyzing. It is always possible to get out of a double bind. It requires no more than a motion, a counterparadox, capable of questioning the premises of a game that has gotten stuck. At times all it needs is some little thing, a little nudge from outside, like the bunch of gladioluses, "beautiful and untidy," which Bateson brought into the meticulously ordered house of one of his patients, whose mother tolerated only plastic flowers that would never wilt.[37] All that is needed is a little fissure that grants us a viewpoint external to the universe in which we are locked. The new might be conceived in a manner unlike that of the differential logic of the modern. But to do so, we must come up with something that has not already been thought. We must reopen the realm of the possible locked up in the vision of history as labyrinth. We must free ourselves from the epochal misrepresentation that characterizes postmodern common sense. This is the gamble that we must now take. This is the challenge facing art and thought today.

37. Bateson 1972, p. 198.

BIBLIOGRAPHY

Adorno, Theodor W. 1967. *Ohne Leitbild. Parva aesthetica.* Frankfurt: Suhrkamp. Translated into Italian as *Parva aesthetica.* Milan: Feltrinelli, 1979.

——. 1991. *The Culture Industry: Selected Essays on Mass Culture,* edited with an introduction by J. M. Bernstein, 85–92. London: Routledge.

Adorno, Theodor W. and Max Horkheimer. 1947. *Dialectic of Enlightenment.* Translated by John Cumming. New York: Continuum, 1982.

Agamben, Giorgio. 1998. *Quel che resta di Auschwitz.* Turin: Bollati Boringhieri.

Alfano Miglietti, Francesca. 1966. *Identità mutanti.* Genoa: Costa and Nolan.

Anceschi, Luciano. 1962. *Le poetiche del Novecento in Italia: Studio fenomenologico e storia delle poetiche.* Milan: Marzorati.

Ardemagni, Marco. 1992. "L'attimo fuggente." In Bufala Cosmica. *Rime tempestose.* Milan: Sperling and Kupfer.

Aristotle. 1947. *Poetics.* Translated by Ingram Bywater in *Introduction to Aristotle,* edited by Richard McKeon. New York: The Modern Library.

Astruc, Alexandre. 1948. "The Birth of a New Avant-Garde: La caméra-stylo." Translated by Peter Graham in *The New Wave,* edited by James Monaco. New York: Oxford University Press, 1976.

Bachelard, Gaston. 1960. *La Poétique de la Rêverie.* Translated by Daniel Russell as *The Poetics of Reverie.* New York: Orion Press, 1969.

Bakhtin, Mikhail. 1975. *Voprosy literatury i estetiki.* Translated by Caryl Emerson as *The Dialogic Imagination. Four Essays,* edited by M. Holquist. Austin: University of Texas Press, 1981.

——. 1979. *Estetika slovesnogo tvorestva.* Translated by Vern W. McGee as *Speech Genres and Other Late Essays,* edited by Caryl Emerson and Michael Holquist. Austin: University of Texas Press, 1986.

Ballestra, Silvia. 1994. *Gli orsi*. Milan: Feltrinelli.

Barth, John. 1967. "The Literature of Exhaustion." *The Atlantic Monthly* 220 (August 1967): 29–34.

Barthes, Roland. 1960. "Ecrivains et écrivant." Translated by Richard Howard as "Authors and Writers," in *Critical Essays*, 142–150. Evanston: Northwestern University Press, 1972.

———. 1966. "To Write, an Intransitive Verb?" English translation in Barthes 1989: 11–21.

———. 1968. "The Death of the Author." English translation in Barthes 1989: 49–55.

———. 1970. *S/Z*. Translated by Richard Miller. New York: Hill and Wang, 1974.

———. 1971. "From Work to Text." English translation in Barthes 1989: 56–64.

———. 1973. *The Pleasure of the Text*. Translated by Richard Miller. Oxford: Basil Blackwell, 1990.

———. 1975. *Roland Barthes/by Roland Barthes*. Translated by Richard Howard. New York: Noonday Press, 1989.

———. 1981. *Camera Lucida: Reflections on Photography*. Translated by Richard Howard. New York: Hill and Wang.

———. 1989. *The Rustle of Language*. Translated by Richard Howard. Berkeley: University of California Press, 1989.

Bataille, George. 1936–1939. *Acéphale*. Translated into Italian as *La congiura sacra*. Turin: Bollati Boringhieri, 1997.

Bateson, Gregory. 1972. *Steps to an Ecology of Mind*. San Francisco: Chandler.

Baudelaire, Charles. 1860. *Les paradis Artificiels*. Translated by Stacy Diamond as *Artificial Paradises*. Secaucus, N.J.: Carol, 1996.

———. 1863. *Le Peintre de la Vie Moderne*. Translated and edited by Jonathan Mayne as *The Painter of Modern Life and Other Essays*. London: Phaidon Press, 1995.

Bazin, Andrée. 1957. *Sur la "Politique des Auteurs."* Translated by Peter Graham as *Cahiers du Cinéma*, edited by Jim Hillier. Cambridge: Harvard University Press, 1985.

Beckett, Samuel. 1967. *No's Knife*. London: Calder and Boyar's.

———. 1970. *Le Dépeupleur*. Translated by the author as *The Lost Ones*. New York: Grove Press, 1972.

Bénabou, Marcel. 1986. *Pourquoi je n'ai écrit aucun des mes livres*. Translated by David Kornacker as *Why I Have Not Written Any of My Books*. Lincoln: University of Nebraska Press, 1998.

Benedetti, Carla. 1984. *La soggettività nel racconto. Proust e Svevo*. Naples: Liguori.

———. 1989. "Sui vincoli della comunicazione." In *Modi di attribuzione. Filosofia e teoria dei sistemi*, edited by R.Genovese, 119–184. Naples: Liguori.

———. 1990. "Il sublime e la non-arte." *Rivista di estetica* 36: 55–64.

———. 1991. "Sull'identità di genere di una letteratura senza generi." *Intersezioni* 1:125–34.

———. 1992. "Come comunichiamo sul mondo." In *Figure del paradosso. Filosofia e teoria dei sistemi 2*, edited by R. Genovese, 173–224. Naples: Liguori.

———. 1993. "Celati e le poetiche della grazia." *Rassegna Europea di Letteratura Italiana* 1:7–33.

——. 1994. " 'Amicizia'. Storia del tempo che non finisce." In *I "Sillabari" di Goffredo Parise*, edited by S. Perrella, 35–49. Naples: Guida.

——.1998. *Pasolini contro Calvino. Per una letteratura impura.* Turin: Bollati Boringhieri.

Benjamin, Walter. 1920. *Der Begriff der Kunstkritik in der deutschen Romantik.* Translated by David Lachterman, Howard Eiland, and Ian Balfour as *The Concept of Criticism in German Romanticism.* In Benjamin 1996, vol. 1, 116–200.

——. 1928. *Ursprung des deutschen Trauerspiels.* Translated by John Osborne as *The Origin of German Tragic Drama.* London: Verso, 1985.

——. 1929. "Robert Walser." Translated by Rodney Livingstone. In Benjamin 1996, vol. 2, 257–261.

——. 1936. *Das Kunstwerk im Zeitalter seiner technischen Reproduzierbarkeit, Zeitschrift für Sozial Forschung.* Translated by Harry Zohn as *The Work of Art in the Age of Mechanical Reproduction.* In Benjamin 1988: 217–251.

——. 1988. *Illuminations.* Translated by Harry Zohn with an introduction by Hannah Arendt. New York: Schocken Books, 1988.

——. 1996. *Selected Writings,* 4 vols., edited by Marcus Bullock and Michael W. Jennings. Cambridge: Belknap Press of Harvard University Press.

Benveniste, Emile. 1956. "La nature des pronoms." Translated as "The Nature of Pronouns." In Benveniste 1971: 217–222.

——. 1958. "De la subjectivité dans le language."Translated as "Subjectivity in Language." In Benveniste 1971: 223–230.

——. 1971. *Problems in General Linguistics.* Translated by Mary Elizabeth Meek. Coral Gables: University of Miami Press.

——. 1973. *Indo-European Language and Society. Summaries, table and index by Jean Lallot.* Translated by Elizabeth Palmer. Coral Gables: University of Miami Press.

Bettini, Filippo, and Roberto Di Marco. 1993. *Terza ondata: il nuovo movimento della scrittura in Italia.* Bologna: Synergon.

Binni, Walter. 1947. *La nuova poetica leopardiana.* Florence: Sansoni; n. ed., 1971.

——. 1963. *Poetica, critica e storia letteraria.* Bari: Laterza.

Blanchot, Maurice. 1955. *L'éspace littéraire.* Translated by Ann Smock as *The Space of Literature.* Lincoln: University of Nebraska Press, 1982.

——. 1959. *Le livre à venir.* Translated by Charlotte Mandell as *The Book to Come.* Stanford: Stanford University Press, 2003.

——. 1986. "Michel Foucault tel que je l'immagine." Translated by Jeffrey Mehlman as "Michel Foucault as I Imagine Him." In Foucault and Blanchot. *Maurice Blanchot—The Thought from Outside; Michel Foucault As I Imagine Him.* Translated by J. Mehlman. New York: Zone Books, 1987.

Bloom, Harold. 1973. *The Anxiety of Influence: A Theory of Poetry.* New York: Oxford University Press.

Booth, Wayne C. 1967. "Distance and Point-of-View: An Essay in Classification." In *The Theory of the Novel,* edited by Philip Stevick, 87–107. New York: The Free Press. Translated in *Poétique* 4 (1970): 511–524.

——. 1983a. *The Rhetoric of Fiction.* 2d ed. Chicago: University of Chicago Press.

——. 1983b. "Rhetorical Critics Old and New: The Case of Gérard Genette." In *Reconstructing Literature,* edited by L. Lerner, 123–141. Oxford: Blackwell.

Borges, Jorge Luis. 1970. *The Aleph and Other Stories*. Translated by Norman Thomas di Giovanni. New York: Dutton.

——. 1993. *Ficciones*. Translated by Norman Thomas di Giovanni. New York: Knopf.

Bourdieu, Pierre. 1992. *Les règles de l'art. Genése et structure du champ littéraire*. Translated by Susan Emanuel as *The Rules of Art: Genesis and Structure of the Literary Field*. Stanford: Stanford University Press, 1996.

Brioschi, Franco. 1983. *La mappa dell'impero. Problemi di teoria della letteratura*. Milan: Il Saggiatore.

Brolli, Daniele, ed. 1966. *Gioventù cannibale. La prima antologia italiana dell'orrore estremo*. Turin: Einaudi.

Bubner, Rüdiger. 1989. *Esthetische Erfahrung*. Frankfurt: Suhrkamp.

Buñuel, Luís. 1983. *My Last Sigh*. Translated by Abigail Israel. New York: Knopf.

Bürger, Peter. 1984. *Theory of the Avant-garde*. Translated by Michael Shaw. Minneapolis: University of Minnesota Press.

Calvino, Italo. 1980. *Una pietra sopra*. Translated by Patrick Creagh as *The Uses of Literature: Essays*. San Diego: Harcourt Brace Jovanovich, 1986.

——. 1984. "Comment j'ai écrit un des mes livres." *Actes sémiotiques-Documents* 6, in *La Bibliothèque Oulipienne*, vol. 2, Paris, Ramsay, 1987, pp. 25–44.

——. 1988. *Six Memos for the Next Millennium*. Cambridge: Harvard University Press.

——. 1991. *I libri degli altri: lettere 1947–1981*. Turin: Einaudi.

——. 1993. *If on a winter's night a traveller*. Translated by William Weaver. Toronto: Knopf.

Carchia, Gianni. 1983. *La legittimazione dell'arte. Studi sull'intellegibile estetico*. Naples: Guida.

Castel, Robert. 1994. " 'Problematization' as a Mode of Reading History." In *Foucault and the Writing of History*, edited by J. Goldstein, 236–252. Cambridge, Mass.: Blackwell.

Celati, Gianni. 1975. *Finzioni occidentali*. Turin: Einaudi, n. ed. 1986.

——, ed. 1992. *Narratori delle riserve*. Milan: Feltrinelli.

Chamarat, Gabrielle, and Alain Goulet, eds. 1996. *L'auteur*. Colloque de Cerisy-la-Salle (October 4–8, 1995). Caen: Press Universitaire de Caen.

Clair, Jean. 1983. *Considérations sur l'état des beaux-arts: critique de la modernité*. Paris: Gallimard. See also François Hauter, interview with Jean Clair and Mare Fumaroli, in *Le Figaro*, January 22, 1997.

——. 1997. *La responsabilité de l'artiste. Les avant-gardes entre terreur et raison*. Paris: Gallimard.

Clair, Jean and Marc Fumaroli. 1997. "Una requisitoria sull'arte contemporanea." *Il giornale dell'arte* 157. See also François Hauter, interview with Jean Clair and Marc Fumaroli, in *Le Figaro*, January 22, 1997.

Compagnon, Antoine. 1998. *Le démon de la théorie: littérature et sens commun*. Paris: Seuil.

Contini, Gianfranco. 1970. *Varianti e altra linguistica*. Turin: Einaudi.

Corti, Maria. 1976. *I principi della comunicazione letteraria*. Bompiani: Milan. Translated by Margherita Bogat and Allen Mandelbaum as *An Introduction to Literary Semiotics*. Bloomington: Indiana University Press, 1978.

Couturier, Maurice. 1995. *La figure de l'auteur.* Paris: Seuil.

Croce, Benedetto. 1902. *Estetica.* Translated by Douglas Ainslie as *Aesthetic as Science of Expression and General Linguistic.* Boston: Nonpareil Books, 1978.

———. 1936. *La poesia. Introduzione alla critica e storia della poesia e della letteratura.* Translated by Giovanni Gullace as *Benedetto Croce's Poetry and Literature: an Introduction to Its Criticism and History.* Carbondale: Southern Illinois University Press, 1981.

———. 1952. *Indagini su Hegel e schiarimenti filosofici.* Bari: Laterza.

Cudini, Piero. 1999. *Breve storia della letteratura itlaliana. Il Novecento.* Milan: Bompiani.

Danto, Arthur. 1992. *Beyond the Brillo Box: The Visual Arts in Post-Historical Perspective.* New York: Farrar Straus Giroux.

De Carli, Lorenzo. 1997. *Internet. Memoria e oblio.* Turin: Bollati Boringhieri.

D'Elia, Gianni. 1993. *Notte privata.* Turin: Einaudi.

Derrida, Jacques. 1972. *Positions.* Translated by Alan Bass. Chicago: University of Chicago Press, 1981.

———. 1986. *Parages.* Paris: Galilée.

Dick, Philip K. 1962. *The Man in the High Castle.* New York: Putnam.

Di Girolamo, Costanzo. 1978. *Critica della letterarietà.* Milan: Il Saggiatore.

Di Girolamo, Costanzo; Berardinelli, Alfonso; and Brioschi, Franco. 1986. *La ragione critica. Prospettive nello studio della letteratura.* Turin: Einaudi.

Doesburg, Theo Van. 1923. *What Is Dada?* Translated and edited by Michael White in *What Is Dada? And Other Writings.* London: Atlas Press, 2003.

D'Oria, Anna Grazia, ed. 1992. *Gruppo 93. Le tendenze attuali della poesia e della narrativa.* Lecce: Manni.

Eco, Umberto. 1962. *Opera aperta.* Translated by Anna Cancogni as *The Open Work.* Cambridge: Harvard University Press, 1989.

———. 1979. *Lector in fabula.* Milan: Bompiani.

———. 1990. *The Limits of Interpretation.* Bloomington: Indiana University Press, 1990.

Ferretti, Gian Carlo. 1994. *Il mercato delle lettere,* 2d reprint. Milan: Il Saggiatore.

Ferroni, Giulio. 1996. *Dopo la fine. Sulla condizione postuma della letteratura.* Turin: Einaudi.

Fish, Stanley. 1980. *Is There a Text in This Class? The Authority of Interpretative Communities.* Cambridge: Harvard University Press.

Foucault, Michel. 1961. *Histoire de la folie à l'âge classique.* Translated by Richard Howard as *Madness and Civilization: A History of Insanity in the Age of Reason.* New York: Pantheon Books, 1965.

———. 1963. *Raymond Roussel.* Translated by Charles Ruas in *Death and the Labyrinth: The World of Raymond Roussel.* Garden City, N.Y.: Doubleday, 1986.

———. 1966. "Fantasia of the Library." Translated by D. F. Bouchard and S. Simon in *Language, Counter-Memory, Practice,* edited by Donald F. Bouchard, 87–111. Ithaca: Cornell University Press, 1977.

———. 1969. "What Is an Author?" Translated by D. F. Bouchard and S. Simon in *Language, Counter-Memory, Practice,* edited by Donald F. Bouchard, 113–138. Ithaca: Cornell University Press, 1977.

——. 1971. "L'ordre du discours." Translated by A. M. Sheridan Smith in *The Archaeology of Knowledge*. New York: Pantheon Books, 1972.

——. 1994. *Dits et écrits*. 4 vols., edited by D. Denfert e F. Ewald. Paris: Gallimard.

Frasca, Gabriele. 1984. *Rame*. Milan: Corpo 10.

——. 1988. *Cascando. Tre studi su Samuel Beckett*. Naples: Liguori.

——. 1992. *La furia della sintassi. La sestina in Italia*. Naples: Bibliopolis.

——. 1995. *Lime*. Turin: Einaudi.

Frixione, Marcello. 1992. *Diottrie*. Manni: Lecce.

Gadamer, Hans-Georg. 1960. *Wahrheit und Methode. Grundzüge einer philosophischen Hermeneutik*. Translated by J. Weinsheimer and D. B. Marshall as *Truth and Method*, 2d ed. New York: Continuum, 1994.

Gadda, Carlo Emilio. 1991. *Saggi giornali favole e altri scritti*. 2 vols., edited by D. Isella. Milan: Garzanti.

Genette, Gérard. 1972. *Figure III*. Translated by Alan Sheridan as *Figures of Literary Discourse*. New York: Columbia University Press, 1982.

——. 1979. *Introduction à l'architexte*. Translated by Jane E. Lewin as *The Architext: An Introduction*. Berkeley: University of California Press, 1992.

——. 1982. *Palimpsestes: la littérature au second degré*. Translated by Channa Newman and Claude Doubinsky as *Palimpsests: Literature in the Second Degree*. Lincoln: University of Nebraska Press, 1997.

——. 1983. *Nouveau discours du récit*. Translated by Jane E. Lewin as *Narrative Discourse Revisited*. Ithaca: Cornell University Press, 1988.

——. 1987. *Seuils*. Translated by Jane E. Lewin as *Paratexts: Thresholds of Interpretation*. Cambridge: Cambridge University Press, 1997.

——. 1991. *Fiction et diction*. Translated by Catherine Porter as *Fiction and Diction*. Ithaca: Cornell University Press, 1993.

——. 1994. *L'oeuvre de l'art I. Immanence et transcendance*. Translated by G. M. Goshgarian as *The Work of Art*. Ithaca: Cornell University Press, 1997.

——. 1997. *L'oeuvre de l'art II. La rélation esthétique*. Paris: Seuil. Translated by G. M. Goshgarian as *The Aesthetic Relation*. Ithaca: Cornell University Press, 1999.

Genovese, Rino. 1989. "L'eredità del romanticismo. Codice dell'arte e codice artistico." *Rivista di estetica* 31.

Goffman, Erving. 1959. *The Presentation of Self in Everyday Life*. Garden City, N.Y.: Doubleday. Translated into Italian with an introduction by Pier Paolo Giglioli as *La vita quotidiana come rappresentazione*. Bologna: Il Mulino, 1969.

——. 1981. *Forms of Talk*. Philadelphia: University of Pennsylvania Press, 1981. Translated into Italian with an introduction by Pier Paolo Giglioli as *Forme del parlare*. Bologna: Il Mulino, 1987.

Grice, H. Paul. 1967. "Logic and Conversation" (William James Lectures, Harvard University). Typescript. A revised version in *Studies in the Way of Words*, 3–143. Cambridge: Harvard University Press, 1989.

Hamburger, Käte. 1957. *Die Logik der Dichtung*. Translated by Marilynn J. Rose as *The Logic of Literature*. Bloomington: Indiana University Press, 1973.

Hegel, Georg Wilhelm Friedrich. 1836. *Vorlesungen über die Ästhetik*. Translated into Italian as *Estetica*, edited by N. Merker. Turin: Einaudi, 1976.

——. 1970. *On Art, Religion, Philosophy.* Translated by Bernard Bosanquet. New York: Harper Torchbooks.

Hirsch, Eric D. 1967. *Validity in Interpretation.* New Haven: Yale University Press. Translated into Italian as *Teoria dell'interpretazione e critica letteraria.* Bologna: Il Mulino, 1987.

Iser, Wolfgang. 1974. *The Implied Reader.* Baltimore: Johns Hopkins University Press.

——. 1978. *The Act of Reading: A Theory of Aesthetic Response.* Baltimore: Johns Hopkins University Press.

Hoy, David C. 1978. *The Critical Circle: Literature, History, and Philosophical Hermeneutics.* Berkeley: University of California Press.

Husserl, Edmund. 1966. *Zur Phänomenologie des inneren Zeitbewusstsein* (1893–1917). Translated by John Barnett Brough as *On the Phenomenology of the Consciousness of Internal Time (1893–1917).* Boston: Kluwer, 1991.

Jakobson, Roman. 1921. "On Realism and Art." In *Readings in Russian Poetics,* edited by Ladislav Matejka and Krystyna Pomorska, 38–56. Cambridge: MIT Press, 1971.

——. 1958. "Linguistics and Poetics." In *The Structuralists: from Marx to Lévi-Strauss,* edited by Richard T. DeGeorge and Fernande M. DeGeorge, 85–122. Garden City, N.Y.: Anchor Books, 1972.

Jauss, Hans Robert. 1970. "Theorie des Gattungen und Literatur des Mittelalters." Translated by Timothy Bahti as "Theory of Genres and Medieval Literature." In *Toward an Aesthetic of Reception,* 76–108. Minneapolis: University of Minnesota Press, 1982.

——. 1972. *Kleine Apologie der ästhetische Erfahrung.* Konstanz: Konstanzer Universitätsreden.

——. 1982. *Ästhetische Erfahrung und literarische Hermeneutick.* Translated by Michael Shaw as *Aesthetic Experience and Literary Hermeneutics.* Minneapolis: University of Minnesota Press, 1982.

——. 1993. "Teoria della ricezione e ermeneutica oggi." An Interview with Hans Robert Jauss by Luca Farulli and Georg Maag. *Iride* 10, 61–75.

Kant, Immanuel. 1790. *Kritik der Urteilskraft.* Translated by J. H. Bernard as *Critique of Judgment.* New York: Hafner, 1951.

Kosuth, Joseph. 1966–1990. *Art after Philosophy and After,* edited by Gabriele Guercio. Cambridge: MIT Press, 1991.

Kristeva, Julia. 1975. *La révolution du language poétique. L'avant-garde à la fin du XIXème siècle: Lautréamont et Mallarmé.* Translated by Margaret Waller as *Revolution in Poetic Language.* New York: Columbia University Press, 1984.

Lacan, Jacques. 1977. *Écrits: A Selection.* Translated by Alan Sheridan. New York: Norton.

Landow, George P. 1992. *Hypertext: the Convergence of Contemporary Critical Theory and Technology.* Baltimore: Johns Hopkins University Press.

La Porta, Filippo. 1995. *La nuova narrativa italiana. Travestimenti e stili di fine secolo.* Turin: Bollati Boringhieri.

Lotman, Jurij. 1970. *Struktura chudozestvennogo teksta.* Translated by Gail Lenhoff and Ronald Vroon as *The Structure of the Artistic Text.* Ann Arbor: University of Michigan, Department of Slavic Languages and Literatures, 1977.

Luhmann, Niklas. 1984. *Soziale Systeme*. Frankfurt a. M: Suhrkamp. Translated by John Bednarz as *Social Systems*. Stanford: Stanford University Press, 1995.

Macrì, Teresa. 1996. *Il corpo postorganico*. Genoa: Costa and Nolan.

Magrelli, Valerio. 1990. *Profilo del Dada*. Rome: Lucarini.

Malraux, André. 1951. *Les Voix du silence*. Paris: Gallimard.

Manganelli, Giorgio. 1969. *Nuovo commento*. Turin: Einaudi.

——. 1994. *Il rumore sottile della prosa*, edited by Paola Italia. Milan: Adelphi.

Marinetti, Filippo Tommaso. 1976. *Teoria e invenzione futurista*, edited by Luciano De Maria. Milan: Mondadori. Partial translation by Robert Brain in *Futurist Manifestoes*, edited and with an introduction by Umbro Apollonio. Boston: MFA Publications, 2001.

Marquard, Odo. 1989. *Aesthetica und anaesthetica: philosophische Überlegungen*. Paderborn: F. Schöningh, 1989.

Medvedev, Pavel Nikolaevich. 1978. *The Formal Method in Literary Scholarship: a Critical Introduction to Sociological Poetics*. Translated by Albert J. Wehrle. Baltimore: Johns Hopkins University Press.

Moresco, Antonio. 1997. *Lettere a nessuno*. Turin: Bollati Boringhieri.

——. 1999. *Il vulcano. Scritti critici e visionari*. Turin: Bollati Boringhieri.

Mukařovský, Jan. 1966. *Studie z estetiky*. Translated by Mark E. Suino as *Aesthetic Function, Norm and Value as Social Facts*. Ann Arbor: Dept. of Slavic Languages and Literatures, University of Michigan, 1970.

Nietzsche, Friedrich W. 1874. *Vom Nutzen und Nachteil der Historie für das Leben*. Translated by Adrian Collins as *The Use and Abuse of History*. New York: Macmillan, 1987.

Orlando, Francesco. 1971. *Lettura freudiana della "Phèdre."* Translated by Charmaine Lee as *Toward a Freudian Theory of Literature: With an analysis of Racine's Phèdre*. Baltimore: Johns Hopkins University Press, 1978.

——. 1973. *Per una teoria freudiana della letteratura*. Turin: Einaudi.

——. 1982. *Illuminismo e retorica freudiana*. Turin: Einaudi.

Ottonieri, Tommaso. 1984. *Conjugativo*. Milan: Corpo 10.

——. 1994. "Parabole di posizionamento." *Allegoria* 18: 129–138.

——. 1995. "Il battito del verso," in *La parola ritrovata*, edited by G. Siçea and M. I. Gaeta. Padua: Marisilio.

——. 1998. *Elegia sanremese*. Milan Bompiani.

OuLiPo. 1973. *La littérature potentielle*. Paris: Gallimard.

——. 1981. *Atlas de littérature potentielle*. Paris: Gallimard.

Pareyson, Luigi. 1954. *Estetica. Teoria della formatività*. Milan: Bompiani.

Pasolini, Pier Paolo. 1975. *Trilogia della vita: "Il Decameron," "I racconti di Canterbury," "Il Fiore delle Mille e una notte,"* edited by G. Gattei. Milan: Mondadori, 1995.

——. 1992. *Petrolio*. Translated by Ann Goldstein. New York: Pantheon Books, 1997.

Paz, Octavio. 1985. *Apariencia desnuda: la obra de Marcel Duchamp*. México, D.F.: Ediciones Era.

Perec, Georges. 1969. *La disparition*. Translated by Gilbert Adair as *A void*. London: Harvill, 1994.

——. 1978. *La vie, mode d'emploie*. Translated by David Bellos as *Life, a User's Manual*. Boston: Godine, 1987.

Pessoa, Fernando. 1979. *Una sola moltitudine*, edited by Antonio Tabucchi and Maria del Lancastre. Milan: Adelphi.

Pingaud, Bernard. 1977. "La non-fonction de l'écrivain." *L'Arc* 70.

Proust, Marcel. 1971. *Contre Sainte-Beuve*. Translated by Sylvia Townsend in *On Art and Literature. 1896–1919*, with a new introduction by Terence Kilmartin. New York: Carroll & Graf, 1984.

———. 1974. *Contro Sainte-Beuve*. Italian edition by Mariolina Bertini. In *Scritti mondani e letterari*. Turin: Einaudi.

Raboni, Giovanni. 1986. *Canzonette mortali*. Milan: Crocetti.

———. 1993. *Ogni terzo pensiero*. Milan: Mondadori.

Riegl, Alois. 1901. *Die spätromische Kunstindustrie nach den Funden in Österreich-Ungarn*. Translated by Rolf Winkes as *Late Roman Art Industry*. Rome: Giorgio Bretschneider, 1985.

Ropars, Marie-Claire, and Pierre Sorlin. 1990. "Voies filmiques pour un procès d'auteur." *Hors cadre* 8: 23–31.

Roscioni, Gian Carlo. 1985. *L'arbitrio letterario. Uno studio su Raymond Roussel*. Turin: Einaudi.

Roussel, Raymond. 1935. *Comment j'ai écrit certaines de mes livres*. Paris: Pauvert, 1963.

Salabelle, Maurizio. 1992. *Un assistente inaffidabile*. Turin: Bollati Boringhieri.

Sartre, Jean-Paul. 1971. *L'idiot de la famille. Gustave Flaubert de 1821 à 1857*. Translated by Carol Cosman as *The Family Idiot: Gustave Flaubert, 1821–1857*. Chicago: University of Chicago Press, 1981.

Schaeffer, Jean-Marie. 1989. *Qu'est-ce qu'un genre littéraire?* Paris: Seuil.

Schiller, Friedrich. 1793. "Uber Amnut und Wurde." Translated by George Gregory as "On Grace and Dignity." In *Friedrich Schiller: Poet of Freedom*, vol. 2, edited by The Schiller Institute, 337–393. New York: Farrar, Straus & Giroux, 1976.

Schlegel, Friedrich von. 1800. *Gespräch über die Poesie*. Translated by Ernst Behler and Roman Struc as "Dialogue on Poetry." In *German Romantic Criticism*, edited by A. Leslie Wilson, 84–133. New York: Continuum, 1982.

Schulz-Buschaus, Ulrich. 1995. "Critica e recupero dei generi. Considerazioni sul 'moderno' e sul 'postmoderno.' " *Problemi* (January–April): 4–15.

Scialoja, Toti. 1994. *Rapide e lente amnesie*. Venice: Marsilio.

Segre, Cesare. 1974. *Le strutture e il tempo*. Turin: Einaudi.

———. 1979. "Generi." In *Enciclopedia Einaudi*, vol. 6, 564–585. Turin: Einaudi.

———. 1993. *Notizie dalla crisi. Dove va la critica letteraria?* Turin: Einaudi.

Shklovsky, Victor. 1929a. "Isjusstvo kak priëm." Translated by Lea T. Lemon and Marion J. Reis as "Art as Technique." In *Contemporary Literary Criticism: Literary and Cultural Studies*, edited by R. Davis and R. Schleifer, 52–63. New York: Longman, 1986.

———. 1929b. *O teorii prozy*. Translated by Benjamin Sher as *The Theory of Prose*. Elmwood Park, Ill.: Dalkey Archive Press, 1990.

———. 1976. *O teorii prozy*. Translated into Italian as *Teoria della prosa*. Turin: Einaudi, 1976.

Sollers, Philippe. 1968. *L'écriture et l'experience des limites*. Translated by Philip Barnab with David Hayman as *Writing and the Experience of Limits*. New York: Columbia University Press, 1983.

Spinazzola, Vittorio, ed. 1999. *Tirature '99. I libri del secolo: letture novecentesche per gli anni duemila*. Milan: Il Saggiatore.

Stempel, Wolf-Dieter. 1979. "Aspects génériques de la reception." *Poétique* 39: 353–362.

Tabucchi, Antonio. 1997. *La testa perduta di Damasceno Monteiro*. Translated by J. C. Patrick as *The Missing Head of Damasceno Monteiro*. New York: New Directions, 1999.

Tel Quel. 1968. *Théorie d'ensemble*. Paris: Seuil.

——. 1974. *Scrittura e rivoluzione, antologia di scritti di "Tel Quel,"* edited by R. Silva. Milan: Mazzotta.

Todorov, Tzvetan. 1984. *Critique de la critique. Un roman d'apprentissage*. Translated by Catherine Porter as *Literature and Its Theorists. A Personal View of Twentieth-Century Criticism*. Ithaca: Cornell University Press, 1987.

Tondelli, Pier Vittorio. 1985. *Rimini*. Milan: Bompiani.

——. 1989. *Camere separate*. Milan: Bompiani. Translated by Simon Pleasance as *Separate Rooms*. London: Serpent's Tail, 1992.

Tynianov, Jurij. 1929a. "O literaturnoj evoljucii." Translated as "On Literary Evolution." In *Readings in Russian Poetics*, edited by Ladislav Matejka and Krystyna Pomorska, 66–78. Cambridge: MIT Press, 1971.

——. 1929b. *Arckaisty i novatory*. Leningrad: Priboj. Translated into Italian as *Avanguardia e tradizione*. Introduction by Victor Shklovsky. Bari: Dedalo, 1968.

Tzara, Tristan. 1918. "Dada Manifesto." Translated in *The Dada Painters and Poets: An Anthology*, edited by Robert Motherwell. Boston: G. K. Hall, 1981.

——. 1920. "Manifeste sur l'amour faible et l'amour amer." Translated by Ralph Manheim as "Dada Manifesto on Feeble Love and Bitter Love." In *The Dada Painters and Poets: An Anthology*, edited by Robert Motherwell, 86–98. Boston: G. K. Hall, 1981.

Valduga, Patrizia. 1989. *Medicamenta*. Turin: Einaudi.

Valéry, Paul. 1952. "Première leçon du cours de poétique." Translated by Jackson Matthews as "The Course in Poetics: First Lesson." In *The Creative Process*, edited by Brewster Ghiselin, 92–105. New York: Mentor, 1952.

Virno, Paolo. 1999. *Il ricordo del presente. Saggio sul tempo storico*. Turin: Bollati Boringhieri.

Wilson, Leslie A., ed. 1982. *German Romantic Criticism*. New York: Continuum.

Wimsatt, William K., and Monroe C. Beardsley, 1946. "The Intentional Fallacy." In *The Verbal Icon: Studies in the Meaning of Poetry*, edited by William K. Wimsatt, 3–18. Lexington: University of Kentucky Press, 1954.

Winckelmann, Johann Joachim. 1755. *Gedancken über die Nachahmung der griechischen Werke in der Malerei und Bildhauerkunst*. Translated by Helfriede Heyer and Roger C. Norton as *Reflections on the Imitation of Greek Works in Painting and Sculpture*. La Salle, Ill.: Open Court, 1987.

Note: *illus.* indicates the section of photographs following page 110.

abstract expressionism, 163–64, 175, 186
Accetto, Torquato, 180
action painting. *See* abstract expressionism
Adorno, Theodor, 1, 24, 182
    aesthetics of, 42n27
    culture industry and, 104–7, 156–57, 187
    on lyric poetry, 190
    on originality, 107n37
advertising, 89, 148
aesthetics, 42–45, 139–47, 173–74
    futurist, *illus.*
    Genette on, 141
    Kant's, 49, 121n13, 137n2, 139, 171
    "material," 147n17
    "negative," 42n27
    poetics and, 14, 24–25, 142
    politics and, *illus.*, 148
    reenchantment and, 187
    romanticism and, 35, 43, 140n7, 169,
        182, 206–8
    sublime and, 183
    See also aisthesis; poetics
aesthetic value. *See* valorization
Affinati, Eraldo, 104

aisthesis, 36, 41–44, 48, 140–42, 145
Alberti, Leon Battista, *illus.*
Aleramo, Sibilla, *illus.*
alienation. *See* estrangement
allegory, 30, 150
alphabetization, 175–76
Anceschi, Luciano, 29n6
antinovel, 34, 101
antiphrasis, 41
antonomasia, 199
apocryphal effect, *illus.,* 17, 18, 21, 22,
    182–87, 203
"architextuality" (Genette), 86, 203
Ariosto, Ludovico, 83, 89, 96, 98–99,
    126–27
Aristotle, 93, 138
    on music, 145
    Poetics of, 38, 84, 90, 91, 142–46
Arp, Hans, 174–75
art
    aesthetics and, 174
    autonomy of, 61–62, 121, 130
    avant-garde, 43
    banalization of, 156–57
    "beautiful," 141
    conceptual, *illus.,* 39, 43–48, 153, 157
    death of, 36, 44, 141, 185–99, 202, 211
    definitions of, 136, 138–40, 154–55

genres of, 90
Hegel on, 35–37, 136, 140–41, 144–45,
    167, 196
"idea" of, 29n5
institution of, 157n29
labeling of, 30–34
"language" of, 174
performance, *illus.*, 139
"posthumous," 44
reflective. *See* reflective art
"science" of, 37
self-referential, 128–32, 207
stochastic, 164
techniques of, 116–19, 123, 132–33, 164
theory of, 43
unity of, 139
verbal, 90, 185
See also aesthetics; poetry
art films. *See* auteur films
artistic freedom, 164, 176–77, 181–82,
    199–200
Hegel on, 167
responsibilities of, 61–62
Sartre on, 192, 194
Tzara on, 173
artistic valorization. *See* valorization
Astruc, Alexandre, 79
"aura," 19n17, 24, 187
auteur films, 24, 78–82
See also films
author
biographical details of, 14, 60
as copyist, 8, 194–95, 201–3
death of, 5, 8, 14–15, 49–54, 159, 188,
    191–203, 211–12
definitions of, 58
disappearance of, 169
"empirical," 57, 60, 69
etymology of, 194
"eye" of, 158–61
fetishes of, *illus.*, 25
functions of, 10, 15, 35, 60–61, 152, 160
genesis of, 19n17
as genius, 26–56, 185–86, 191–94, 198
genre and, 11, 77–78, 83–84, 153
as guardian of meaning, 67–70
ideal/implied, 13–14, 19, 57, 59–68, 72
image of, 9, 51–56, 65–67, 159, 183, 195
labeling of, 30–34
malaise of, 21–22, 159
merchandising of, 8–10, 23–25, 75
naming of, 58–59, 71
problematization of, 17, 19–20, 184–85
role of, 83, 158, 190, 194–95
sign of, *illus.*, 71, 186

strategies of, 9, 48–51, 195
text and, 2–4, 11–16, 77–78, 200, 204
war against, 16–20
writer's block and, 3, 46
writer versus, 8, 192, 197–98
authored versus generic text, 11, 77–78,
    83–110, 153
authorialism, 8–12, 16–17, 20–22, 51, 75
automatic writing, 163, 170, 175
autonomy, artistic, 61–62, 121, 130
"autotelism" (Todorov), 121, 148, 149
avant-garde, 30–31
convention and, 99, 114
craftsmanship and, 61
dadaism and, 21
"neo," 29n6, 34, 53, 190
poetics of, 34–35, 40–41, 125, 149, 156,
    197
postmodernism and, 189–90
Shklovsky on, 125, 171–72
See also specific groups, e.g., dadaism
axiology. *See* valorization

Bacchylides, 130
Bachelard, Gaston, 205
Bakhtin, Mikhail, 30, 64
on aesthetics, 147
on author intentionality, 63n16
dialogism of, 7, 131
genre and, 105, 111–13, 126
on indirect discourse, 63
"novelization of literature" of, 81, 109
Baldaccini, César, 187n48
Balestrini, Nanni, 29n6, 31, 164
Ballestra, Silvia, 32n13
Balzac, Honoré de, *illus.*
Baricco, A., 102n25
Barilli, Renato, 29n6
Barth, John, 45, 47, 190
Barthes, Roland, *illus.,* 9, 191, 201
    Camera Lucida of, 54–55
on death of the author, 5, 50–54, 192,
    194–95, 197
on narcissism, 131
Pleasure of the Text of, 55, 200
on "provocative" language, 206–7
Bataille, Georges, 196
Bateson, Gregory, 20n21, 210–12
Baudelaire, Charles, 62, 105, 193n9
Bazin, André, 79–80
Beckett, Samuel, 5n3, 56, 99, 178
Bénabou, Marcel, 165
Benigni, Roberto, 104
Benjamin, Walter

on allegory, 30
on aura, 19n17, 24
on defining art, 153n25
on genre, 114
on intentionality, 183
on Proust, 197
on romanticism, 35
on subjectivity, 184
Benveniste, Emile, 5, 51–52, 194n12
Bertini, Mariolina, 58
Beuys, Joseph, *illus.*
Binni, Walter, 29n5
bipolar disorders, 203
Blanchot, Maurice, 5
  on *désoeuvrement*, 159, 196–97, 199
  on Foucault, 15n15
  on genre, 92, 94, 96, 109
Blanco, Matte, 148n19
Blisset, Luther (pseudonym), 7n6, 8–9,
  75
Blok, Aleksandr, 133–34
Bloom, Harold, 131
Boiardo, Matteo, 126
Booth, Wayne, 57, 62–67
Borges, Jorge Luis, 26–27, 154
  Ficciones of, 44–48, 197–98, 201–2, 204
  on memory, 200
  on originality, 47
bound writing, 17, 22, 50, 103, 161–69,
  175–76, 182, 185
Bourdieu, Pierre, 62n11
brand name. *See* merchandising
Breton, André, 173, 206, 210
bricolage, 8, 194–95
Brunelleschi, *illus.*
Buñuel, Luis, 181, 206, 209–10
Bürger, Peter, 164n7
Burroughs, William, 164, 193
Butor, Michel, 165

Cage, John, 162–63
Cahiers du Cinéma (journal), 79–80
Calvino, Italo, 27, 61, 64, 114, 155, 186–87
  "authorial experience" of, 133
  on authorship, *illus.*, 17, 53–54, 184, 209
  Borges and, 46, 47
  Castle of Crossed Destinies of, 166
  Comment j'ai écrit un de mes livres of,
    165–66
  "Cybernetics and Ghosts" of, 59
  If on a winter's night a traveler of, 9, 27,
    47, 53, 67, 101, 160, 165n13, 167
  Marcovaldo of, 107–8
  on originality, 116, 184

as Oulipian, 161n3, 167
Palomar of, 183
Pavese and, 135
poetics of, 34
on readers, 9, 53
"Sign in Space" of, 116, 130, 158–60
on style, 66–67
Camus, Renaud, 165
"cannibal" fiction, 28, 31, 103, 104, 106
canon, literary, 84–85, 96, 99, 125–26
  exploitation of, 124
  freedom from, 167–68, 173
  Kristiansen on, 123–24
  novels and, 112–13
Carrà, Carlo, 43
Carver, Raymond, 31–32
Castel, Robert, 19n18
categories. *See* classification
catharsis, 38, 42, 56, 143, 196–97
Celati, Gianni, 27–28, 33, 34, 61, 159, 183,
  185
censorship, 61–62
Cervantes, Miguel de, 112–13, 126–27,
  197–98, 201–4
César (artist), 187n48
chance
  intentionality and, 161–64, 171, 174–75,
    186
  "mathematization" of, 164
choice, 17, 49–50, 159
  postmodernism and, 184–86
  recipes for, 161–64, 167–77, 185
  unconscious, 163
  valorization of, 182–83
cinema. *See* films
Clair, Jean, 32n12, 61
classification, 30–34, 141, 150–51
  Genette on, 138
  genre and, 84–85
  hidden, 100
  techniques and, 118
claustrophilia, 199–205
coherence, hypothesis of, 70
comedy, 90, 138, 142–43
commercialization. *See* merchandising
Compagnon, Antoine, 12n13, 69–70
conceptual art, *illus.*, 39, 43–48, 153, 157
Conte, Giuseppe, 30n8
Contini, Gianfranco, 30, 124n17
Coover, Robert, 32
copyist, author as, 8, 194–95, 201–3
copyright, 9
Corti, Maria, 72–73, 86, 87, 94, 126–27
Couturier, Maurice, 15, 64n18, 191
creativity. *See* originality

criticism
  film, 14, 82n44
  genre, 111–13
  intertexuality and, 205
  liberation of, 199–200
  poetics and, *illus.*, 31–32, 146
  Proustian, 58
  reader-oriented, 19–20, 53–54, 69
  romantic, 29n5
  self, 21
  "Western," 61
Croce, Benedetto, 29n5, 40
  on genre, 84–86, 92, 126, 139
  on poetics, 35–36
  on unity of art, 139
cubism, 171, 173
Cudini, Piero, 179n39
cult movies, 81
culture industry, 8–10, 23–25, 104–7,
  156–57, 187
"cunning of tradition" (Jauss), 98–99
cutup method, 164
cyperpunk fiction, 106n35

dadaism, 21, 153, 161, 163, 169–76, 186,
  206
Daniel, Arnaut, 179n38
D'Annunzio, Gabriele, 124
Dante Alighieri, 177, 178
Danto, Arthur, 36n21, 208n33
De Amicis, Edmondo, 166
death-of-author myth, 5, 8, 14–15, 49–54,
  159, 188, 191–203, 211–12
De Carli, Lorenzo, 7n6
deconstructionism, 6, 69, 201–2
De Dominicis, Gino, 32n12
defamiliarization, 118, 120, 122, 125–26
D'Elia, Gianni, 179
De Longis, Franco, 2n1
De Quincey, Thomas, 193
Derrida, Jacques, 5–6, 87n7, 200–202, 205
Derzhavin, Gavrila, 122
désoeuvrement, 159, 196–97, 199
deutero-learning, 20, 21, 205–7, 209
dialogism, 7, 131
diaries, 145–46
Dick, Philip K., 96, 163n5, 211
Dickinson, Emily, 60
Di Girolamo, Costanzo, 70n29, 149n20
Dilthey, Wilhelm, 6
discourse theory, 57, 61–64
dithyrambic poetry, 142–43
Doesburg, Theo van, 173n24
Duchamp, Marcel, *illus.*, 43, 162, 163, 174

  bottle rack of, 10, 151
  Fountain of, 156
Durante, Lorenzo, 180

Easton Ellis, Bret, 32
Eco, Umberto, 28–29, 38, 70
  Limits of Interpretation of, 69
  Name of the Rose of, 101, 108
  on text, 68
  Varaldo and, 168n20
Einstein, Albert, 134
Elkin, Stanley, 32
Emilia, Reggio, 31, 32
Enlightenment, 48–49, 85
epic, 75, 90, 116, 138, 152
  Ariosto and, 126–27
  Aristotle and, 142–43
  oral tradition and, 185
epigonism, 8, 23, 125, 132, 198–99
  Borges on, 47, 204
  Calvino on, 209
  death of author and, 194, 202
  innovation and, 209–12
  internalized, 194–96
  ironic, 202–3
  Nietzsche on, 200n22
epistemological breaks, 201, 205
Ernst, Max, 206
estrangement, 42, 120, 122, 130, 152
exhaustion, literature of, 45, 47, 119–23,
  190–91
existentialism, 192, 194
expectations
  horizon of, 85, 93, 98n18, 101, 122
  structures of, 83n1
expressionism, 42, 152
  abstract, 163–64, 175, 186
  dadaism and, 171, 173
  neo, 182
  poetics of rupture and, 30

Faulkner, William, 32, 79
Ferroni, Giulio, 36n21
fetishization, *illus.*, 25
Filippini, Enrico, 29n6
films, 16, 146, 153
  auteur, 24, 78–82
  criticism of, 82n44
  genre, 80–82
  Holocaust, 103–4
Fish, Stanley, 70n29, 149n20, 150–51
Flaubert, Gustave, 64
  Bouvard et Pécuchet of, 194–95, 202

censorship of, 62
Dictionnaire des idées réçues of, 175n28, 195n14
Foucault, Michel
  Blanchot on, 15n15
  Histoire de la folie of, 196n16
  on problematization, 19
  "What Is an Author?" of, 14–15, 56n49, 70–75
"found object," 161
Frasca, Gabriele, 102, 176–83
freedom. *See* artistic freedom
Freud, Sigmund, 192, 203
Frixione, Marcello, 180
futurism, *illus.*, 125, 171–73, 206, 209

Gadamer, Hans-Georg, 6, 12, 193n11
  on genius, 19, 50, 199
  on readers, 19–20
  relativism in, 68
  See also hermeneutics
Gadda, Carlo Emilio, 13, 71, 120n10
game(s)
  genius and, 50, 168–69
  Goffman on, 56
  writing recipes as, 164–65, 168–69
Gass, William, 32
generic versus authored text, 11, 77–78, 83–110, 153
Genette, Gérard, 43n28, 46, 62
  on authorship, 60n8
  on genre, 86–87, 89, 93, 138–41
  on narrator, 64
  Paratexts of, 77n41
  on poetics, 142n11
genius, 26–56, 185–86, 191–94, 198
  chance and, 171, 174–75
  Gadamer on, 19, 50, 199
  as game, 168–69
  Hegel on, 193, 199
  irony and, 193
  Kant on, 49
  romanticism and, 193n10
Genovese, Rino, 137n2
genre(s), 11–12, 39, 83–110, 137–39, 151–52
  Aristotle on, 144–45
  artificial, 103, 166–68
  author and, 11, 77–78, 83–84, 153
  Bakhtin on, 105, 111–13, 126
  Benjamin on, 114
  Blanchot on, 92, 94, 96, 109
  cinematic, 80–82
  of consumption, 106n36
  Corti on, 86, 94

Croce on, 84–86, 92, 126, 139
  freedom from, 167, 173
  functions of, 84–90, 97
  Genette on, 86–87, 89, 93, 138–41
  industrial, 97, 100, 103–7
  Jauss on, 85–87, 94, 96, 109, 127–28
  "open," 105
  postmodernism and, 92n12, 94, 101–2
  recycled, 101–3
  romanticism and, 85, 93, 138
  Schlegel on, 113, 207n32
  structuralism and, 85–86
genre criticism, 111–13
genre films, 80–82
Giuliani, Alfredo, 29n6
Goethe, Johann Wolfgang von, 112n2
Goffman, Erving, 56, 59
gothic fiction, 77, 95, 101
grace, poetics of, 17, 50, 176, 182–85, 187
Greimas, A.J., 165n13
Grice, H. Paul, 103n29
Gruppo, 63, 29, 31, 33, 101n23
Gruppo 93, 29–31
Guglielmi, Guido, 29n6

Hamburger, Käte, 140
Hawks, Howard Winchester, 80–81, 103
Hegel, Georg Wilhelm Friedrich, 39
  on art, 35–37, 136, 140–41, 144–45, 167, 196
  on genius, 193, 199
  on romanticism, 167n18, 193
hermeneutics, 68–69, 191
  desubjectivization and, 199
  Gadamer and, 6, 12, 19–20, 50, 68, 193n11, 199
  genre and, 85
  intending author of, 61
Hirsch, Eric D., 68
Hofstaedter, Douglas, 168
Holocaust, 103–4, 190
homosexuality, 60
Horace, 38
"horizon of expectations" (Jauss), 85, 93, 98n18, 101, 122
Husserl, Edmund, 93n14
"hypersemanticity" (Corti), 72
"hypersign," 3
hypertexts, 3, 4, 7, 9, 46, 203

I Ching, 163
identity
  authorial, 159
  Goffman on, 56, 59

identity (*Continued*)
    literary, 89–94
    See also self
image(s), 16–18, 24
    author, 9, 51–56, 65–67, 159, 183, 195
    museum of, 195
    Shklovsky on, 118–19
impressionism, 173n24
innocence, 7–8, 175, 185
innovation. *See* originality
intentionality, 10–12, 24, 61, 68–70, 151n23,
    154
    artistic technique and, 118
    Bakhtin on, 63n16
    Benjamin on, 183
    chance and, 161–64, 171, 174–75, 186
    in film, 79
    interpretation and, 13, 69, 160
    New Criticism and, 5
interpretation
    author intent and, 13–14, 69–70
    community, 150–51
    hypotheses of, 68–70
    readers', 19–20, 53–54, 69, 191
intertextuality, 6–8, 131, 203–5
    Barthes on, 200
    genre and, 85
    history and, 208
Ionesco, Eugène, 207
irony, 18, 22, 98, 115, 174, 198n19
    apocryphal effect and, 184, 203
    genius and, 193
    metric schemes and, 180–81
    of romanticism, 194
    tragedy and, 202

Jakobson, Roman, 72, 73, 117, 120
    poetics of, 136–39, 142, 144–48
    on realism, 129
Jakubinsky, L. P., 121
James, Henry, 64
Jauss, Hans Robert, 42n27
    "cunning of tradition" of, 98–99
    on genre, 85–87, 94, 96, 109, 127–28
    "horizon of expectations" of, 85, 93,
        98n18, 101, 122
Judd, Donald, 136

Kant, Immanuel, 49, 121n13, 137n2, 139,
    171
Khlebnikov, V., 122
Khomeini, Ayatollah Ruhollah, 61
Kierkegaard, Søren, 66n20
kitsch, 104n33

Kosuth, Joseph, 43–44, 153–54, 157n28,
    173–74
Kristeva, Julia, 5, 72, 131, 148n19, 201
Kristiansen, S. V., 123–24
Kuhn, Thomas S., 201n25

labyrinth, 23, 32n13
    Borges on, 47
    history as, 201–2, 207–9
Lacan, Jacques, 5, 52n43
Landolfi, Tommaso, *illus.*
Landow, George P., 7n6
Lang, Fritz, 80
late modernity, 5–8, 20–23, 202–12
    authorialism of, 17–18, 20–22
    poetics of, 20–21, 24–25, 34–35
    See also modernity; postmodernism
learning
    double-binds of, 23
    secondary, 20, 21, 205–7, 209
Leavitt, David, 32
Le Lionnais, François, 161n3, 166–67
Lem, Stanislaw, 96
Leopardi, Giacomo, 38–39
Lescure, Jean, 164n9
Levi, Primo, 104
lipograms, 162, 167–68
literature
    Barthes on, 131
    conceptual, 39, 44–48
    definitions of, 136–40
    epochs of, 188–89
    of exhaustion, 45, 47, 119–23, 190–91
    as genre, 39, 107–10
    identity of, 89–94
    madness and, 196n16
    metacommunication and, 88–90
    "novelization" of, 81, 109
    popular, 24–25, 77–82, 95, 97, 100–103,
        145
    psychoanalysis and, 192
    "reconfigured," 203–5
    reenchantment of, 186–87
    theories of, 146
    work of, 6–7, 11, 56
    See also novels; poetics
Lombardo, Sergio, 164
Lotman, Jurij, 73, 87, 149n21
Lubitsch, Ernst, 80, 103
Luhmann, Niklas, 83n1

Mácha, Karel Hynek, 145–46
Mallarmé, Stéphane, 149, 196n16

Malraux, André, 195n15
Manganelli, Giorgio, 166, 180n40, 184, 192, 198, 200n21
manic depression, 203
mannerists, 180
Manzoni, Piero, *illus.*, 186
Marinetti, Filippo Tommaso, 206
Marra, Alfonso Luigi, *illus.*, 1–2, 4
Marx, Karl, 201
Masaccio (Tommaso de Giovanni di Simone Guidi), *illus.*
Masolino da Panicale, *illus.*
"mathematization of chance," 164
Maupassant, Guy de, 28
McInerney, Jay, 32
melancholy. *See* mourning
melodrama, 77
memory, 83, 200
merchandising, of authors, 8–10, 23–25, 75
Merleau-Ponty, Maurice, 54
metacommunication, 84, 88–90, 97
    and "art," 151, 153, 155–58
    definition of, 154–55
    in popular fiction, 101
metaliterature, 128n23
metatexts, 6–7
    See also texts
metric schemes, 168, 174–85
mimesis, 143
modernity, 20–23, 34–35
    authorialism and, 17, 21–22
    differential logic of, 111–35
    fashion and, 105
    malaise of, 21–22, 159
    See also late modernity
Montale, Eugenio, 27, 124
Moresco, Antonio, 32n13, 61n9
Moro, Aldo, 70
mourning, 98, 187–89, 202–3, 205
movies. *See* films
Mukařovský, Jan, 99–100, 139n4, 172
Mussolini, Benito, *illus.*
myth(s)
    Aristotle on, 143
    bourgeois, 201
    death-of-author, 5, 8, 14–15, 49–54, 159, 188, 191–203, 211–12
    identity and, 59
    Schlegel on, 189n2
    terminal, 188–91
    Winckelmann on, 196n15

Nadar (Félix Tournachon), *illus.*
Napoleon Bonaparte, 181

narcissism, 56, 131
neo-avant-garde, 29n6, 34, 53, 190
    See also avant-garde
neoexpressionism, 182
neo-realism, 38, 53
networks, creative, 3–4, 6–7, 10
New Age novel, 77, 95, 101
New Criticism, 5, 68
Nietzsche, Friedrich, 200
noesis, 41–44
    See also aisthesis
Novalis (Friedrich von Hardenberg), 116
novels
    anonymous, 75–77
    anti, 34, 101
    Bakhtin on, 111–12
    Barth, 190
    canon and, 112–13
    genres of, 109, 111–13, 126, 138, 166
    serial, 24, 77
    See also literature

objet trouvé, 161
Oliva, Achille Bonito, *illus.*, 31
oral tradition, 90, 185
originality, 12, 20, 154, 185–86, 190, 193–96
    Adorno on, 107n37
    Barthes on, 194–95
    Borges on, 47
    Calvino and, 116, 184
    creative networks and, 3–4, 6–7, 10
    dadaism and, 170–72
    genre and, 107, 123
    impossibility of, 40, 132, 199, 202–3, 207–12
    Jakobson on, 144n13
    postmodernism and, 98, 184, 206
Orlando, Francesco, 148n18, 192n5
ostraneniye, 120
    See also estrangement
Ottonieri, Tommaso, 31, 184, 180
OuLiPo (Ouvroir de Littérature Potentielle), 161–69, 176
    See also specific authors, e.g., Calvino

Pagliarani, Elio, 29n6
painting
    action, 163–64, 175, 186
    "rebirth" of, 141n9
    stochastic, 164
    See also art *and specific movements, e.g.,* surrealism
Pareyson, Luigi, 29n5

Parise, G., 175–76, 183
parody, 113
Pascoli, Giovanni, 124
Pasolini, Pier Paolo, *illus.*, 34, 47–48, 60, 131
Pavese, Cesare, 135
Paz, Octavio, 151n24
Perec, Georges, 161n3, 163
    La disparition of, 162
    La vie, mode d'emploi of, 165
performance art, *illus.*, 139
photography
    Balzac on, *illus.*
    Barthes on, 54–55
Pingaud, Bernard, 8
Plato, 143
Poe, Edgar Allan, 29n5
poetics, 27–30, 105–10
    aesthetics and, 14, 24–25, 142
    anticipatory, 39–41
    Aristotlean, 38, 84, 90, 91, 142–45
    avant-garde, 34–35, 40–41, 125, 149, 156, 197
    criticism and, *illus.*, 31–32, 146
    Croce's, 35–36
    dadaist, 161, 171–74, 206
    definitions of, 3, 28, 38, 137, 142
    Eco's, 28–29, 38
    of grace, 17, 50, 176, 183–85, 187
    Hegel's, 35–37, 136, 140–41, 144–45, 167, 196
    Horace's, 38
    Jakobson's, 136–38, 142, 144–48
    late-modern, 20–21, 24–25, 34–35
    mediation of, 37–38
    of rupture, 30, 73, 128, 201, 202, 205
    self and, 29n5, 182, 188
    Shklovsky's, 117–22, 132–35
    Valéry's, 29n5, 38, 142n11
    Verlaine's, 28
    See also aesthetics; literature
poetry, 77, 89
    lyric, 190
    meter of, 168, 174–85
    oral tradition of, 90, 185
    prose versus, 100, 121–22, 136, 140, 144–49, 181–82
    recipes for, 167, 170–71, 185
    Schlegel on, 188n1, 189n2, 207n32
    schools of, 125, 171–72, 207n32
    science versus, 134
popular fiction. *See* pulp fiction
Porta, Antonio, 29n6
postmodernism, 21–25, 208

avant-garde and, 189–90
    "critical," 30
    genre and, 92n12, 94, 101–2
    ironic detachment of, 18, 22
    originality and, 98, 184, 206
    self-referentiality of, 130, 207
    See also late modernity
poststructuralism, 13, 50, 202
Potebnya, A. F., 118–19
prïem, 117–18
prose, 100, 121–22, 136, 140, 144–49, 181–82
    See also poetry
Proust, Marcel, 57, 183–84, 197–99, 203
    Barthes on, 200
    Contra Sainte-Beuve of, 58, 192
    Remembrance of Things Past of, 60, 81
psychoanalysis, 192, 203
pulp fiction, 24, 77–82, 95, 97, 100–103, 145
Pushkin, Aleksandre, 122

Q (novel), 7n6
Queneau, Raymond, 161n3, 163, 164n9

Raboni, Giovanni, 179
Raimi, Sam, 81
Ray, Man (Emanuel Rabinovitch), *illus.*
reader, 9, 48
    Barthes on, 53–54
    "eye" of, 160
    Gadamer on, 19–20
    "horizon of expectations" of, 85, 93, 98n18, 101, 122
    "instructions" for, 67–68
    narrator and, 63–64
    strategies of, 68
    text appropriation by, 19–20, 54, 69, 191
    as vampire, 9, 53
readymades, 156, 161, 170, 174
realism, 42, 129–30, 152
    neo, 38, 53
    self-referentiality of, 128n23
recipes, writing, 161–64, 167–77, 185
reenchantment, 185–87
reflective art, 20–21, 34–38, 114–16, 152
    Borges and, 45–46, 154
    dadaism and, 171
    Hegel on, 35–37, 141
    modernism and, 17
    See also self-referentiality

rhyme schemes, 177–82
Riegl, Alois, 29n5
Rimbaud, Arthur, 60, 207
romanticism, 81
  aesthetics of, 35, 43, 140n7, 169, 182, 206–8
  criticism of, 29n5
  formalists and, 120
  genius and, 193n10
  genre and, 85, 93, 138
  Hegel on, 141, 167n18, 193
  irony of, 194
  Novalis on, 116
Romero, George, 81
Ropars, Marie-Claire, 82n44
Roussel, Raymond, 165, 176
rupture, poetics of, 30, 73, 128, 201, 202, 205
Rushdie, Salman, 61

Sainte-Beuve, Charles Augustin, 58, 60
Salabelle, Maurizio, 161n2
Sanguineti, Edoardo, 29n6
Sartre, Jean-Paul, 175n28, 192, 194
Schaeffer, Jean-Maire, 91, 93
Schiller, Friedrich von, 35, 183, 189
schizophrenia, 211
Schlegel, Friedrich von, 113, 188n1, 189n2, 207n32
Schwarz, Arturo, 174
Scialoja, Toti, 179n39
science fiction, 77, 95, 101, 105
  cyperpunk, 106n35
secondary learning, 20, 21, 205–7, 209
second-level art. See reflective art
Segre, Cesare, 46n32, 69, 87
self, 21, 52–53, 72
  deep versus worldly, 57
  Goffman on, 56, 59
  poetic, 29n5, 182, 188
  sacrifice of, 196–97
  second, 62, 65–67
self-consciousness, 132–35
self-referentiality, 121–22, 128–32, 207
  definition of, 128n23
  See also reflective art
semiotics, 3, 6, 57, 70, 73
  genre and, 85–86
  ideal author of, 13–14, 19, 57–61, 67–68
sestinas, 102, 176–79
Sherman, Cindy, illus.
Shklovsky, Victor, 9, 40n26, 205, 206
  on avant-gardes, 125, 171–72

Blok and, 133–34
  "differential sensations" of, 123–26
  poetics of, 117–22, 132–35
  on self-referentiality, 128–29, 132
  short stories, 33, 75, 77
Silva, R., 198n18
Simmel, Georg, 153n25
simplicity, 184–85
sociolinguistics, 59–60
Sollers, Philippe, 5, 163n5, 201
sonnets, 11, 102, 108, 166–67, 176, 179
Sorlin, Pierre, 82n44
Spielberg, Steven, 103
S + 7 method, 164
Stempel, Wolf-Dieter, 99
stochastic art, 164
structuralism, 13–14, 57, 85–86, 117
style, 14, 29n5
  auteur, 24, 79–82
  Booth on, 65–67
  Calvino on, 66–67
sublimity, 183
surrealism, 161, 163, 175, 209–10

technique, artistic, 116–19, 123, 164
  definition of, 118
  liberalization of, 132–33
Tel Quel (journal), 8n8, 201
terrorism, 209–10
terza rima, 177–78
text(s)
  author and, 2–4, 11–16, 77–78, 200, 204
  Eco on, 68
  function of, 13, 61
  generic versus authored, 11, 77–78, 83–110, 153
  "law" of, 73n36
  meaning of, 45–46
  reconfiguration of, 203–5
  transcendence and, 86–87
  work versus, 6–7, 70, 196–99, 204–5
Todorov, Tzvetan, 72, 121, 142n11, 148–49
Tolstoy, Lev, 120, 132
Tomashevsky, B., 117
Tondelli, Vittorio, 33, 102n24
tragedy, 11, 75, 90, 91, 138, 152, 166
  Aristotle on, 142–43
  catharsis and, 38, 42, 56, 143, 196–97
  irony and, 202
  rules of, 163n6, 166
"transtexuality" (Genette), 86–87
Tynianov, Jurij, 117, 121n13, 122–23, 128
Tzara, Tristan, 170–73

unconscious, 134, 192n5, 202
  choices by, 14, 163
  creation and, 193
utopianism, 14–15, 183, 186, 189–90,
  197–99

Vaillant, A., 193n10
Valduga, Patrizia, 179
Valéry, Paul, 19, 29n5, 38, 142n11, 144
valorization, 11–14, 39, 42–43, 72–77,
  81–82, 97–98, 182–85
  culture industry and, 156
  interpretation and, 69
  postmodernism and, 102
  realism and, 128n23
Varaldo, Giuseppe, 168
verbal art, 90, 185
Verlaine, Paul, 28
Virno, Paolo, 200n22
voice, 18, 34, 62n14, 192

Walser, Robert, 183
Warhol, Andy, 158

Weil, Simone, 188
Welles, Orson, 79
West, Jessamyn, 66n20
westerns, 80, 95, 106
Wilson, Jan, *illus.*
Winckelmann, Johann Joachim, 195n
  15
wishful thinking, 51
work, 11–16, 56, 136–37
  absent, 14, 67, 196–99
  "open," 101
  text versus, 6–7, 70, 196–99, 204–5
writer's block, 3, 46
writing
  automatic, 163, 170, 175
  bound, 17, 22, 50, 103, 161–69, 175–76,
    182, 185
  recipes for, 161–64, 167–77, 185
  "science" of, 201n24
  text and, 11, 204
  "truth" of, 195
  See also author

Zanzotto, Andrea, 179